GCSE Economics

GCSE Economics

NN Proctor and J Pratten

TUDOR

First published in Great Britain in 1996 by Tudor Business Publishing Ltd.

Sole distributors worldwide,
Hodder and Stoughton Ltd.,
338 Euston Road, London, NW1 3BH

© 1996 NN Proctor and J Pratten

The right of the authors of this work has been asserted by them in accordance with the Copyright, Designs and Patents Act, 1988.

All rights reserved. No part of this publication may be reproduced or transmitted in any form or by any means, electronically or mechanically, including photocopying, recording or any information storage or retrieval system, without prior permission in writing from
Tudor Business Publishing Ltd at Stanton House, Eastham Village Road, Eastham, Wirral, Merseyside L62 8AD.

British Library Cataloguing in Publication Data
A catalogue record for this book is available from the British Library

ISBN 1-872807-41-0

1 2 3 4 5 96 97 98 99

Typeset in Novarese by GreenGate Publishing Services, Tonbridge, Kent
Printed in Great Britain by The Bath Press, Bath, Avon

Contents

List of Figures ... vi

Introduction ... ix

1 The Economic Problem ... 1
Scarcity ... 1
Choice ... 3

2 Economic Behaviour ... 8
Group behaviour ... 8
Organisational behaviour ... 10
National behaviour ... 17

3 Economic Theory ... 28
The price mechanism and the market ... 28
Elasticity ... 38
Costs, revenues and profit ... 43
Circular flow of income ... 47
Monetary and fiscal policy ... 51
The gains from trade ... 56
The problems of trade ... 60

4 Economic Terminology ... 65
Money and the money supply in the UK ... 65
Income and wealth ... 68
Expenditure patterns ... 72
National income and the standard of living ... 77
Government revenue and expenditure ... 81
The balance of payments ... 85
Currency exchange ... 89
Economic issues ... 93

5 The Economic Institutions ... 99
Business organisations ... 99
Trade unions and employers' associations ... 103
The financial institutions ... 106
The role of central and local government ... 110
Taxation in the UK ... 112
The European Union and other international institutions ... 116

6 The Assessment of Economic Behaviour ... 120
Economic growth ... 120
The standard of living and the quality of life ... 124
Economic performance ... 128

7 Coursework ... 134
Coursework titles ... 134
Presentation, evaluation and analysis of data ... 137
Coursework sources and general guidelines ... 141

8 The Examination ... 144
The examination paper ... 144
Sample questions (with answers and advice) ... 147

Index ... 155

List of Figures

Chapter 1

1.1	What are people's basic needs?	1
1.2	The economic problem	2
1.3	Economic choices	3
1.4	Opportunity cost	4

Chapter 2

2.1	Specialisation	8
2.2	Division of labour	9
2.3	Economies of scale	11
2.4	The principles of multiples	12
2.5	The forces of location	13
2.6	Diseconomies of scale	15
2.7	Income distribution UK 1991– before housing costs	18
2.8	Income distribution UK 1991– after housing costs	19
2.9	Marketable wealth UK 1991	20
2.10	Gross domestic product per head for the more developed countries of the world	20
2.11	Gross domestic product per head – international comparison 1991	21
2.12	The origins of UK trade – 1992	22
2.13	UK commodity trading – 1982 and 1992	22
2.14	Trade on a Balance of Payments basis	23

Chapter 3

3.1	The demand curve	28
3.2	Extension and contraction of demand	29
3.3	Changes in demand	30
3.4	Factors affecting demand	30
3.5	The supply curve	32
3.6	Changes in quantity of supply	32
3.7	Changes in supply	33
3.8	Market disequilibrium	33
3.9	Market equilibrium	34
3.10	Changing market equilibrium	35
3.11	Extremes of elasticity	38
3.12	Elasticity of supply graphs	41
3.13	Total costs	44
3.14	The simple two sector economy	48
3.15	Three sector circular flow	49
3.16	The open model	50
3.17	Monetary policy	52
3.18	UK base rates 1980–1994	53
3.19	Public money 1995–96	
3.20	The Public Sector Borrowing Requirement in the UK	54
3.21	Reasons for trade	56
3.22	Trade problems	61
3.23	The effect of exchange rates on prices	62

Chapter 4

4.1	Functions of money	66
4.2	UK notes, coins and bank deposits	67
4.3	The composition of UK national income	69
4.4	The composition of household income – UK 1992	69
4.5	The composition of wealth UK	70
4.6	Consumer goods and services	73
4.7	Weekly family expenditure – UK 1992	73
4.8	UK government revenue 1995–96	83
4.9	UK government expenditure 1995–96	83
4.10	Government intervention in the foreign exchange market	90
4.11	The floating exchange rate	91
4.12	The demand-pull spiral	93
4.13	The cost-push spiral	93
4.14	Policies to cure inflation	94
4.15	The causes of unemployment	95
4.16	Policies to cure unemployment	96

Chapter 5

5.1	The private sector	100
5.2	Union action	103
5.3	Working days lost through strikes	103
5.4	Number of trade unions 1950–1995	104
5.5	Membership of trade unions 1950–1995	104
5.6	The role of the Bank of England	108
5.7	UK government expenditure – 1995/96	110
5.8	Local government expenditure – 1994	111
5.9	UK government central revenue – 1995/96	113
5.10	Local government revenue – 1994	115

Chapter 6

6.1	The benefits of growth	120
6.2	The costs of growth	121
6.3	Factors affecting the quality of life	125
6.4	Economic growth and quality of life	126
6.5	UK inflation 1985–1994	129
6.6	Unemployment in the UK 1985–1994	130
6.7	UK GNP growth 1985–1994	130
6.8	UK balance of payments account 1985–1994	131

Chapter 7

7.1	Factors affecting price	135
7.2	Factors affecting demand	135
7.3	Organising your work	138
7.4	Student price survey	139
7.5	General guidelines for your report	142

Chapter 8

8.1	Sample examination paper instructions	144
8.2	Allocation of marks on an examination paper	145
8.3	Allocation of time on an examination paper	145
8.4	Supply and demand for bottles of lemonade per day in a school shop	147

To
Lesley
Amanda, Zoë and Gregory

Introduction

This book has deliberately been written to meet all of the needs of students following the 1995 GCSE Economics syllabus. It should also be an ideal introduction to the subject for those not following an examination course.

Throughout the book we have integrated coursework and case study material. As experienced examiners and moderators we feel that too many students fail to achieve their full potential in the coursework and examination situation due to a lack of guidance. To this end we have also deliberately added chapters on 'Coursework' and 'The Examination'. Knowledge of these areas is as important as the knowledge of economics itself.

All of the case study material is based upon a fictional village, 'Barengo'. This village has been developed to experience all of the economic situations a student needs to cover. We hope that this makes learning more enjoyable and that students will want to follow the progress of Barengo.

We decided, along with the publishers, to set the case study questions at three different levels rather than the two prescribed by SCAA. The intention is to provide questions for the less able and A* candidates, many of whom are neglected.

The varying degree of difficulty should provide testing questions for every student.

Nigel Proctor and John Pratten

ACKNOWLEDGEMENTS

The authors thank the following for granting permission to reproduce photographs in the book:

Universal Pictorial Press and Agency Ltd pages 5, 24, 126 and 127
Vauxhall Motors Ltd page 11
Liverpool Daily Post and Echo and The Press Association Ltd pages 18 and 19
Philip Micheu page 31
Liverpool Daily Post and Echo pages 34 and 35
Porsche GB page 58
F Loughlan page 75
The Press Association Ltd page 122
T Kenwright page 96
Camera Press Ltd page 108

1

The Economic Problem

> The basic economic problem and decisions that give rise to economics as a discipline
>
> 1.1 SCARCITY • 1.2 CHOICE
>
> This section should enable students to:
> - explain the nature of the economic problem
> - demonstrate that this arises from the finite nature of resources and people's unlimited wants
> - understand the concept of opportunity costs
> - recognise the potential effects of solutions to economic problems.

1.1 SCARCITY

Wants and needs

People all over the world have different wants and needs. All countries have basic needs for items such as food and water. In Less Developed Countries (LDCs) these basic needs are often in very short supply. In the more advanced countries the basic needs are usually ample and are replaced with a desire for other things. These items are not really necessary for survival: they are what people **want** rather than what they **need**.

As the basic needs are satisfied people turn their attention to new items that they think they need. People are never satisfied with what they have and this is true of the rich as well as the poor. If you rent a house you want to buy your own. If you own your own house you want a bigger one and then one with bigger grounds and a double garage, maybe even a swimming pool.

It is possible for everyone to produce a list of what they want. If these wants were satisfied it would be a simple task to produce another list and then another. This happens because even when the requirement is just food and shelter there is a big difference between a basic need and what is wanted. Stale bread is food but so is caviar; a wooden hut is shelter but so is Buckingham Palace.

A family of six will need a larger house than a single person; could they therefore say that a four-bedroomed detached house is a basic need? It is clearly difficult to show the difference between people's wants and needs.

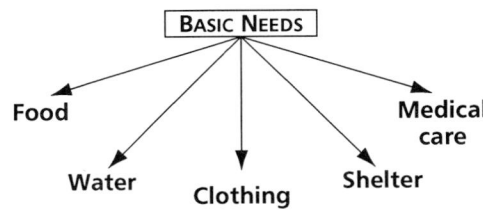

Figure 1.1 What are people's basic needs?

The confusion between what human beings need and what they think they want creates a desire for more and more. This desire can be described as ambition, trying to improve one's lifestyle, or greed.

However it is described the presence of this desire in people produces a never-ending demand for goods and services. This is increased by the fact that goods are used up or wear out and need replacing, or are replaced by better versions. The result is that the human race possesses an **unlimited demand** for goods and services.

ACTIVITY 1

Produce a list of ten items that you would like. Imagine that these have been given to you. Can you produce a list of ten more? How many lists do you think you could make?

Using your first two lists can you say how many items you want and how many items you really need?

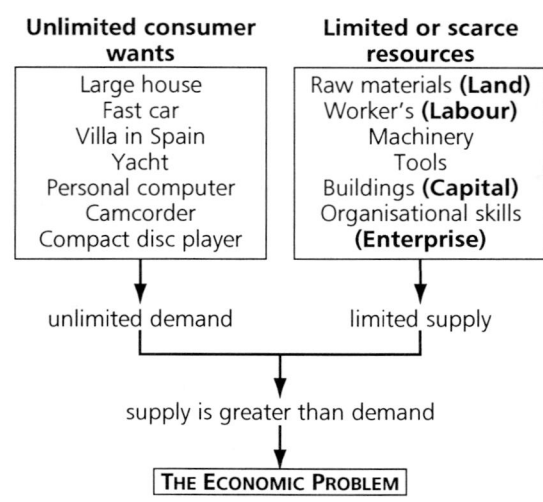

Figure 1.2 The economic problem

If everyone's wants and needs are to be satisfied a constant supply of goods and services must be produced. This is only possible if there are enough resources, an unlimited supply of resources, to produce everything that is demanded. In other words unlimited demand should be matched by unlimited supply.

The problem is that the resources needed for production, raw materials, workers, machinery and buildings, are **limited in supply.**

Factors of production

The resources, known as the **factors of production,** are described as the factors **land, labour, capital** and **enterprise.** The factor land is used to describe all the raw materials beneath the ground and in the seas and rivers, as well as on the surface of the land and grown on the earth's surface.

Labour is human effort, work performed by the workforce. The workforce includes all of those willing and able to work. Capital is the machinery, factories and buildings used to help and increase output.

Enterprise is the organising factor, in other words, the person who makes the decisions and takes the risks, the 'boss'.

All these factors are limited in supply. We do not possess a never-ending supply of labour or oil or land on which to build.

If the factors of production are limited or **scarce** then the supply of goods and services will be limited and the unlimited demand cannot be satisfied. This creates a problem, the **economic problem,** how can people's unlimited demand be satisfied?

If limitation or scarcity of resources means that not all demand can be satisfied then choices have to be made. The role of economic decision making becomes important. It must be decided how best to satisfy as many of the wants and needs as possible.

The whole reason for the existence of economics is the existence of this economic problem.

ACTIVITY 2

List as many raw materials as possible. How many of these can be found in the UK?

Try to find how many years supply of oil and coal the UK has.

Using official statistics try to calculate the size of the UK workforce in one, five and ten years time.

 Review terms

Wants; needs; unlimited demand; limited supply; scarce resources; the factors of production; land; labour; capital; enterprise; the economic problem.

1.2 CHOICE

What to produce?

The economic problem is faced by every country and community. Everywhere resources are limited or scarce and demand is unlimited but in some countries the problem is more obvious than in others. A commodity that is scarce in one country, or in one community, is not necessarily scarce in another. For example, food is scarce in many African countries but in the UK it is plentiful.

If resources are scarce and all the people's wants and needs cannot be satisfied, what is needed is organisation, a way of producing as much as possible with the resources available to satisfy as many of the wants and needs as possible. This form of organisation is called an **economy.**

Different economies around the world exist because there are many different solutions to the economic problem. Economic decisions are made by different groups or in different ways and this produces entirely different types of economic system.

If it is impossible to produce everything that people want and need then the first economic decision to be made is **what to produce.**

The government can decide what to produce. This would produce a **planned** or **command economy** where the ruling body decides what to produce instead of letting the people decide for themselves.

An alternative way of deciding what to produce is to let the people, the consumers, make the decision through their demand for goods and services. This allows the consumer to dominate the system, giving **consumer sovereignty,** and produces a **market economy** (also known as a capitalist or *laissez faire* economy).

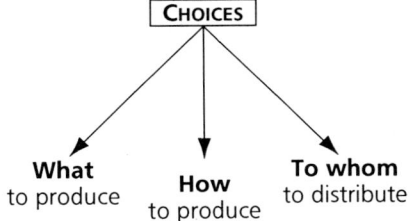

Figure 1.3 The economic problem

A third solution is to use a combination of the two methods already described. In this economy, the mixed economy, decisions about what to produce are taken by the consumers and the government together. The UK is an example of a **mixed economy.** Some goods such as food are provided by the **private sector** according to what the consumer wants, and some goods and services, such as education and health care, are provided by the **public sector** according to what the British Government believes the people need.

The method used to decide what to produce is a major factor in determining the type of economy that exists. Every economy tends to solve the problem in a different way.

Opportunity cost

Whatever the method used to decide what to produce a choice has to be made and that choice involves a cost. For every item (good) or service produced something has to be given up, a sacrifice has to be made. This cost is explained in economics as the **opportunity cost.**

The opportunity cost of any item is '**the next best alternative that has to be given up**'. If an individual has five hours of spare time and decides to watch the television rather than finish their homework, the opportunity cost of watching the television is the homework that has not been finished.

Opportunity cost is a part of everyone's life. All economic goods have an opportunity cost. Every day everyone makes choices in their life: what to buy, what to eat and how to spend their time. All of these involve an opportunity cost.

Firms have to make the choice of what to produce and it is very important for them. If they use their raw materials, labour and capital to build offices they cannot build houses with the same resources; this is the opportunity cost.

Governments have to make decisions about the way in which they spend their money: should it be on education, health, defence, reducing the tax rate or increasing unemployment benefits? If they have £20 billion the opportunity cost of spending £10 billion on defence is the £10 billion they could have spent on health.

One of the biggest decisions that has to be made is whether an economy should produce

ACTIVITY 3

Produce a list of all the things you could do instead of reading this chapter. What is the opportunity cost of reading this chapter?

It is often said that there is no such thing as a 'free meal'. If this is true what is the 'cost' of a 'free school meal'? Try to calculate the 'cost'.

List all of those goods or services that are 'free'. What makes these goods or services so special?

consumer goods and services or capital goods. Capital goods, such as factories and machines, increase output in the future giving everybody more to enjoy. The cost, the opportunity cost, of increasing output in the future is a decrease in the output of consumer goods and services now. Consumer goods and capital goods cannot both be produced using the same resources; a choice has to be made.

Figure 1.4 shows how the concept of opportunity cost actually works. If a country has a set amount of the factors of production then it can either produce all consumer goods (point A) or it can produce all capital goods (point B). It cannot produce at point A and at point B.

Between points A and B are a number of different combinations of consumer goods and capital goods that can be produced with a set amount of the factors of production. These combinations are shown by the line joining points A and B together, known as the **production possibility frontier.**

If this country produces at Point F they can produce 'OD' units of consumer goods and 'OE' units of capital goods. If they then decide to move to point B increasing consumer good output and decreasing capital good output an opportunity cost is involved. The opportunity cost of increasing consumer goods by 'DJ' units is 'HE' units of capital that are lost.

In some communities the decision between consumer and capital goods is extremely serious. If resources are used to produce capital goods the opportunity cost is those people who will not have enough food to eat. If capital goods are not produced the opportunity cost of producing food now is those people who will die in the future due to a lack of food as the population increases.

How to produce

Once the decision of what to produce has been made the next step is to decide **how to produce?** This will be decided by the type of produce or service to be produced, the amount of labour available and the amount of capital available.

Production can be **capital intensive,** using more machinery than labour, or **labour intensive,** using more labour than capital. If the community has a large supply of labour and very little capital, or a poor level of technology, then a labour intensive method would make more sense. However, if the level of technology in the country was very advanced and a small highly skilled population lived there a capital intensive method would be better.

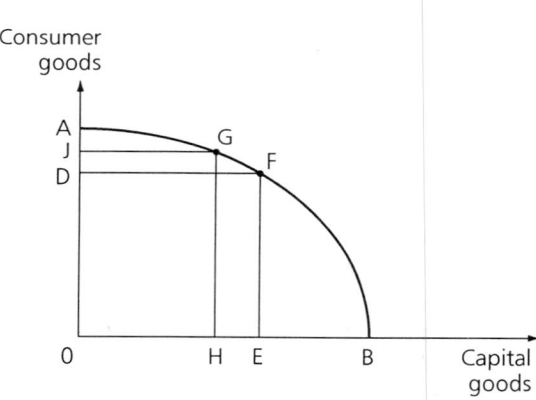

Figure 1.4 Opportunity cost

In some cases the choice of production method is determined by the good or service itself. Delivering letters or cutting people's hair cannot be done by using capital intensive methods. Hand-made furniture needs skilled craftsmen, not machines. If only small quantities of a good are required capital intensive methods would again not be suitable.

The decision 'how to produce' is not influenced by the type of economy but by other factors. The production method used does not determine, or influence, the type of economy.

Distribution

The final decision that has to be made to overcome the economic problem is **how to distribute** the goods and services produced.

All the goods and services produced can be shared out according to tradition: the elder comes first, the worker comes first, the religious leader takes precedence, and so on.

A second solution would be for everything to be shared out according to people's ability to pay. Those that can afford the goods and services can have them, those that cannot go without. This would be a market economy.

A third solution would be for everyone to have an equal share of everything produced. This would need the state to own the factors of production and individuals to have total equality. In this command economy the state would also decide what should be produced.

The final alternative is that some goods such as health and education should be shared equally, and other goods, consumer durables, according to people's ability to pay. This would give a mixed economy in which private enterprise and market forces share out goods according to people's ability to pay while the government, through the public sector, provides everyone with zero priced goods and services paid for through the collection of taxes.

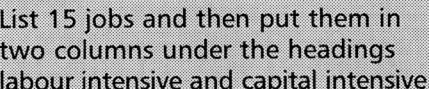

ACTIVITY

List 15 jobs and then put them in two columns under the headings labour intensive and capital intensive.

Using the two columns of jobs, try to find:

a) any similarities between the jobs within each column
b) any differences between the jobs in the different columns.

Draw a line of 15 cm. Mark the left hand side planned economies, the centre mixed economies and the right hand side free market economies. Place the countries of the European Union on the line according to the type of economy they have.

Review terms

Command economy; market economy; mixed economy; consumer sovereignty; public sector; private sector; opportunity cost; consumer goods; capital goods; production possibility frontier; capital intensive; labour intensive.

Modern example of scarcity: effects of the Ethiopian famine

THE DAILY NEWS

Famine in Barengo

It was reported yesterday that aid lorries had finally reached the remote settlement of Barengo in Southern Ethiopia. It has been three months since the last aid convoy delivered any food and over this period the population of the small settlement has shrunk from 120 adults and 60 children to 96 adults and 39 children.

Faminaid reports that the problem this community faces is a shortage of water. They have the tools, seeds and skills to grow their own food, but they do not have enough water to drink as well as to water the crops.

Stark choice

As a result they face a stark choice. If people drink the water, no food can be grown. If the water is used to grow the crops, then there is none left to drink.

Faminaid plans to help this settlement to drill a well to find another source of water. If this can be done then it is hoped there will be enough water for the people to drink and to ensure that the crops grow.

Inevitable delays

The project, funded by Faminaid, will require 40 workers from the settlement and is expected to take a month to complete. Due to the problems of communication in this region and the heavy demand for Faminaid's resources it is expected that the project will begin two months from now. Unfortunately, these are the driest two months of the year in this part of the world.

Data questions

Foundation level

1 (a) How many adults were there in the settlement three months before the aid lorries arrived?
(b) How many were there when the aid lorries arrived?
(c) What was the main problem that Faminaid reported?
(d) What solution to this problem did Faminaid suggest?
(e) How long will it take for the problem to be solved?

2 Paragraph three of the text gives an example of the concept of opportunity cost. Explain the meaning of the term, and give two other examples of the concept.

3 Is the community capital intensive or labour intensive? Explain the meaning of the terms, and use the information in the text to provide the answer.

4 What problems might Faminaid experience in trying to solve the problem?

Intermediate level

1 Extract the five most important pieces of information from the text.

2 Paragraph three of the text provides an example of an important economic concept. Identify the concept, explain its meaning, and give two other examples.

3 Using the information in the text, what do you know about the type of production to be found in the community?

4 What problems might Faminaid meet when it begins its project?

Higher level

1 Summarise the contents of the text.

2 Find two basic economic concepts contained in the text, and explain their meanings.

3 What does the text tell us about the community in terms of its productive potential?

4 What problems might the community experience in the period between the delivery of aid which is described in the text and the harvesting of its crops?

Coursework Suggestions

Idea

What would people do if they had more money? Would different groups of people spend it in different ways?

Suppose you were given £1,000 or £10,000 or even £100,000:

- How would you spend it?
- How would other people spend it?
- Why would different people make different choices?

Interview different types of people, and ask them what they would do with the money. Make sure that you interview distinct groups of people. For instance, you could ask ten people who are single but in their 20s, ten young married couples, and ten pensioners. Or you could ask ten people with well paid jobs, ten people with moderately paid jobs, and ten who are unemployed. Or you could ask ten people who work in a large town or city, and ten who work in a village or small town, and ten who work from home.

Analyse the answers to see if there are differences between the groups.

Idea

Different people have different wants. Why is this? Think of a variety of items that people can buy, such as:

- designer clothes and a car or a house
- designer clothes or a compact disc system
- a mountain bike or a television set.

Find out why they have made their choices, and take other information about them, so as to see if different age groups, or occupations, or marital status or age or anything else helps to shape their choices. Analyse answers, and draw conclusions.

2

Economic Behaviour

The economic behaviour of individuals, groups, organisations and Governments within local, national and international communities.

2.1 GROUP BEHAVIOUR • 2.2 ORGANISATIONAL BEHAVIOUR
2.3 NATIONAL BEHAVIOUR

This section should enable students to:
- explain specialisation and exchange whilst understanding the benefits and limitations
- identify external and internal economies of scale whilst appreciating the reasons for the location of industry
- understand the pattern of trade in the UK and how government controls international trade
- explain the distribution of wealth and income in the UK and the world.

2.1 GROUP BEHAVIOUR

Specialisation and exchange

In poorer countries, (Less Developed Nations – LDCs), throughout the world it is usual to find people supplying all their own needs. They build their own shelter, grow their own food and make their own clothes. This lifestyle makes these people self-sufficient. They look after themselves and do not need the help of anyone else; they are **economically independent**.

In the developed nations people very rarely provide for their own wants and needs. Everyone tends to produce one good or provide one service. The money earned from production is then used to buy the other things that people need. This means that people in the developed nations cannot survive on their own; they are **economically dependent**.

Two of the biggest differences between the developed and less-developed world are that in developed nations individuals are economically dependent and that these developed nations have a good money system. Money is a vital part of any country's development.

If people produce only for themselves then no extra goods are available. This stops people storing goods for the future and so accumulating wealth. It is the accumulated wealth that allows countries to grow rich because resources can be diverted from the production of consumer goods to the production of **capital goods** – (see pages 4 and 21). Capital allows countries to produce more in the future and so increase their wealth even more.

If individuals specialise it means they either produce a complete good or service or perform

Figure 2.1 Specialisation

ACTIVITY

Produce a list of ten jobs, occupations or professions in which people specialise.

Choose two from the list of ten and see how far the jobs can be broken down.

Produce a list of five jobs in which it is not possible to specialise. List the reasons why these jobs cannot benefit from specialisation.

one task in the production of a good or service. For example, very few car workers produce a whole car, they concentrate on one particular operation such as fitting doors. Teachers in senior schools concentrate upon teaching one subject.

Because people specialise they become very good at what they do and produce more than they actually need. The extra that they produce can then be exchanged for other goods and services that they want.

This system works well if people are making bread for example. They take the loaves that they need and then exchange the remainder for what they want. A problem occurs when people only produce part of a good or if the product is very large and cannot easily be exchanged. A builder cannot take a house into the market place and exchange it for goods and services; civil engineers could not swop a bridge for their wants.

In this situation the only answer is to reward these individuals for their labour. If the reward is in the form of tokens then these can be exchanged for goods and services. These tokens are known by everyone as **money.**

Without money people would not specialise because they could not survive. They would have to provide for all of their wants. Therefore a good money system is vital if specialisation is to take place. Specialisation leads to exchange and the accumulation of wealth and this allows countries to develop and grow.

Division of labour

Specialisation is a process; it means that people concentrate upon producing that good or service, or part of it, at which they are best. Jobs and processes are divided between the workers and this gives specialisation the alternative title of **division of labour.**

The benefits of division of labour were first noticed by Adam Smith, in his book The Wealth of Nations. (Your librarian will help you find a copy.) He described how a pin making factory employing ten men could increase its output from 200 pins per day, 20 pins per man per day, to 4,800 pins per day, 240 pins per man per day. This was achieved by splitting the process of pin making into 18 different operations with men specialising in one or two operations.

The great advantage of specialisation is that output is greatly increased because everyone is more efficient at their job. This allows goods and

Figure 2.2 Division of labour

services to be produced on a large scale. The fact that larger quantities can be produced with the same amount of labour and capital also means that these goods are cheaper. More people can enjoy a wide range of goods and services.

Figure 2.2 shows that the basic advantages gained from the division of labour are economic. They all lead to reduced costs and greater output. By contrast the disadvantages are social, affecting the workers rather than the companies.

Although the division of labour has the benefit of increasing output and decreasing prices it does have its limitations. As previously stated the division of labour will not work if a good money system does not exist. If people do not accept and trust the money that is given to them they will go back to producing everything for themselves.

The division of labour greatly increases output and so large quantities of goods are produced. This is good if the demand for the good is high. However, if the demand is only for a small quantity then this method is not appropriate.

Some goods and services cannot be **mass produced,** for example services such as hairdressing and dentistry would be difficult to divide even further into small tasks. The same applies to General Practitioners in medicine; if they specialised even more, each patient would need to know what was wrong with them before they attended the surgery in order to select the right doctor. Some products such as hand-made furniture cannot be mass produced. It is purchased because it is made by one person by hand.

Specialisation has enabled economies to move away from **self sufficiency** and **subsistence** living (i.e. each person producing his or her most basic needs and no more) to a more developed economy which relies upon excess production being exchanged.

Review terms

Economically independent; economically dependent; capital goods; specialisation; division of labour; mass production; self sufficiency; subsistence.

2.2 ORGANISATIONAL BEHAVIOUR

The major aim of every business is to be successful. Success can mean huge profits, selling more than any other firm or simply becoming a household name. Whatever a firm's view of success it needs to make a profit. Profits are essential to produce a living for owners and keep shareholders happy. If a business fails to earn a profit and makes a loss instead it will soon go out of business.

Economies of scale

For a company to ensure that it makes a profit it must organise itself so that its costs are as low as possible and so that it can sell as many goods and services as possible. A method of achieving both of these objectives is to produce goods on a large scale. Large scale production not only increases output but at the same time ensures certain cost advantages. This means that the company can produce more while the cost per unit, the average cost, can actually decrease. These cost advantages are known as **economies of scale,** the benefits of producing on a large scale.

Economies of scale can be both internal and external. Internal economies of scale are obtained when the individual firm expands. External economies of scale are gained by all firms in an

ACTIVITY

Using a map of the UK mark on it the regions that specialise in particular goods or services. See if you can discover why.

List the 12 members of the European Union. Try to allocate products or services for which each country is well known.

Using the car industry as an example, try to find which jobs have been lost in the last ten years. Can you find out how the car industry has tried to overcome the problems of specialisation?

ECONOMIC BEHAVIOUR 11

Figure 2.3 Economies of scale

industry when that industry is concentrated in a certain location. The most important are usually the internal economies of scale which are under the control of the company itself, unlike external factors. All six categories lead to decreased production costs for a large firm.

Technical economies allow the firm to use a division of labour and unit of capital that would not be practical on a small scale.

The rule of increased dimensions explains why supertankers and container lorries are used for transport. In the following example, if the

Robotic production in a car factory: An example of specialisation in the car industry and a reason for increased unemployment

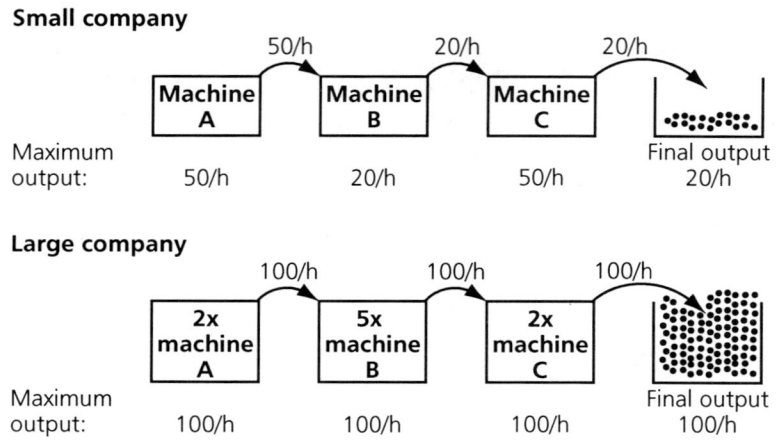

Figure 2.4 The principle of multiples

dimensions of a tanker are doubled, then the capacity increases by a factor of eight, not two.

- A tanker 300 m × 200 m × 100 m
  = 6,000,000 cubic metres.

if this is doubled:

- A tanker 600 m × 400 m × 200 m
  = 48,000,000 cubic metres.

Thus carrying capacity has increased by a factor of eight:

- 48 million = 8 × 6 million.

A tanker twice the size would not need eight times the number of staff and even if twice as many staff were needed the cost per unit of oil carried would still decrease.

A further technical economy is the principle of multiples (see Figure 2.4). Machines often work together, performing part of a task. This often means that production is limited to the least efficient machine. Small firms can often only afford one of each machine type but larger firms are able to employ a number of machines for each process, that is, multiples. These machines can be arranged in such a way that the maximum for each one is gained. Using each machine to its maximum reduces waste and costs.

In the small company machines A and C will only be running at 40% capacity which is a waste of resources and will increase costs. The large firm can afford to buy quantities of each machine. If they buy two of machine A, five of B and two of C all machines will work at their maximum capacity. Output will increase by 400% whilst cost for A and C will increase by only 100%, although they will increase by 400% for B.

Financially large companies have many advantages. Not only do they have access to more sources of finance but usually they are offered lower rates of interest than small companies. It is only practical for large companies to raise finance through shares and debentures (see pages 100 and 108) so again large companies gain through **financial economies.**

If output is increased more workers are needed but the number of supervisors and managers need not necessarily increase in proportion. Specialists can also be employed making further cost savings, hence **management economies** can be made.

Commercial economies exist when firms are able to buy in bulk at cheaper rates and only large companies can afford to buy in such quantities. Packaging and administration costs also decrease per unit as the quantity of goods increases.

A large company has better market information and is therefore aware of changes in the market before the small company. In this way the large company can avoid potential problems and has the resources to diversify into different products and markets. They can also buy from a variety of suppliers. All of these factors are **risk bearing economies** which avoid potential problems and reduce costs.

ACTIVITY 3

Find out the rate of interest charged for (a) mortgages of £40,000, £75,000 and £100,000; (b) overdrafts of £40,000, £75,000 and £100,000.

Visit either (a) a cash and carry or (b) a large butcher's. Compare the prices charged for large and small quantities of the same good. Why are the two activities examples of economies of scale?

Finally **Research and Development** (R and D) is only practical for large companies. Its benefit is that it can produce more competitive products or new production processes, all helping to cut costs.

Location of firms

Another very important business decision that also has an influence on a firm's costs is where it should locate its factories, plants and offices. A bad decision can cause many problems and could lead to a decrease in sales or an increase in costs.

There are many factors that influence where a firm locates its premises. These factors have changed over time; some that were very important are now no longer vital.

The existence of a source of power was at one time the most important influence on the location of firms. The main industry that existed was heavy manufacturing industry and the main, often the only, source of power was coal. It was therefore quite obvious that all major heavy industries should be situated near coalfields.

The situation is now very different. Heavy industry does not dominate the UK economy, services and technologically advanced light industry are major parts of the economy. Their demands for power are not as great but at the same time alternative sources of energy now exist. The UK has a national grid for gas and electricity and both are clean and efficient. The UK has its own source of oil, the North Sea, and it can be transported using the motorway network. This means that power is no longer a major influence when firms are locating their factories.

Access to raw materials was once a strong influence on the location of industry. The woollen and steel industries had to be close to ports for the import of the raw materials. Again, over time, this influence has diminished, synthetic materials have replaced natural products and the improved transport system has meant that other influences are now more important. For those industries still dependent upon imported raw materials the ports are still a major attraction but many more firms now use components produced by other smaller firms and so their location is a factor to consider.

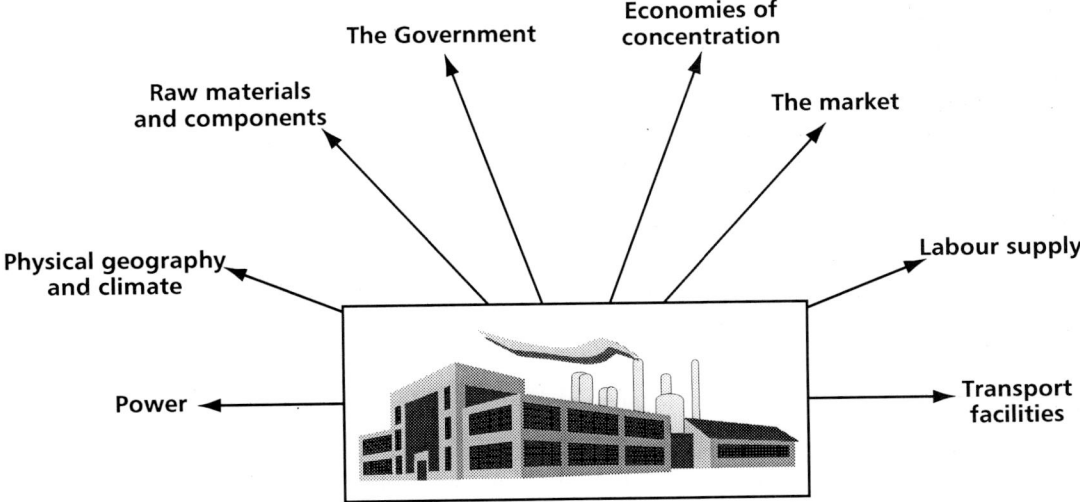

Figure 2.5 The forces of location

The nature of the product is still important. Some products are weight-losing, an example being steel. In this case the finished product is lighter than the raw materials and so it makes sense to produce near the source of the raw materials. However, some industries are weight-gaining, an example being beer. The finished product is heavier than the essential ingredients because water is added. Water can be obtained anywhere, therefore it is better to produce near to the market so that the heavy product has a short distance to travel.

Transport facilities have always been important and still remain so. What has changed is the nature of transport. At one time rail transport was the most important but this has gradually been overtaken by road transport and an increasing influence is the nearness of airports rather than ports. For the modern firm it is the **infrastructure,** the existence of a varied transport system, that is important so that whatever the situation, or nature of their product, they can deliver efficiently at the least cost.

The physical geography and climate of an area are important for certain industries. Agriculture must take account of the contours of the land and the soil, coal mining must be over coal seams, shipbuilding must be near to the water and factories cannot be built on the side of a mountain. It is well known that climate influenced the location of the cotton industry: the damp climate of Lancashire reduced the chance of the cotton thread breaking and so decreased the chances of stoppages, which increase costs.

The **supply of labour** has always been a consideration for firms when deciding where to locate. Labour is a very valuable yet scarce resource. There are many classic examples of firms, and even whole industries, locating in certain areas because of the supply of labour that exists, for example the car industry located initially in the West Midlands because there existed a supply of labour in the motorcycle industry that had similar skills. The textile industry located in Lancashire because of an abundant supply of cheap female labour, among other things.

A more modern influence has seen firms locate in areas where the labour supply has a good reputation for labour relations or where a large supply of unemployed labour exists. This has been shown by the siting of new Japanese car firms in Washington, Tyne and Wear and Burnastone.

The market has also become a very important influence in the location of modern industries. As the UK has moved closer to becoming a **tertiary** based economy, producing services, then the consumers have become the most important factor influencing firms. There is little point siting a bank away from the people and so they are found in the middle of densely populated areas. Many firms that produce perishable foods, such as bread, have to be close to the market because the product does not travel well. It is a feature of many modern towns that bakeries and market gardens are located on the outskirts. All retail establishments need to be close to the market, as do any items that are bulky to transport. Goods that are for export are often found close to a port or airport. The building of the channel tunnel will see more firms locate to the south of London to take advantage of the easy access to France and the rest of Europe. The rail links to the channel tunnel will also attract those firms exporting to Europe.

When an industry is concentrated in an area certain advantages are enjoyed by the firms who are situated there. These advantages are called **economies of concentration,** or **external economies of scale.** These external advantages decrease a firm's costs in the same way that internal economies of scale decrease costs.

To begin with, if an industry is concentrated in a particular area then the labour force tends to acquire the skills that are needed: local educational institutions also provide courses. For example, all further education colleges along the coast have always provided courses on tourism and catering, it is only now that other colleges have begun to provide the same courses. In Northampton, once the centre of the shoe industry, there are many courses on shoe manufacture and technology as well as leather technology. This effectively means that those firms situated within the area of concentration have a ready trained supply of labour. This decreases costs because training is virtually complete and the workers can produce almost immediately.

A further advantage is that the many support services, such as banking, insurance, repair, and so on, gain a specialist knowledge of the industry

ECONOMIC BEHAVIOUR 15

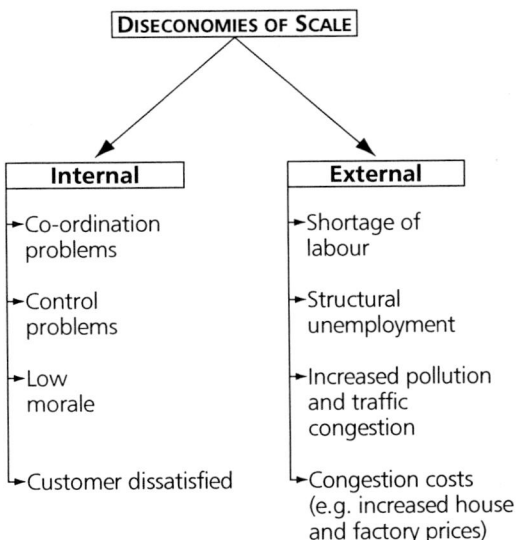

Figure 2.6 Diseconomies of scale

because the majority of their customers will be in that industry. For the firms it means that they will provide specialist services for the same cost but the specialist knowledge will ultimately provide a better and more efficient service.

The concentration of an industry provides many opportunities for enterprising businesses. For example, the waste leather from one shoe factory might not be of much use but if it is from twenty factories then the waste could be useful. For the shoe firms who had to pay to have their waste removed they might now be able to charge someone for it. This will turn cost into a revenue. Service specialists and information services will move to this area all helping to decrease costs. If the firms are close together they might even collaborate on Research and Development, again reducing their individual costs.

Finally, the concentration of an industry in an area often leads to that area gaining a reputation. The Potteries are known for china and Sheffield for cutlery. Firms can gain from this reputation with increased sales and preferential treatment from banks and other financial institutions.

Economies of scale and the forces of location explain why firms make the decisions that they do. However, firms often make the wrong decision or over time situations change. Firms initially increase their size to gain the cost advantages but

ACTIVITY 4

Choose five products and list the most important factors of location for each product. Put these in order of priority.

Using a modern motorway map, plot the major growth industries in the UK. Do you notice any patterns, and if so, why?

Using a map of your local area, plot any major firms or industries. What do you think influenced their location decision?

once a firm begins to grow and goes public it becomes difficult to stop the growth. At this point **diseconomies of scale** can set in. These are the disadvantages of being too large.

A large firm is difficult to co-ordinate. The management do not know the workers and the workers feel as if they are unimportant; this lowers morale and decreases output. Customers are faced with a large bureaucratic structure and also feel as if they are only a number. These problems lead to increased costs and a breakdown in the smooth running of the company.

There are also **external diseconomies of scale** and these occur when an industry becomes too concentrated in an area. An example of this is the City of London. When an over concentration occurs, overcrowding creates a shortage of labour, higher house prices, congestion and pollution which all increase costs. The initial advantages all disappear because the demand for the original location factors becomes greater than the supply thus increasing the price.

✓ Review terms

Economies of scale; technical, financial, management, commercial; risk-bearing; research and development; infrastructure; supply of labour; tertiary; economies of concentration; external economies of scale; diseconomies of scale; external diseconomies of scale.

THE DAILY NEWS

Faminaid update

Faminaid was able to complete the well at Barengo in Southern Ethiopia ahead of schedule. Our last report on the situation there resulted in a great many readers sending donations which gave Faminaid the extra money that allowed them to begin work early.

Paying the water bill

The water problem was solved by sending tankers full of water to the area. This would not have been possible without the money sent by you, our readers. This varied from a cheque for £1,000 from a businessman, who simply said that he could afford it and hoped that it would do the people some good, to 50p from a schoolgirl, who said that it was her week's pocket money, and all that she could afford.

The well is now providing enough drinking water and also allows the crops to be grown.

Unfortunately, the size of the settlement has again fallen, to 74 adults and 30 children, but they are now starting to reorganise their lives. There are those who work in the fields, and others who look after the animals, and yet others who are making clothes and repairing the homes, while three people spend all their time looking after the well, so as to make sure that it will continue to supply the water that is needed to keep everyone alive.

Another charity, ELDC (Education for Less Developed Countries) has sent a teacher, so that the children are at last receiving a basic education.

Dress material

The teacher has been very impressed with the quality and colours of locally-made dress material, and is persuading the villagers to make more than they need, so that it may be sold elsewhere. The money for this could be used to buy better agricultural equipment.

There is also a temporary nurse in the settlement. She is pleased with the improvements in the health of the people; she has been training one of the villagers in first aid so that someone can assist the sick when she leaves next year.

Data questions

Foundation level

1 (a) Why was the well completed earlier than expected?
  (b) How was the water problem solved?
  (c) What is the size of the settlement?
  (d) Who has provided a teacher?
  (e) What else does the teacher want to do?

2 List the different occupations that are mentioned in the text.

3 What are the major changes that have taken place in the settlement?

4 If Barengo could have one more skilled person to live there, who should it be, and why?

Intermediate level

1 Give five important pieces of information from the text relating to the well and the settlement.

2 Explain the meaning of the term 'division of labour' and give four examples from the text.

3 What are the major economic changes that have taken place in the settlement?

4 What problems might the settlement experience in the future?

Higher level

1 Describe the changes that have taken place in the settlement.

2 Explain the meaning of the term 'division of labour' and give examples from the text. What other specialisms might take place in the future in the settlement?

3 Identify the ways in which the settlement is showing evidence of economic development.

4 What could hinder the economic development of the settlement?

Coursework Suggestions

Idea

Different people do different jobs. How is a firm organised?

- Find a firm that will allow you to look round and answer your questions. It needs to be a large firm – or perhaps your school.
- Collect information about the types of jobs that there are.
- Examine the information so that you can explain the system of division of labour in the organisation.
- Show why some of the jobs can easily be split up, whereas others cannot.

Idea

Years ago, the reasons for the location of industry was more obvious than today. However, many firms are still able to explain their locations. Why are firms where they are?

- Go to a firm that will help you, and ask the reasons for its location.
- Compare the reasons with those that you have been taught.
- Would there be greater economies if the firm was situated elsewhere?

Idea

Firms often specialise in a small range of products. Why is this?

- What is made in the area where you live?
- If you live in an agricultural area, farming is the major industry, but there are a lot of firms providing goods and services to the farming industry.
- Finance is at the centre of the City of London, so there are many firms locally providing equipment and support for the finance industry.

Look at your own area, and decide the main industry.

- Discover the other firms and industries that support the main industry.
- Explain how they are connected.
- Show how they have come to depend on one another.

2.3 NATIONAL BEHAVIOUR

The distribution of **income** and **wealth** both within the UK and the rest of the world greatly influences the level and the pattern of trade internationally.

Income

In the UK the way in which income is distributed determines not only the amount of goods produced but also the type of goods produced.

People on low incomes tend to spend all of their income, and often more than they have, on **necessities**, basic foods and goods required for living. As income rises then **consumption**, the purchase of goods and services, moves away from the basic goods, necessities and **inferior goods**, to luxury items such as cars, personal computers and high quality foods such as champagne and caviar. As incomes rise still further then a greater proportion of income is saved and consumption decreases as a proportion of total income, although the actual amount spent remains about the same.

Figure 2.7 shows the result of a survey by the Department of Social Security which looks at individual's incomes within the UK. The figures represent **net disposable income** before the costs of housing, such as mortgages and rent, have been deducted. Individual's incomes can also be given as net disposable income after the cost of housing has been deducted, as in Figure 2.8.

If the range of income is found, via the family expenditure survey, then this can be divided into groups representing high income earners, low income earners and a range in between. In the case of Figure 2.7 the income range has been split into fifths, known as quintile groups; the five categories are the bottom fifth, the lower fifth, the middle fifth, the upper fifth and the top fifth. The top fifth would be those people whose income is within the top fifth of the income range. The bottom fifth is those people whose income falls within the bottom fifth of the income range.

The next stage in this process is to calculate how much of the total disposable income available in the UK is received by each of the five categories listed.

Close investigation of Figure 2.7 shows that the top fifth of income earners actually receive 41% of all the disposable income obtained in the UK. Put a slightly different way the top 20% receive almost 50% of all the disposable income available. This is in contrast to the bottom 20% who receive only 7% of all the disposable income available.

It can be seen that as we move from the bottom fifth to the top fifth the share of disposable income received by each group increases:

- The bottom fifth receive 7%.
- The lower fifth receive 12% which is 70% more than the bottom group.

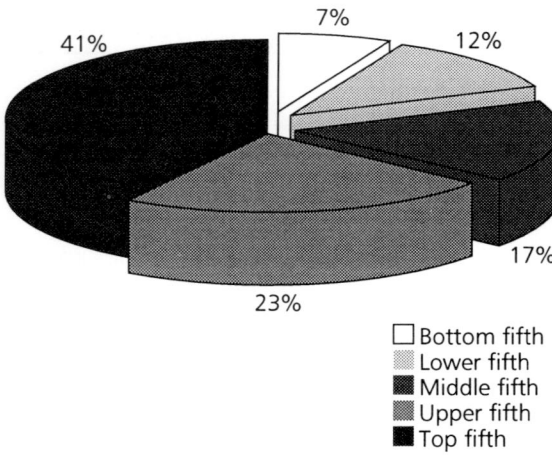

Figure 2.7 Income distribution UK 1991 – before housing costs

- The middle fifth receive 17% of the disposable income available which is 42% more than the lower fifth.
- The upper fifth receive 23% of the disposable income available and this is 35% more than the middle fifth.

Contrasting levels of wealth and lifestyle

ECONOMIC BEHAVIOUR

- The top fifth receive 41% of the disposable income, a massive 78% more than the upper group.

Sixty four per cent of all disposable income is therefore received by the top 40% of the income earners. If this is extended to the top three groups then they receive 81% of all the disposable income available.

The picture in Figure 2.8 is not very different, the only change is that the top fifth now receive an extra 1%, 42% instead of 41%, and the bottom group receive 1% less, 6% instead of 7%, of the disposable income available. The other groups remain unchanged, exactly as in Figure 2.7.

The distribution of income is important as previously mentioned, because it determines the quantity and type of goods produced as well as such things as the level of savings. From the information produced in Figures 2.7 and 2.8 it can be seen that the top fifth of income earners have a far greater influence on the type and quantity of goods produced and therefore have more economic power. These figures do not show the impact of taxes and benefits, as disposable income is being compared. It is also significant that housing costs have very little influence except for the top and bottom groups.

An important point to remember is that the bottom fifth, the lowest income group, have the least economic power.

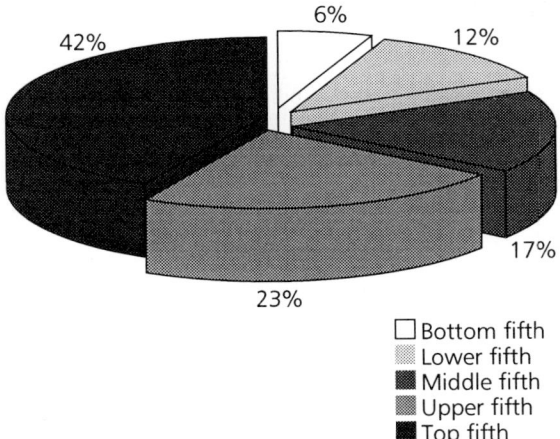

Figure 2.8 Income distribution UK 1991 – after housing costs

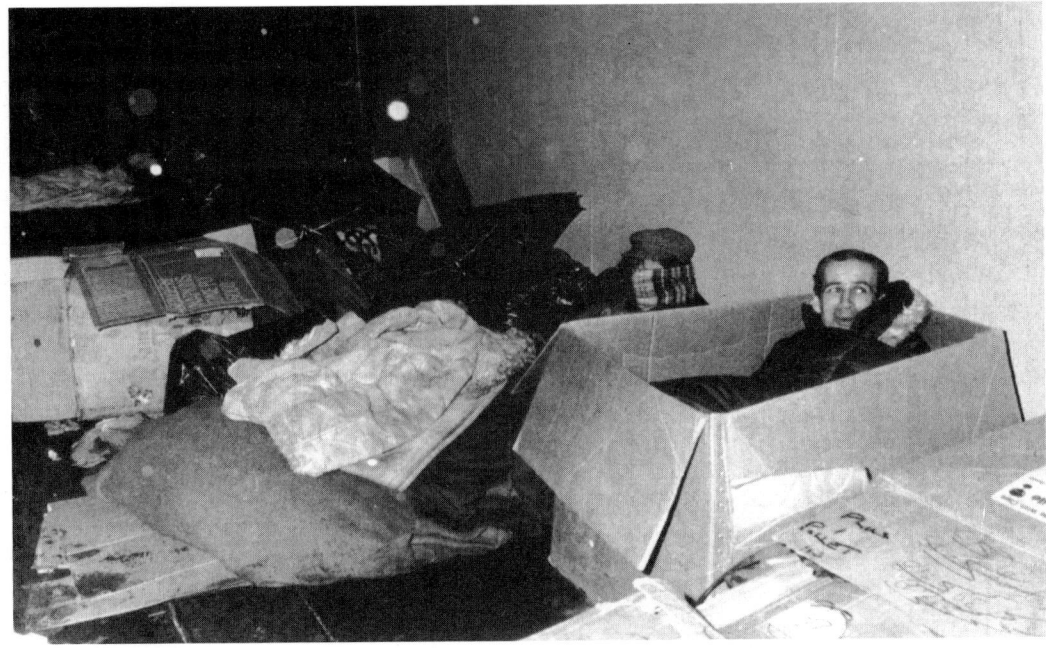

Contrasting levels of wealth and lifestyle

Wealth

The distribution of wealth within the UK is equally significant. Wealth is measured in terms of marketable wealth, that is the value of assets owned that could be sold, examples being property, life assurance, stocks, shares, unit trusts, pensions, etc. Figure 2.9 shows clearly that the most wealthy 1% own 18% of the nation's total wealth:

- The most wealthy 10% of the population own 50% of the nation's total wealth.
- The most wealthy 25% of the population own 71% of the nation's wealth.
- The most wealthy 50% own 92% of the country's wealth.

The significance of the final statement is that the remaining 50% of the population have only 8% of the entire wealth of the country between them. This shows that the distribution of wealth is even more unequal than the distribution of income.

The second part of Figure 2.9 shows the marketable wealth less the value of their property, dwellings. This shows an even more unequal distribution of wealth. Using this measurement, 50% of the nation's wealth is owned by the wealthiest 5% of the population, instead of the wealthiest 10% as previously stated. The top category remains the same with the wealthiest 50% of the population owning 92% of the nation's wealth, leaving 8% of the wealth for the remaining 50% of the people.

Marketable wealth	per cent
Most wealthy 1%	18
Most wealthy 5%	37
Most wealthy 10%	50
Most wealthy 25%	71
Most wealthy 50%	92
Marketable wealth less dwellings	**per cent**
Most wealthy 1%	28
Most wealthy 5%	50
Most wealthy 10%	63
Most wealthy 25%	79
Most wealthy 50%	92

Figure 2.9 Marketable wealth UK 1991 (percentage of wealth owned by persons over 18)

Once again this distribution has a real effect on the economy: wealth is economic power (see chapter 4.2, p.70). It signifies control over the factors of production and with it the means of production. Figures 2.7, 2.8 and 2.9 clearly show that within the UK income and wealth are not evenly distributed.

International income and wealth

The distribution of income and wealth around the world is also very uneven. On an international scale there are basically three categories of country: the developed nations, generally the western industrialised world, who are the richest in terms of income and wealth, the developing nations and the less developed nations (LDCs). The LDCs are often wealthy in terms of natural resources, but are unable to exploit this wealth and so have a very low income. The LDCs also tend to concentrate upon the production of primary products which poses another problem. The developed world has managed to produce many synthetic substitutes for natural materials and the price of primary products is very volatile unlike the manufactured goods of the developed nations.

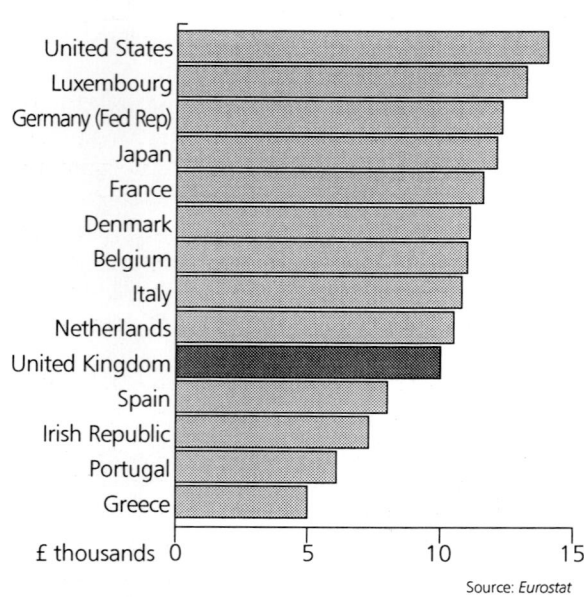

Figure 2.10 Gross domestic product per head for the more developed countries of the world

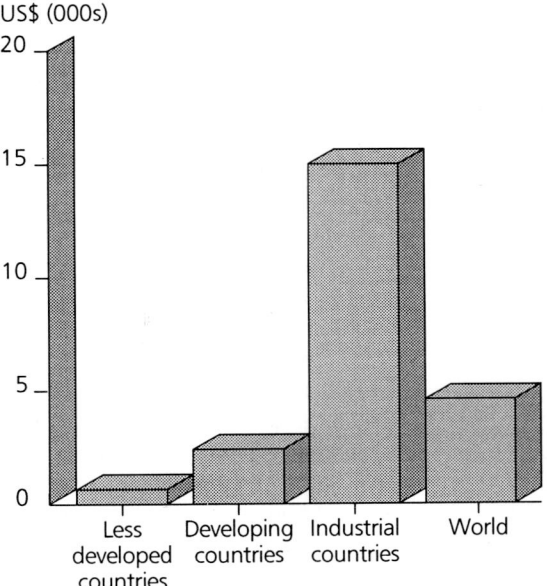

Figure 2.11 Gross domestic product per head – international comparison

This further depresses the income of the LDCs. Figure 2.10 shows the **Gross Domestic Product** (GDP) per head of the population for the more developed nations of the world. Even within this developed sector the GDP per head is wildly different. The USA is at one extreme with a GDP/head of nearly £15,000, and Greece is at the other extreme with a GDP/head of £5,000.

Figure 2.11 also gives a comparison of GDP/head for LDCs, developing nations and industrial, or developed, nations. A world figure for GDP/head, which is an average of all nations, provides a further comparison for the different groups of countries. In 1991 the average GDP/head for the LDCs was only US$719 but in the industrial nations the figure was US$15,043, both compared to a world average of US$4,662.

This means that the world average is US$3,903 greater than the LDC average, 542% more. The industrial countries' average is US$10,421 more than the world average, 225% more. The difference between the rich industrial nations and the LDCs is US$14,324 per head of the population.

The GDP of a nation includes items such as **gross domestic fixed capital formation.** Fixed capital includes machines and factories that aid production and increase output and income in the future. The wealth of a nation depends not only on the natural resources it possesses but also on the capital, both fixed and social, that exists. If the GDP/head is low then it is likely that GDP itself is relatively low and so the production of capital is merely to replace what is worn out. Without new capital it is unlikely that the wealth of these nations will increase. Thus the wealth of a nation and its GDP per head produce similar patterns.

It can clearly be seen that, just as in the case of the UK, the wealth and income between nations is very unevenly distributed.

ACTIVITY

Find the regional distribution of income in the UK and place this on a map. (Average weekly income would be the most appropriate.)

Find the sources of household income for the latest period available and present these in an appropriate manner.

Using the most recent figures available present the composition of 'net wealth' in a visual format for one year. Compare this with a previous year.

The pattern of UK trade

Trade between the UK and the rest of the world has developed over hundreds of years. An important factor is the state of the UK economy and the distribution of income and wealth within it. A further factor is the development of other countries and the state of their economy. However, there is much more to international trade than this.

There are many reasons why countries trade with one another. Resources are unevenly distributed around the world. So, if a country requires a resource such as oil that it does not possess then it must trade for it with the resources it does have. Climatic conditions around the world are very different, so some countries are unable to grow or produce certain products and so must trade for them. A shortage of skills or lack of technical expertise also produces variations in what countries are

22 GCSE ECONOMICS

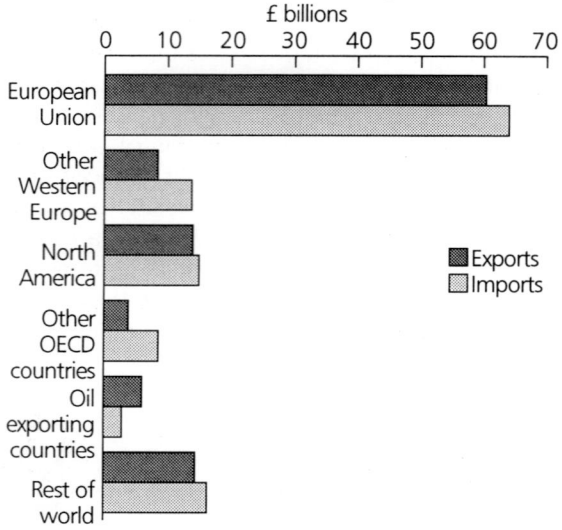

Figure 2.12 The origins of UK trade 1992

able to produce. It is also a fact that trading with another country improves relations between those countries, so politics is a strong motive for trade.

When a country trades it obtains a greater variety of goods and services than it would be able to produce itself; this improves the **standard of living** of the people within the country. Possibly the single greatest reason for trade is provided by the theory of **comparative advantage** (see section 3.6 – page 56). Briefly explained, the theory states that if countries specialise in producing that good or service at which they are most efficient, and trade freely, then every country will benefit. The world output of goods and services will increase.

Figure 2.12 shows that the majority of trade undertaken by the UK is with the European Union (formerly the EC). The total value of all exports and imports outside of the EU do not amount to the total trade with the EU. The main reason for this is that the EU is a **customs union,** set up to encourage and increase free trade between its members. If free trade exists then the theory of comparative advantage works. Competition between member countries increases and the prices of goods should decrease. The existence of a free trade area, closer relationships with other member countries and the movement towards a **Single European Market** all explain why the UK trades so much with the other members of the EU.

For the other areas trade is more modest. The links between the UK and North America are historical and the North American continent has an abundance of raw materials. The USA is also the most developed of all the nations and so its production of manufactured goods has always been high. Trade with the oil exporting countries is low

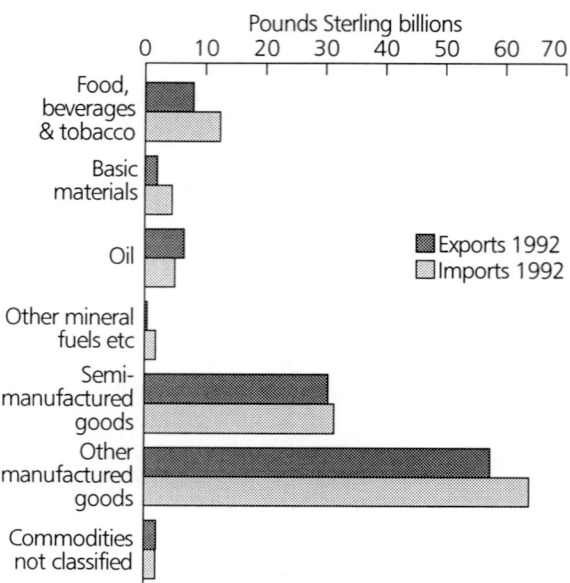

Figure 2.13 UK commodity trading – 1992

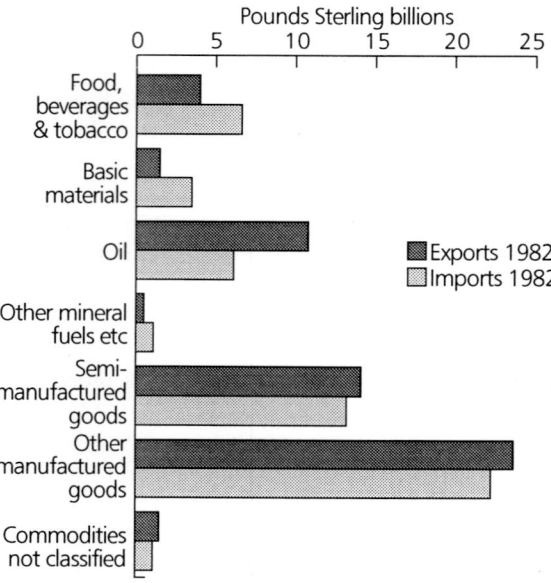

UK commodity trading – 1982

but in the 1960s and early 1970s it was high. Then we needed oil and had none of our own. Now we have North Sea oil and need little from elsewhere.

Trade with the rest of the world reflects the fact that the UK has very few raw materials, oil and coal being the exceptions. It is also a fact that as the UK becomes more of a tertiary based economy our need for imported manufactured goods has increased and these are increasingly being produced by the developing nations.

Examining the pattern of UK trade by commodity reveals a very clear picture. In Figure 2.13 the UK's imports for all commodities, except oil and the unclassified grouping, exceed its exports for 1992. However, if this is compared with the same commodity groupings for 1982 it can be seen that imports only exceeded exports in three out of the seven categories; these being food, beverages and tobacco, basic materials, other mineral fuels, etc.

This shows that the groupings of semi-manufactured goods and finished manufactured goods have actually changed between 1982 and 1992. In 1982 exports of semi-manufactured goods totalled £13,980m and imports £13,143m giving a surplus of £837m. For finished manufactured goods exports totalled £23,334m and imports were £22,077m, a surplus of £1,257m. In 1992 semi-manufactured goods had a deficit of £803m with finished manufactured goods becoming a deficit of £6,547. This shows a change of £1,640m for semi-manufactured goods and a change of £7,804m for finished manufactured goods.

	1982	1983	1984	1985	1986	1987	1988	1989	1990	1991	1992
Exports											
Food, beverages, tobacco (HCIV)	3940	4230	4677	4937	5450	5523	5450	6455	6995	7654	8673
Basic materials (CGJX)	1387	1653	2069	2199	2112	2246	2124	2343	2241	2008	1946
Oil (BOPX)	10671	12486	14834	16115	8189	8423	5971	5873	7486	6757	6566
Other mineral fuels and lubricants (HDVE)	551	602	457	662	464	303	242	256	324	353	304
Semi-manufactured goods (HCJK)	13980	15864	18134	19921	20818	22380	23984	26689	28795	29195	30354
Finished manufactured goods (HBTG)	23334	24284	28421	32319	33618	38117	40620	48241	53613	55604	57144
Commodities and transactions not classified according to kind (BOPF)	1468	1581	1673	1838	1976	2161	1955	2297	2264	1842	2060
Total (CGJP)	55331	60700	70265	77991	72627	79153	80346	92154	101718	103413	107047
Imports											
Food, beverages, tobacco (HCJB)	6598	7259	8297	8660	9436	9553	9988	10765	11606	11604	12609
Basic materials (HCNN)	3468	4251	50574	5041	4636	5223	5468	5934	5526	4588	4613
Oil (BPAX)	6033	5514	7901	8014	4119	4262	3221	4616	5964	5549	5079
Other mineral fuels and lubricants (HDVN)	1081	1274	2029	2257	1877	1561	1470	1482	1471	1613	1555
Semi-manufactured goods (HBTK)	13143	16003	18696	20338	21761	24330	28031	31036	31555	30391	31157
Finished manufactured goods (HCJB)	22077	26878	32386	35667	38825	44460	51874	61159	62497	58035	63691
Commodities and transactions not classified according to kind (BPAF)	1021	1058	1218	1359	1532	1346	1774	1845	1908	1917	1749
Total (CGGL)	53421	62237	75601	81336	82186	90735	101826	116837	120527	113697	120453
Visible balance											
Food, beverages, tobacco (HBXU)	−2658	−3029	−3620	−3723	−3986	−4030	−4538	−4310	−4611	−3950	−3936
Basic materials (HBUO)	−2081	−2598	−3005	−2842	−2524	−2977	−3344	−3591	−3285	−2580	−2667
Oil (HDSD)	4638	6972	6933	8101	4070	4161	2750	1257	1522	1208	1487
Other mineral fuels and lubricants (HDVX)	−530	−672	−1572	−1595	−1413	−1258	−1228	−1226	−1147	−1260	−1251
Semi-manufactured goods (HCHB)	837	−139	−562	−417	−943	−1950	−4047	−4347	−2760	−1196	−803
Finished manufactured goods (HDIU)	1257	−2594	−3965	−3348	−5207	−6343	−11254	−12918	−8884	−2431	−6547
Commodities and transactions not classified according to kind (HCLW)	447	523	455	479	444	815	181	452	356	−75	311
Total (HCHL)	1911	−1537	−5336	−3345	−9559	−11582	−21480	−24683	−18809	−10284	−13406

Figure 2.14 Trade on a balance of payments basis: commodity analysis, UK. (In £millions)

In this ten year period the UK has moved from being a country that sold more manufactured goods than it bought, to a country that now purchases more manufactured goods than it sells. This indicates that the UK is no longer competitive in the production and sale of manufactured and semi-manufactured goods. The UK has lost its comparative advantage in these areas; it can no longer produce them more cheaply than other countries. In fact, the only category in which the UK still have a comparative advantage is in the production of oil, and this is only because very few countries actually possess oil within their borders.

Whilst the UK has lost its comparative advantage in the production of finished manufactured and semi-manufactured goods another country must have gained a comparative advantage in these categories. They can now produce them more efficiently than the UK and so countries are buying from them instead of the UK.

Government control of trade

When countries find themselves in the position where their imports are greater than their exports they have a problem. Exports earn income for a country but imports are expenditure. If imports are greater than exports this means that a country is spending more than it earns and just as any individual a country cannot do this. They must try to do something about the situation. One option is to try to increase exports and the other option is to decrease imports.

Trying to increase exports is very difficult: it is impossible for one country to force another one to buy its goods. The best that can be done is to try to persuade other countries that your exports are the best. This is done by attending trade fairs, getting MPs and other prominent people to promote the products of your country.

Dealing with imports is easier: there are a number of different policies to decrease or stop imports being purchased.

To begin with a government can impose a **tariff** on all imports. A tariff is an import tax which has to be paid by the importer. The effect is to increase the price of the import which should decrease the quantity demanded and so decrease the amount imported. The tariff can be a set amount or a percentage of the value of the good.

An alternative measure is to impose a **quota.** A government using a quota system would physically restrict the number of goods allowed into the country. The decrease in supply would lead to an increase in price but no matter what price people were prepared to pay there would be a limited number of imported goods available.

The problem with both of these methods is that other countries may retaliate. One country's imports are another country's exports and so by

Border controls: HM Customs' check points at the Channel Tunnel

reducing your imports you are decreasing another country's income and they might then decide not to buy your goods. In this situation nobody wins.

Another policy that can be used by a government is to impose **exchange controls.** This is when the government limits the amount of foreign currency that can be purchased. When countries sell their goods (exports) they want to be paid in their own currency. Therefore, if you wish to buy imports you have to buy the foreign currency first before you can purchase the goods. If you cannot buy the currency, you cannot purchase the goods.

This method is not particularly effective in a modern world. Currency can be moved around the world very easily and quickly, companies have accounts in foreign banks, and currencies such as the US Dollar are accepted by almost everyone as payment for goods and services.

An alternative policy is for the government to **subsidise** the production of all home produced goods that compete against imports. This should make the home goods cheaper than the imports and so the demand for imports should decrease.

This policy is very expensive and does not guarantee that people will not buy the imports. The imports might be of better quality or have a better reputation. The home producers might become more inefficient because part of their costs are being paid for and not sell any more goods.

The fear of retaliation and the problems associated with all of these policies plus the movement towards greater free trade, supported by the General Agreement on Tariffs and Trade (GATT), (see page 117), has led many countries to look for other less expensive and less obvious policies that are effective. This has produced a group of policies known as **non-tariff barriers.** This involves the country in question using its rules, regulations and laws to stop the import of goods.

The need for all imported goods to be checked thoroughly slows down the import process considerably. Other examples include border checks with too few border guards that take days instead of hours. The UK, when threatened by the import of EC milk, tested the milk and declared that it contained too much water. The UK's health and safety laws stated the amount of water permitted per litre of milk and this exceeded the limit. Technically, as far as the UK was concerned, it was water and so we refused to import it.

The strength of this type of policy is that it is not unfair. You cannot ask a country to change its laws to suit your imports; that would be unreasonable. The best that you can do is obey their laws and change your product to meet them.

The expansion of free trade areas and customs unions, such as the European Union, has made all these policies redundant. Trade restrictions between members are not permitted and in the EU we are slowly moving towards a single European market.

A final method of controlling imports and increasing exports is to alter the exchange rate. This is discussed in more detail in section 4.7 (page 89). Briefly stated, if the value of a country's currency decreases, or is devalued, then its exports become cheaper. At the same time imports into the country become more expensive. This combined effect should increase exports and decrease imports, assuming that the elasticity of demand is favourable.

ACTIVITY 6

At home choose 12 household items and check where they were made. How many were produced in the UK? Does this tell you anything?

What non-tariff barriers exist between the UK and the rest of Europe if we export electrical goods to Europe?

With which European country do we do the most trade, both exports and imports? What was the amount of trade, in pounds, with this country last year? Why do you think this is so?

✓ Review terms

Income; wealth; necessities; consumption; inferior goods; net disposable income; gross domestic product; gross domestic fixed capital formation; standard of living; comparative advantage; customs union; single European market; tariff; quota; exchange controls; subsidies; non-tariff barrier.

THE DAILY NEWS

Barengo

Our series of reports on the drought in the Southern Ethiopian settlement of Barengo, the sinking of the well, and the development of a small textile industry produced a massive response at the time.

Now, one year on, we decided to send a reporter to Barengo to see for himself how the people are faring. As you will see from his report in the supplement, it seems that everyone there appears happy and well-fed. Faminaid's well is producing enough water to allow crops to grow, and the farmers in the community are now producing enough food for everyone.

Those people who are specialising in production of the locally-made textiles are earning enough money to buy all the food that they need.

As a result, families in Barengo now clamour to explain how much better off they are than other people in the region.

A good life

That does not mean that they are rich by western standards. There are no televisions, no cinemas, no pubs or restaurants. No-one owns a car, or even a bicycle, but everyone has somewhere to live, a job, and enough to eat, while the children receive an education, and there is some medical help available. The entire community feels it is enjoying a good life, which can improve even further if they continue to work hard.

Data questions

Foundation level

1 **(a)** Give two reasons why the inhabitants of Barengo believe that they are wealthy.
   (b) List three items which we in the western world enjoy that are not available in Barengo.

2 Explain what you understand by the term 'wealthy'.

3 Using information in the text and your own knowledge, why do you think that people such as those in Barengo believe that they are wealthy, when they are not rich by western standards?

4 Give five pieces of information that you could use to decide how wealthy people are and explain how you would use the information.

Intermediate level

1 From the text, list the factors that make Barengans feel that they are wealthy.

2 Explain the meaning of the term 'wealth'.

3 Why would inhabitants of less well-developed countries such as Barengo feel that they are wealthy when, by western standards, they could be considered poor?

4 What factors should be taken into consideration when discussing a person's wealth?

Higher level

1 On what evidence have Barengans assessed their wealth?

2 Define the term 'wealth'.

3 Why are some countries wealthier than others?

4 What are the problems associated with discussing wealth simply in money terms? What other factors should be considered?

Coursework Suggestions

Idea

Find out the income distribution of the country, and compare it to the area in which you live, so that you can estimate how typical your area is to the country as a whole.

The local and national information is available in government publications, and then you can describe the socio-economic area in which you live, and draw comparisons to the national picture.

Warning

It would be really interesting to compare Britain with another country in terms of wealth, happiness, etc., but it would be very difficult to find the information for another country.

Avoid starting on a piece of work like this unless you know that you can obtain the information quickly and with little difficulty. Unfortunately, it is most unlikely that you can, so do be careful. It is easy to think of topics that would be great fun to do, but all too often it causes you problems when you find that you cannot obtain the data that you need to finish the work properly.

Idea

People earn different amounts of money, and spend it in different ways. How much you earn depends on the type of job you have; it may also depend on your age.

How you spend your money can depend on your age, whether or not you are married, and if you have a family.

The total of your possessions is your wealth.

- Select a group of people who have different wages, and are of a variety of ages, etc., and find out their wealth.
- At the same time, see how content they are with their lives – do they want a better car, bigger house, more holidays, etc.?
- Analyse the results, to see if wealth brings happiness.

3

Economic Theory

The concepts, theories and methods needed to analyse issues from an economic perspective

3.1 THE PRICE MECHANISM AND THE MARKET • 3.2 ELASTICITY
3.3 COSTS, REVENUES AND PROFIT • 3.4 CIRCULAR FLOW OF INCOME
3.5 MONETARY AND FISCAL POLICY • 3.6 THE GAINS FROM TRADE
3.7 THE PROBLEMS OF TRADE

This section should enable students to understand:
- the workings of the market and the importance of elasticity
- the significance of the circular flow of income
- what policy weapons are available to the government and how they work
- the importance of trade and the problems that it creates.

3.1 THE PRICE MECHANISM AND THE MARKET

Demand

Individuals have different wants and needs and if they are to be satisfied a variety of goods and services must be produced. The problem is which goods and services? How do the producers know which items to provide? What is required is a method of giving the producers the information they need, what to produce, how many and at what price.

There are people who want goods but are unable to purchase them. This is of no use to a producer. There are also those people who are able to purchase a good or service but have no desire to do so. They are also of no use to a producer of goods and services.

What a producer needs is people who wish to buy and have the money to buy his good, or service. This is known as **effective demand**:

- Effective demand exists when people are *willing* and *able* to purchase a good or service.

If people do not have the ability to purchase, as well as the willingness, then their wants and needs are little more than a dream and of no practical use to producers. It is their desire as well as their ability that provides the producer with the right information to produce the goods and services that people want and can afford to buy.

People demanding goods and services act as a sophisticated information system; they can register what type of goods and services they require, in what quantities and at what prices. If any of these preferences change then they alter their demand to change the signals that are being given.

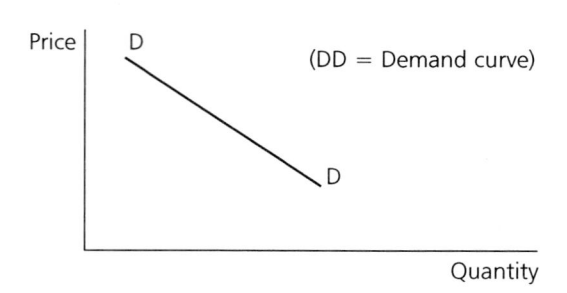

Figure 3.1 The demand curve
(DD = Demand curve)

The demand that a person has for a particular good or service can be represented graphically. If a person demands a set quantity of a good, for example bottles of milk, then, if the price of that good increases, they will buy less. The opposite is also true that if the price of that good decreases they will buy more. This shows a relationship between price and quantity demanded for a particular good.

Figure 3.1 shows the relationship between price and quantity and this is called an **individual demand curve**:

- A **demand curve** shows the *quantity* of a good or service *demanded* by an individual at each and every price during a specified time period

The convention is that price is plotted on the vertical axis and quantity along the horizontal axis. The individual curve usually slopes down from left to right. Price and quantity are said to be inversely related; that means as price increases the quantity demanded decreases and as price decreases then the quantity demanded increases.

If individual demand curves are added together (aggregated) for the same good or service they form a **market demand curve**. The market demand curve is also usually downward sloping from left to right, even though some individuals may have different shaped demand curves. Thus the market demand curve looks exactly like the individual demand curve shown in Figure 3.1.

There are exceptions to this rule. In special circumstances the demand curve can be horizontal, vertical or sloping up from left to right. The vertical and horizontal demand curves are explained in section 3.2 (page 38), but the backward sloping demand curve, known as the **perverse demand curve**, occurs in special situations where the quantity demanded increases as price increases. This can be found with 'snob value' goods such as jewellery, furs and cars such as Rolls Royces. The more expensive they are the more they are demanded because they are a statement of your wealth. The other situation is rising share prices. As share prices go up the more they are demanded because purchasers believe that this company must be doing well.

Changes in the quantity demanded

The normal shaped demand curve can produce a number of different situations. It is possible to move along the demand curve or the whole demand curve can move. A movement along the demand curve is caused by a change in price. This is known as a change in the quantity demanded. Figure 3.2 shows the effect of the price changing from P_0 to P_1; this creates a **change in the quantity demanded,** decreasing from Q_0 to Q_1. The movement along the demand curve is from point 'a' to point 'b': this can only happen when the price of the good or service changes. This creates the general rule that '*changes* in the *price* of a good create a *change* in the *quantity* demanded, which is a movement along the demand curve'.

The movement along the curve from point 'a' to point 'b' creates a decrease in the quantity demanded, this is known as a **contraction in demand.** A movement from point 'b' to point 'a' would create an increase in the quantity demanded, described as an **extension in demand** or an expansion of demand.

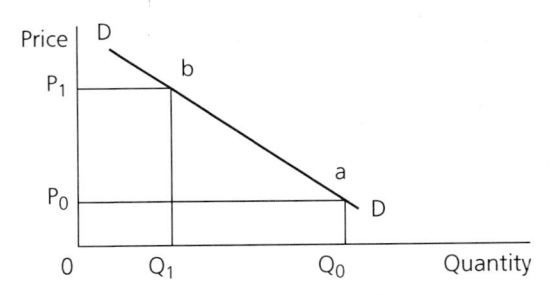

Figure 3.2 Extension and contraction of demand

Changes of demand

When the whole demand curve moves it means that at each and every price people are demanding more or less of the good in question; this must be due to influences other than price. A major factor that influences demand is **income.** If an individual's income increases then they can afford more goods and services, assuming that the prices of these goods and services remain unchanged. Thus at each and every price the quantity they demanded would increase. This would be an increase in demand shown by a movement of the whole curve to the right, as in Figure 3.3.

If income were to decrease then an individual would decrease his or her demand for a good or service at each and every price. This in turn would move the whole curve to the left, as in Figure 3.3.

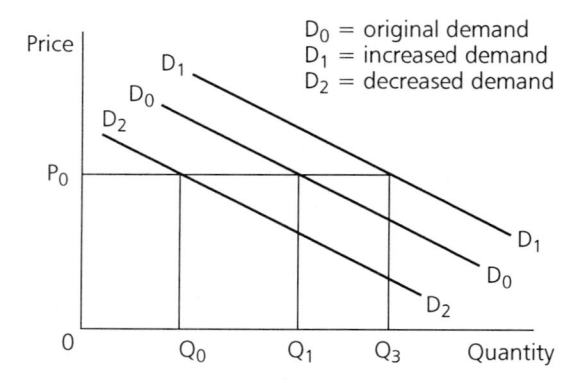

Figure 3.3 Changes in demand

A movement of the whole curve to the **right** is an **increase in demand**. A movement of the whole curve to the **left** is a **decrease in demand**.

Another factor that influences demand is changes in **taste** and **fashion**. When goods become fashionable people wish to buy more. The demand for these goods increases and the curve moves to the right.

The **season** or **climate** can increase or decrease demand. In the summer the demand for sun cream increases, although the price is the same throughout the year. At the same time the demand for umbrellas and wellingtons decreases but, once again, not because of a change in price. Other examples of seasonal products include Christmas trimmings and lights and turkey, Easter eggs, and beach wear. All of these experience an increase in demand at certain times of the year, people have a need for them and so demand increases.

A situation that links together Figure 3.2 and Figure 3.3 is the **change in price of a substitute**. Substitutes are goods that are an acceptable replacement for one another. For example, chicken and beef are substitutes for each other as are Ford and Rover cars.

If the price of holidays abroad increases the quantity demanded would decrease. This is shown in Figure 3.2 by a movement from point 'a' to point 'b'. The people that stop buying holidays abroad (quantity Q_0 to Q_1) would then buy the substitute: holidays in the UK. The demand for UK holidays would therefore increase and the whole curve would move to the right, as in Figure 3.3. Similarly if the price of butter decreased then more people would buy butter and the demand for margarine would decrease, the curve moving to the left. The change in the price of one good creates a transfer of demand for another product, an acceptable substitute. This is known as the **income and substitution effect**.

Some goods are **complementary**, for example cars and petrol. Cars will not run without petrol and petrol itself has very few uses except to drive a car. If the price of cars were to increase the quantity demanded would decrease. If less cars were purchased then the demand for petrol would decrease and the demand curve would move to the left.

Advertising is a deliberate attempt by producers to move the demand curve to the right. They try to influence people by convincing them of the value and special qualities of their good, hoping they will buy more. Bad publicity has the opposite effect, moving the demand curve to the left. A good example is the press coverage on 'mad cow disease' which decreased the demand for beef.

Expectations of price changes create a change in demand. If it is known that the price of coffee is to rise next month because of a shortage of coffee beans then people will go out and buy

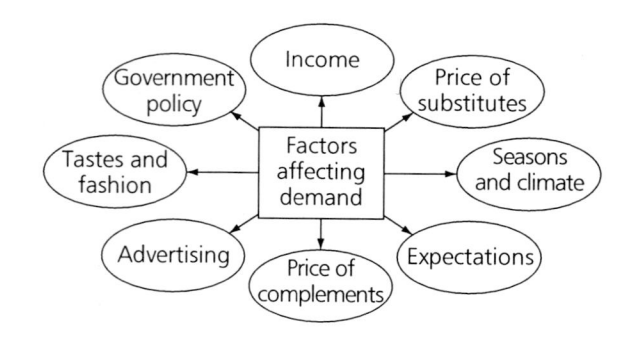

Figure 3.4 Factors affecting demand

The price mechanism in action

more coffee now before the shortage occurs. This will increase demand even though it is only temporary.

Finally **government policy** can change demand. If the government decided to ban smoking for everyone under 25 the demand for cigarettes would decrease. The policy that all new cars must be fitted with catalytic converters has increased the demand for them. The effect can also be indirect; a few years ago the government decreased the tax on new cars which increased the quantity purchased. The indirect effect was to increase the demand for petrol, a complementary good.

Supply

Demand is of little use unless someone is prepared to produce the goods and services that people are willing and able to buy. The fact that people are prepared to produce goods and services creates a **supply**. Supply only exists if people want to produce the goods and services and are able to do so:

- **Supply** exists when *producers* are *willing* and *able to offer* goods and services for sale.

As with demand it is important that producers are willing and able to supply. Without both elements supply will not exist.

The supply of goods and services provided by any one individual, or single firm, can be represented graphically. A firm offers goods and services for sale because they believe that they will make a profit from the transaction. The higher the price paid for an item the more profit will be made and the more items firms are willing to supply. This produces the opposite relationship to that of demand, as the price increases the quantity offered for sale by the producers also increases.

Once again the convention is that quantity is plotted on the horizontal axis and the price is on the vertical axis therefore the supply curve is upward sloping from left to right:

- A *supply curve* shows the quantity of a good or service offered for sale at each and every price during a specified period of time.

In this case price and quantity are positively related: as price increases so does the quantity supplied.

If individual supply curves are added together a **market supply curve** can be produced. This is the same shape as the individual supply curve, Figure 3.5, with a few exceptions which are discussed in section 3.2 (page 38). The major difference is that the quantities along the horizontal axis are much greater.

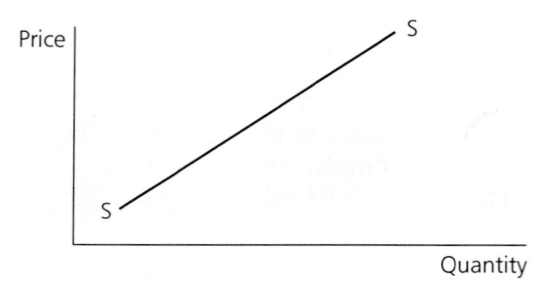

Figure 3.5 The supply curve

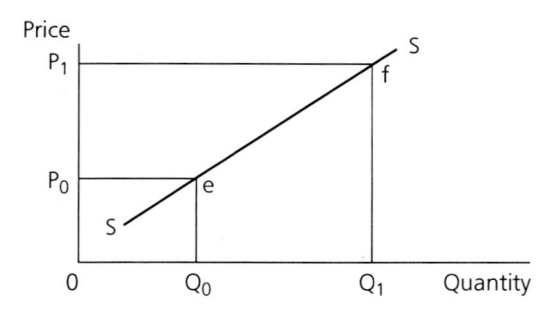

Changes in the quantity supplied

When price changes it causes a movement along the supply curve, as with demand in Figure 3.2 (page 29).This is known as a **change in the quantity supplied**. Figure 3.6 shows the effect of price moving from P_0 to P_1, this creates a change in the quantity supplied, increasing from Q_0 to Q_1. The movement along the supply curve is from point 'e' to point 'f', which can only happen when the price of the good or service changes. This creates a general rule for supply:

- *Changes in the price* of a good or service *create a change in the quantity* supplied, which is a movement along the supply curve.

Movement from point 'e' to point 'f' is an **extension** or **expansion of supply** (Q_0 to Q_1). A decrease in price from P_1 to P_0 would create movement along the supply curve from point 'f' to point 'e', this would be a **contraction of supply** (Q_1 to Q_0).

Figure 3.6 Changes in the quantity supplied

Changes in supply

Whilst changes in price create a movement along the supply curve there are factors that move the whole supply curve, either to the left (a decrease in supply) or to the right (an increase in supply). The supply curve is heavily influenced by a firm's ability to produce the item concerned and the costs of production. Thus changes in either of these will move the whole supply curve.

The **cost of labour** (wages) is possibly the biggest cost faced by any producer. If wages increase the costs of production increase which moves the whole supply curve to the left (an upward shift), which shows a decrease in supply. The same would happen if the **cost of raw materials** and **equipment** also increased. If any of the costs of production decreased, whilst the rest remained the same, then the whole curve would move to the right producing an increase in supply at the set price.

Changes in technology, such as new inventions or new methods of production, usually allow producers to make an item more cheaply or at a faster speed. The result is to increase the supply of the good at the present price, moving the curve to the right.

The **weather** has a special influence on the supply of agricultural products. Good weather usually means an increased supply of goods, because of the right growing conditions, whereas poor weather often affects the growing season and so decreases the supply.

Natural disasters, such as earthquakes, floods and fires, all have an adverse effect on the supply of goods and usually move the curve to the left, due to a decreased supply.

ECONOMIC THEORY

Taxes on production, such as VAT (value added tax), or **government subsidies** either decrease or increase the costs of production and in turn affect the supply of a product. VAT is added to the cost of production and so increases the costs of production. This decreases supply, moving the curve to the left. A government subsidy is used to help output by decreasing the cost of production. If the cost of production decreases then output will increase, moving the curve to the right.

Strikes and **inefficient management** will decrease output, or make the firm less productive which will increase the cost of production. The result in both of these cases is that the supply curve will move to the left, a decrease in supply.

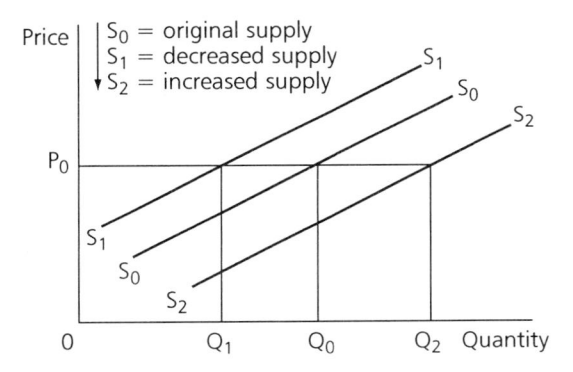

Figure 3.7 Changes in supply

The market

Demand for a product without supply or the supply of a product without demand produces nothing. Both elements need to exist at the same time. It is only when demand and supply exist for the same product that a market is formed:

- a market exists whenever *buyers* and *sellers* come into *contact* with each other

This can be a physical contact, over the telephone, via a fax or by using the pages of a local newspaper, where sellers advertise their goods and buyers scan the pages to find the product that they wish to buy.

Buyers create a demand, and sellers create a supply. A market exists when demand and supply interact. This interaction creates an **equilibrium** which in turn creates a **market price**. Figure 3.8

ACTIVITY 1

Choose a good you normally buy. Write down its price and the quantity you buy. Imagine the price increases in multiples of 20p. Write down how many you will buy at each price. Imagine that the price decreases in multiples of 20p, down to zero. Write down how many you will buy at each price. Plot each price and quantity and join the points together.

Ask you friends to do the same exercise for the same good. Add together all quantities at each price. Construct a market demand curve.

Imagine that you are a producer and repeat the exercises above.

Produce a list of 20 goods. How many relationships can you find, are they substitutes, complements, etc.? How could you test these relationships?

shows a demand and a supply for Christmas cards. If we assume that demand and supply does not change (*ceteris paribus* – all other things remain equal) then the market will find its own equilibrium and a market price will be determined.

Using Figure 3.8, if the Christmas cards are offered for sale at price P_0 then demand will equal quantity Q_0 and supply will equal quantity Q_1. Supply will be greater than demand and the

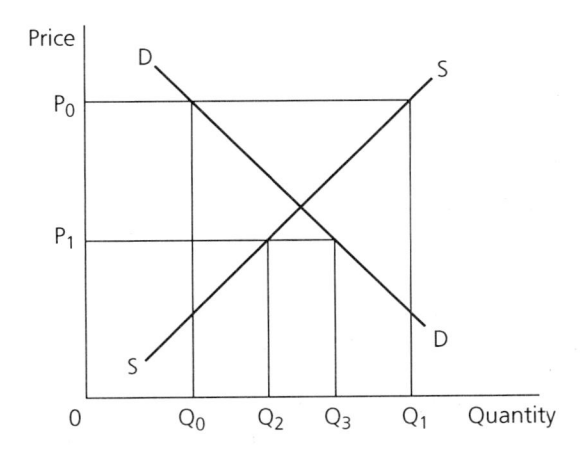

Figure 3.8 Market disequilibrium

A typical retail fruit and vegetable market. As a result of recent European Union integration weights now are given in kilograms.

producers will have spare unsold cards on their hands, an excess supply. In this situation the supplier will have to decrease the price of the cards in order to encourage people to buy them. Thus the price will drop from P_0. If the price was to be set at P_1 then demand, at quantity Q_3, would be greater than supply, at quantity Q_2, and there would be a shortage of cards. The supplier in this case would increase the price, selling them to the highest bidder. If price is at P_1, it will increase.

The point at which price neither increases nor decreases is where demand equals supply. At this point all of the cards being offered for sale are being purchased. The market is said to be in equilibrium, balanced until either demand or supply changes. Figure 3.9 shows the market equilibrium. Equilibrium will exist as long as neither demand nor supply changes.

At this point the signals given by the consumers have been correctly received by the producers and the correct quantity of resources have been allocated to the production of the good or service. The result is that the right quantity has been produced at the right price.

If demand were to increase (see Figure 3.10) due to an increase in consumers' income, possibly due to a reduction in the income tax rate, more goods would be demanded. This would disturb the equilibrium situation and the resources would need to be allocated because of the new messages being given out.

If Figure 3.10 represents the market for a product then equilibrium exists when the price is P_0 and the quantity demanded and supplied equals Q_0, at point 'a'. Everything in the market is balanced. If demand increases to D_1D_1, as previously described, then the equilibrium is disturbed. The quantity demanded is now $0Q_2$, and the quantity supplied equals $0Q_0$. This creates a new set of messages for the market:

- Demand is greater than supply.
- More resources are needed to produce this good.

The producers are not prepared to produce $0Q_2$ units at P_0. If they supply more they want a

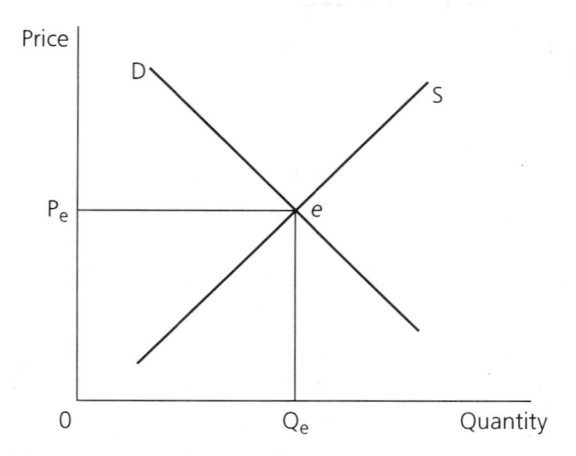

Figure 3.9 Market equilibrium

higher price. Therefore, the price will increase and the quantity supplied will also increase. The increase in price attracts new resources and enables more to be produced. Gradually the market will produce more at a higher price until demand equals supply at point 'b'. At this point the quantity demanded equals $0Q_1$ and the quantity supplied also equals $0Q_1$. Equilibrium is restored and the market has successfully attracted new resources, rationing the goods available to the highest bidders, at price P_1.

If new technology is introduced which decreases the cost of production, then the supply curve moves to the right, an increase in supply. In this situation supply is greater than demand, the price drops as the excess supply is sold and resources are diverted to more profitable uses. Eventually a new equilibrium is achieved at a lower price but at an increased quantity.

It is the role of the market to transmit signals between consumers and producers in order to allocate resources according to need. The price signals the value of output and as price increases more resources are directed to the production of that good. As price decreases the resources are taken away and used for more profitable production. The signals of demand, supply and price should eventually achieve an equilibrium where all of the resources are allocated efficiently.

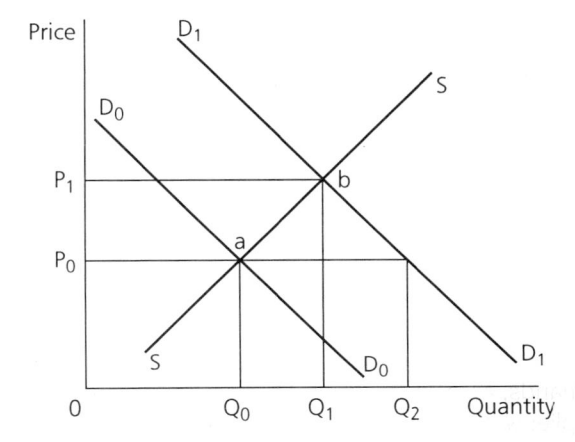

Figure 3.10 Changing market equilibrium

The London Stock Exchange – a modern example of a market

In the real world, because things are constantly changing, markets are rarely in equilibrium. They are usually trying to reach an equilibrium. Also many markets are not free to work properly; they are influenced or restricted by forces such as the government or trade unions.

This does not mean that the market is inefficient but that it is often unable to work in the way that it should.

Review terms

Effective demand; individual demand; market demand; perverse demand; extension/contraction of demand; substitutes; complements; income and substitution effect; expectations; market supply; extension/contraction of supply; excess supply; market equilibrium; market price.

ACTIVITY

Using a copy of your local evening newspaper, look at the classified section. How many markets can you find? Produce a list.

Draw a diagram of a market where the government set a maximum price below the market equilibrium. What would happen in this market?

If the government changed the maximum price to one above the equilibrium, how would this change the situation?

Use the Stock Exchange as an example of a market. Track the movement of share prices using the Financial Times Share Index 100 (FTSE 100), and try to explain in terms of supply and demand why fluctuations occur.

THE INTERNATIONAL ECONOMIST

Barengo learns about supply and demand

The growth of the Barengan textile industry has provided students of economics with a good example of the application of economic theory to a real life situation.

Amazement
The Barengans have discovered that the more they offer for sale, the less people are prepared to pay, while if they limit the amount for sale, the price remains high. They are amazed to discover this pattern of demand.

They were prepared to produce as much as they could sell when the price was high, but they could not persuade their workers to make any cloth if the price was very low.

Of course, it is worth noting that this would not always be the case. Every time that Barengo is reported in the newspapers, it creates interest in the region, and leads more people to want to buy their cloth – this interest leads to an increase in demand.

Study
In the same way, students of economics may surmise, when the workers have no money left, that they are likely to produce the cloth at a low price, thereby creating an increase in supply.

Data questions

Foundation level

1 Using the information in the text and your own knowledge, explain the meaning of the terms 'supply' and 'demand'.
2 Draw and label a graph to show supply and a graph to show demand.
3 Explain the meaning of the term 'equilibrium'.
4 How would changes in supply and demand change the equilibrium?

Intermediate level

1 Explain the meaning of the terms 'supply' and 'demand'.
2 Draw and label a diagram to show supply and demand in equilibrium.
3 What factors can affect supply and demand?
4 How would changes in supply and demand influence the equilibrium?

Higher level

1 Explain the meaning of the terms 'supply' and 'demand' and draw and label a diagram to illustrate the relationship between the two.
2 What factors can change supply and demand in the Barengan textile industry?
3 Outline the possible consequences of such changes on the Barengan economy.
4 Why is it that Barengans might have been surprised to discover the realities of the price mechanism?

Coursework Suggestions

Idea

Demand curves slope downwards, and move from left to right.

Decide on a product, and consider your own demand for it. This will give you an individual demand.

- Find out the demand for the same product with a group of people, such as everyone in your class.
- This will allow you to produce a group demand schedule, and a demand curve.
- Find out from each of those you have used what would make them change their demand.

This will allow you to comment on the factors that influence demand. You can then comment on your original assertion.

Idea

The classical concept of demand is not always correct. Sometimes, people will not buy an item because it appears to be too cheap to afford good value. Perfume could be an example, as could certain items of clothing.

Think of a product like this, and then conduct a survey to see at what price people would make a purchase.

- Ask them why they would not buy at a low price, if that is what they have said.
- Construct a demand curve. It may not follow the traditional shape.
- Explain the reasons for the difference from basic economic theory.

3.2 ELASTICITY

The slope of the demand curve is very important: it determines the relationship between price and quantity. In a market situation, if supply changes the slope of the demand curve will decide how the market will react. The slope determines by how much quantity changes when price changes. This is known as the **price elasticity of demand**:

- price elasticity of demand shows the responsiveness of the quantity demanded to changes in price

The amount by which the quantity demanded changes, when price changes, can be important to producers, considering price rises, or governments looking at increases in VAT or sales taxes.

There are two extremes. Firstly, for a change in price there can be a very small change in the quantity demanded and secondly, for the same change in price, there can be a very large change in the quantity demanded. It is also possible that as price changes the quantity demanded can change by an equal proportional amount.

Figure 3.11 shows the two extremes of price elasticity of demand. Figure 3.11(a) shows a **perfectly inelastic demand curve** which is a vertical straight line: as price changes the quantity demanded remains constant. Figure 3.11(b) shows the more usual situation with a demand curve that **tends towards the inelastic**. In this situation as price changes the quantity demanded changes by a smaller amount in the opposite direction. For example, if price increased by 10% then the quantity demanded would decrease by less than 10%.

Figure 3.11(c) shows a **perfectly elastic** demand curve. This is a horizontal straight line, showing an infinite demand at the set price. Once again Figure 3.11(d) is the more usual situation where a small change in price gives a larger proportional change in demand in the opposite direction. A ten per cent increase in price would produce a decrease in the quantity demanded of more than ten per cent.

At the extremes it is easy to determine whether a curve is price inelastic or price elastic, but the majority of curves lie between these two extremes. It is here that the third curve, the **unitary curve**, is useful. The unitary curve has **unit elasticity**, and is the middle curve which is either a straight line at 45° to both axes or a rectangular hyperbola.

The demand curve with unit elasticity gives an equal but opposite proportional change in the quantity demanded for every change in price. This is because of its 45° slope. A 10% increase in price will give a 10% decrease in the quantity demanded. This curve is the 'watershed': any demand curve with a slope of more than 45° tends towards the inelastic and any curve with a slope of less than 45° tends towards the elastic. Degrees of elasticity include:

- perfectly inelastic – vertical line – change in P = 10%, then change in Q < 10%
- perfectly elastic – horizontal line – change in P = 10%, then change in Q > 10%
- unitary elasticity – 45° line – change in P = 10%, then change in Q = 10%.

Measurement of elasticity

Looking at a demand curve to estimate the price elasticity of demand is not accurate enough for producers or the government. It is necessary for many reasons to get an accurate view of the relationship between changes in price and the quantity demanded, especially when demand is not perfectly elastic or inelastic.

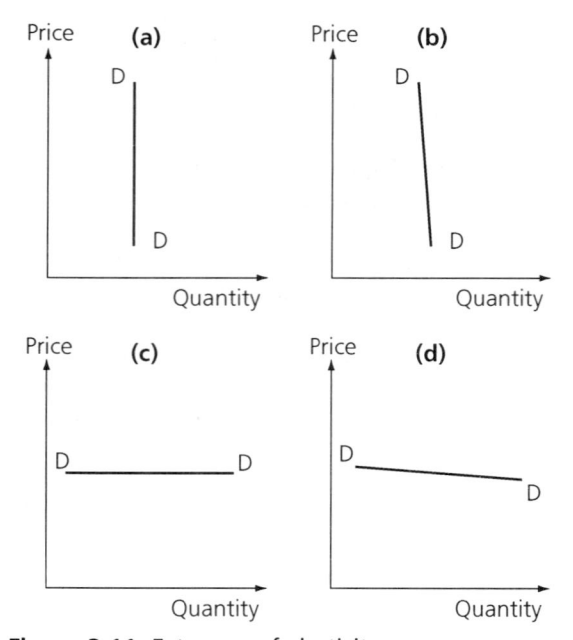

Figure 3.11 Extremes of elasticity

The amount by which quantity actually changes when price changes can mean extra revenue for a firm or a loss of revenue: the same applies to a government. The need for an accurate assessment of the relationship between quantity and price has produced a number of methods of measurement for the price elasticity of demand.

The most commonly used method is the equation for price elasticity of demand:

$$P_e = \frac{\text{change in quantity demanded}}{\% \text{ change in price.}}$$

This produces a coefficient, a value, which can be used to judge the slope of the demand curve:

- For a perfectly inelastic demand curve the quantity demanded does not change as the price changes, therefore the top half of the equation is zero. Zero divided by anything equals zero. Therefore the coefficient is zero (0).
- For the perfectly elastic demand curve the bottom half of the equation is zero. Anything divided by zero equals infinity.

This provides the values at two extremes:

- P_e equals zero for the inelastic curve.
- P_e equals infinity for the elastic curve.
- The unitary curve has an equal but opposite change in price and quantity. If price increases by 10% then the quantity demanded will decrease by 10%: thus the price elasticity coefficient will equal one, and will always equal one. To be strictly accurate it will equal one because the quantity demanded will always decrease when price increases. All price elasticity coefficients will be negative because the slope of the demand curve is normally negative.

Re-stated, the price **elasticity coefficients** are:

Inelastic – $P_e < 1$
Elastic – $P_e > 1$
Unitary – $P_e = 1$.

Factors affecting elasticity

There are a number of factors that influence the price elasticity of demand. Some of these factors make the demand curve more inelastic whilst the absence of some factors make the curves more elastic.

Real income: the greater a person's real income the more inelastic will be their demand for most products. Because their income is high then the price of most goods is insignificant and therefore they can afford large price increases without decreasing their demand by any large amount. If income is low then the price elasticity of demand tends to be elastic.

The availability of substitutes: products that have good substitutes have elastic demand curves because any small change in price will mean that people will buy the substitute good and the quantity demanded of the original good decreases by a large amount. Goods without an acceptable substitute tend to have demand curves that tend towards the inelastic.

Necessities and luxuries: goods that are considered to be luxury items tend to have an elastic demand curve. They are not vital to a person's survival and so as price increases the quantity demanded rapidly decreases. The opposite is true of necessities, these are the basic needs for survival and even if price increases people will continue to buy them. Thus the demand curve tends towards the inelastic. The problem with this classification is that what is a luxury to one person may be a necessity to another.

Low priced goods: those goods that are very cheap tend to have an inelastic demand curve because they take up such a small proportion of a person's income. An example would be a box of matches; if the price doubled very few people would stop buying them because a 100% increase would be very small in terms of the cost.

Habit forming goods: these are goods that people feel they cannot live without, or believe they cannot. The examples are cigarettes and alcohol. In both of these cases demand tends towards the inelastic; as price increases very few people will stop drinking or smoking because they are unable to. The quantity demanded changes very little.

> ### ACTIVITY 3
>
> Calculate the price elasticity of demand (P_e) if price rises by 15% and the quantity demanded falls by 10%. Is the curve tending towards the elastic or inelastic?
>
> A firm wishes to increase its price from £1.60 to £2.00. It has a P_e of 0·6 and produces 10,000 items per year. If it produces fewer than 8,000 units it will need to make some staff redundant. Should they increase the price to £2.00?
>
> Some products can have different elasticities at different times of the year, e.g. Christmas cards. Produce a list of other products like this and try to explain why this happens.

Income elasticity

Over time incomes in most Western industrialised countries increase, as countries become wealthier and produce more goods and services. As income increases individuals tend to change the type and quantity of goods and services that they buy. This has an effect upon individual firms as well as the government which collects VAT

The relationship between changes in income and the quantity demanded is very important to the market. It helps firms to predict what will happen to the demand for their product in the future.

As with price elasticity of demand, it is important to calculate the relationship between changes in income and the quantity demanded. This relationship is known as the **income elasticity of demand (Y_e)**. It is:

- the *responsiveness* of the *quantity* demanded *to changes in income*

An equation provides a coefficient which indicates what will happen to the quantity demanded for a product as income increases.

$$Y_e = \frac{\text{change in quantity demanded}}{\text{\% change in income.}}$$

Generally as income increases the demand for almost all goods, except those classified as inferior, will increase but not all by the same amount.

Table 3.1 Income elasticity coefficients

Value of Y_e	Description
Negative	Demand (D) for the good decreases as income (Y) increases (inferior good)
Zero	D for the good is constant as Y increases
> 0 but < 1	D for the good increases by a smaller amount than the increase in Y
= 1	D for the good increases in the same proportion proportion to the increase in Y
> 1	D for the good increases by a greater proportion than the increase in Y

Using this table, we know that if our product has a Y_e of 4 and incomes are due to increase by 10% next year then the demand for our product should increase by more than 10%. In fact it should increase by 40%.

Alternatively, if we know that incomes have increased by 5% this year and the quantity demanded of our product has decreased by 4%, over the year, then we have a Y_e of 0·8. This indicates that our good is inferior and will continue to decline as incomes increase in the future.

Elasticity of supply

Supply curves, just like demand curves, have different slopes. When the prices of some goods increase firms may be more willing, or in most cases, more able to increase the supply. However, in other situations they may be unable or unwilling to increase supply.

For supply, **time** is very important. In the **momentary run** everything is fixed in supply. The moment is now, this instant, and in this time period nothing can be produced, therefore the supply curve is perfectly inelastic. In the **long run**, which is an infinite period of time, everything can be increased in supply. Thus the supply curve is perfectly elastic. In between these two situations, in the **short run**, the supply of some products can be increased whilst others, such as the supply of oil, cannot be increased. The slope of the supply curve is therefore determined more by the type of product or by the producer's willingness to increase supply. The **elasticity of supply** is:

- the responsiveness of the quantity supplied to changes in price.

It can be calculated accurately to gain a precise relationship between changes in price and the quantity supplied:

$$Y_e = \frac{\text{change in quantity supplied}}{\text{\% change in price.}}$$

As with demand:

- A value of S_e equals zero gives a perfectly inelastic supply curve.
- S_e equals infinity gives a perfectly elastic supply curve.
- The unitary curve, which cuts through both axes at zero quantity, is a 45° line sloping up from left to right and has a value of S_e equals one.

Any curve with a value greater than one is therefore tending towards the elastic, and any curve with a value of less than one tends towards the inelastic.

Other factors that affect the elasticity of supply, apart from time, are the cost of entering the market; the diversity of a firm's production and the ease with which firms can alter supply between products. If the costs of entering and leaving a market are small, supply can more easily be increased and tends towards the elastic. Where a firm produces for several different markets and can divert supplies or can move production between several different products, supply also tends to be inelastic.

The relevance of price elasticity of demand and the elasticity of supply is the influence both can have on the market. A change in demand or supply changes the market price and quantity; however, the elasticity of the two curves determines by how much, if at all, the price and quantity changes.

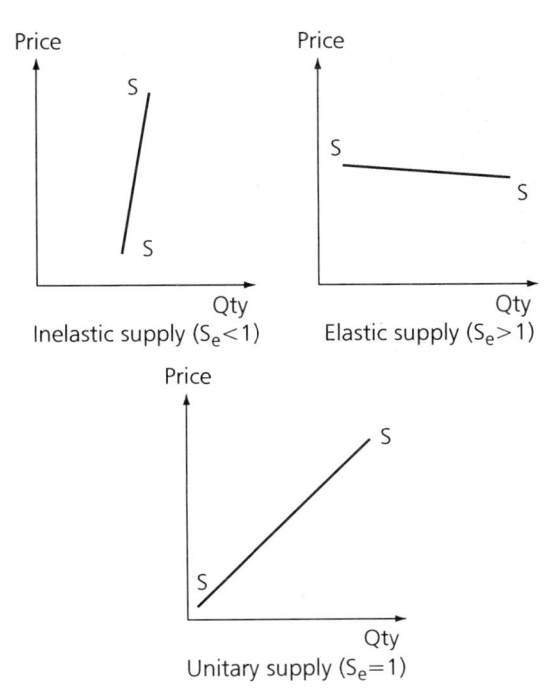

Figure 3.12 Elasticity of supply graphs

ACTIVITY 4

Produce a list of the first ten items that come into your mind. Place these ten items into two columns, price elastic and price inelastic. Check your ideas with a friend or your teacher.

Imagine your income, or that of your parents, increased by 25%, then 50% and finally 100%. How would this extra income be spent, what items would you buy more of and what would you buy less of? Use Figure 3.15 to put each item into one of the five categories.

The Chancellor wishes to raise more tax revenue from the sale of cigarettes: they have a price elasticity of –0.1. If he raises the price of cigarettes 10% by taxing them, will he raise extra revenue for the government? What other products could he use to raise extra revenue? What products should he avoid? Why?

THE INTERNATIONAL ECONOMIST

Economic Lessons Continue

As representatives of the textile industry in Barengo negotiate over the price of cloth, they are rapidly learning the lessons of western economics.

They have just discovered two key facts of economics; first, if the price of cloth is increased, then the amount sold will fall.

Second, if the amount of cloth available increases, the price will drop, but different colours will fall by different amounts depending on popularity of the cloth in question. They have had some experience.

Popularity

One cloth – a dark purple with darker irregular markings – is not popular within Barengo itself, but in the UK it sells very well. When 1,000 kilos were available, buyers would pay £10 a kilo. However, when the quantity available rose to 2,000 kilos, the price fell to £8 a kilo.

By contrast, when the red cloth doubled in price, the amount bought only halved. When the amount of white cloth doubled, the price fell by three quarters. It seems that the more ordinary colours show greater falls in price. This has sent the Barengans away to ponder on western tastes.

Different cloths take differing amounts of time to make, and fetch different prices, so they are going to have to think about production costs

Data questions

Elasticity is probably too difficult a concept to examine as a single topic at GCSE. That is not to say that candidates should not have a knowledge of the subject, and may well be able to use this knowledge to demonstrate a high level of understanding of market issues.

It is possible that some examiners may select the topic of elasticity for a general topic, but little could be expected from the Foundation Level candidate.

Foundation level

1 The concept outlined in the text is known as the 'elasticity of demand'. Use your own words to explain what it means.

2 Why is it important to producers to understand this concept?

3 Economics contains other terms relating to elasticity, apart from 'elasticity of demand'. Explain any other elasticity that you know.

4 Why do you think customers were prepared to pay more for some types of cloth than others?

Intermediate level

1 Explain the meaning of the concept of 'elasticity of demand' outlined in the text.

2 Give a formula to measure elasticity of demand, and calculate the elasticities of purple, red and white cloth.

3 Draw and label diagrams to show the elasticity of demand.

4 Explain the significance to producers of knowledge of elasticity of demand.

Higher level

1 Measure the elasticity of demand for purple, red, and white cloth.

2 Draw diagrams to illustrate elasticity of demand.

3 Explain the significance of each type of elasticity to a cloth producer.

4 What information other than elasticity of demand might a cloth producer need in determining what colours to produce?

Review terms

Price elasticity of demand; perfectly inelastic demand; perfectly elastic demand; inelastic demand; elastic demand; unitary demand; unit elasticity; elasticity coefficients; substitutes; necessities; luxuries; income elasticity of demand; elasticity of supply; time; momentary run; long run; short run; elastic supply; inelastic supply.

Coursework Suggestions

Idea

Just as you can look at the demand for a product, you could also measure its elasticity.

- Find out why consumers respond as they do to the product by asking.

Thus, you can show the elasticity of demand of a product with a group of people, and offer an explanation for the figure that you calculate.

Idea

If you know a shopkeeper or a producer, then you can do the same sort of piece of work, but from a different viewpoint.

- Look at particular products, and see if the supplier knows what would happen to demand when price changes.
- Find out what sort of market research is undertaken to ensure that the customer is able to buy what is really wanted.
- Find out how the supplier is able to respond to changes in demand.

3.3 COSTS, REVENUES AND PROFIT

The aim of every firm is to make a **profit**. For most it is the major aim but for some it is one of many aims. If a firm is to make a profit it must make sure that the revenue it collects for selling its goods and services is greater than the cost of producing those goods and services. Profit is the excess that is left after all of a company's costs have been paid:

Profit = Total revenue (TR) − Total cost (TC).

Total revenue is quite simply the price of each item sold multiplied by the quantity sold:

TR = Price × Quantity.

Total cost is split into two parts: **fixed costs** and **variable costs**. Fixed costs are those costs that are constant as output increases. Fixed costs are the same if output equals zero or if it equals 10,000. These are costs such as rent, insurance and business rates.

A second element of fixed costs is **normal profit**. This is the wage the owner could earn elsewhere for the same number of hours, plus the return on the money invested in the business if it were to be put into a financial institution at the market rate of interest.

Variable costs are those costs directly related to output and these do vary as output increases. Variable costs equal zero when production is zero but gradually increase as the quantity produced increases. Examples of variable costs include wages, the purchase of raw materials and the cost power.

Total cost = Fixed costs + Variable costs

Variable costs are influenced by economies of scale, (see section 2.2, page 10) and so do not increase in perfect proportion to the increase in output.

The increase in variable costs is at first quite rapid and then begins to slow down, due to the economies of scale, but beyond an ideal level of output variable costs begin to increase at a faster rate.

The fact that fixed costs remain the same throughout production means that as total costs

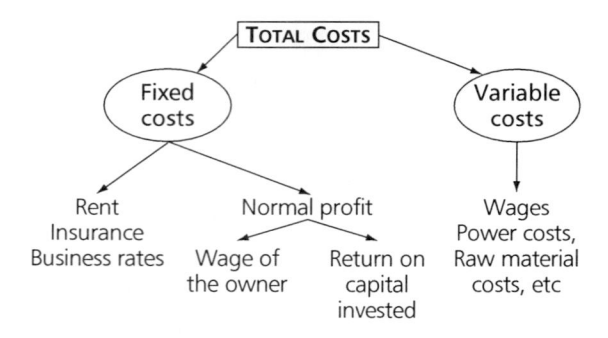

Figure 3.13 Total costs

increase, the increase is due to extra variable costs.

Average costs and average revenue

Firms are able to calculate their total profit by taking their total costs away from their total revenue, but often this simple equation is not enough. At other times they may need to know how much profit they are making from each unit or whether they could increase their profit by producing a greater quantity or a smaller quantity of their product. The profit per unit is especially important if they are producing several different items or they have just put a new product onto the market.

Table 3.2 Fixed and variable costs

Quantity	Fixed costs (FC)	Variable costs (VC)	Total cost (TC)
0	145	0	145
1	145	30	175
2	145	55	200
3	145	75	220
4	145	105	250
5	145	155	300
6	145	225	370
7	145	315	460

Therefore,

TC = FC + VC.

To find the profit per unit it is necessary to find the cost per unit and the revenue per unit. To work out the individual cost per unit would be virtually impossible, but it is possible to calculate the **average cost** (AC). This is a cost per unit spread over all of the units produced. It is not strictly accurate because it is an average but it does provide an acceptable measurement.

Average cost, the cost per unit, is calculated like any average by taking the total cost and dividing it by the appropriate quantity, therefore average cost is:

$$\text{Average cost} = \frac{\text{Total cost}}{\text{Quantity}}$$

Average revenue (AR) is calculated in the same way, by taking total revenue and dividing by the quantity sold:

$$\text{Average revenue} = \frac{\text{Total revenue}}{\text{Quantity}}$$

If total revenue minus total cost gives the total profit, then:

Average revenue − Average cost = Profit/unit.

In order to gain the average cost at each quantity the total cost is divided by the quantity, for example, at quantity 2 total cost equals 200 and when divided by 2 this gives an average cost of 100.

The same process is used to produce the average revenue, total revenue divided by the quantity. The profit per unit is then calculated by subtracting the average cost from the average revenue.

Table 3.3 shows that the maximum profit per unit is at quantity 3, at £66·67 per unit. However, if total profit is taken the maximum is when 4 units are produced with a total of £230. This presents two conflicting pictures: what should the firm actually do? The question is, what is the aim of the firm?

If the quantities given in Figure 3.20 are in thousands rather than units then it is unlikely that maximum profit will be exactly equal to 3,000 or 4,000 units, it could lie in between. Therefore, a method is required that looks at the maximum profit situation to the nearest unit produced rather than the nearest thousand.

Table 3.3 Profit per unit calculation

Quantity	Price	TR	TC	Total profit	AR	AC	Profit/unit
0	200	0	145	–	–	–	–
1	180	180	175	+5	180	175.00	5.00
2	160	320	200	+120	160	100.00	60.00
3	140	420	220	+200	140	73.33	66.67
4	120	480	250	+230	120	62.50	57.50
5	100	500	300	+200	100	60.00	40.00
6	80	480	370	+110	80	61.60	18.40
7	60	420	460	+40	60	65.70	–5.70
8	40	320	570	–250	40	71.25	–31.25

Marginal revenue and marginal cost

The method used to find the maximum profit output is **marginal revenue (MR)** and **marginal cost (MC)**. The marginal cost is:

- the extra cost of producing an extra unit of output.

It looks at producing one extra unit and the extra cost of producing that unit and only that unit. All of the other costs such as fixed costs are ignored. To calculate this the difference between total costs is used. The marginal revenue is:

- the extra revenue received from the sale of an extra unit.

This again only looks at the revenue for that one extra unit, everything else is ignored. To calculate the marginal revenue the difference between the total revenue at each quantity is used.

Because both marginal cost and marginal revenue represent the difference between the totals the marginals are plotted at the mid-points. For example, the difference between TR at quantity 1 and quantity 2 is at quantity 1·5.

The fact that marginal values deal only with individual units allows a more accurate calculation of maximum profit output to be made. For every unit that has marginal revenue above marginal cost a profit is being made. When marginal cost is *greater* than marginal revenue a loss is being made on that unit. The aim is to find the output where marginal cost is equal to marginal revenue for then maximum profit is being made: if MC = MR then every single bit of profit is being made from every single unit and is therefore at a maximum. In the example of Table 3.4, MC = MR between quantity 3·5 and 4·5, and is actually at quantity 4. This is the maximum profit output.

Table 3.4 Maximum profit output

Quantity	TR	MR	TC	MC
0	0		145	
		180		30
1	180		175	
		140		25
2	320		200	
		100		20
3	420		220	
		60		30
4	480		250	
		20		50
5	500		300	
		–20		70
6	480		370	

FINANCE MONTHLY

Costs, revenues and profits in Barengo's textile industry

When the textile industry of Barengo began to export, there was little attention paid to the profitability of particular items and elasticity of demand was not considered. Now, a higher level of sophistication has developed.

Administrative costs and shipping charges are fixed at £2·00 a kilo.

Production costs to date have remained constant at £3·00 a kilo for the purple cloth, £2·50 for the white cloth, and £2·00 for the red cloth. When sales are 2,000 kilos a month of the purple cloth, the price is £8·00 a kilo. With sales of red cloth at 1,500 kilos a month, the selling price is £5·00 a kilo. When sales of white cloth are at 1,000 kilos a month, the price is £6·00 a kilo.

The shops that buy the cloth are happy to stock all three colours. They say it is important that they are able to offer the variety, because the availability of choice that brings customers into the shops, even though there is a clear preference for purple.

Profit

Profit is important for the Barengan economy, but it is also important that the large number of textile workers, who would otherwise be without an income, are employed.

It seems that the industry may well need to expand and offer a wider range of products; the issue of profitability is now under consideration.

Data questions

Foundation level

1 (a) Explain the term total revenue.
  (b) Showing all your workings, calculate the total revenue that the Barengan textile industry would receive for the sale of: (i) purple cloth; (ii) red cloth; (iii) white cloth.
2 (a) Explain the meaning of the term total costs.
  (b) Showing all your workings, calculate the total costs that the Barengo textile industry would pay out for the production of: (i) purple cloth; (ii) red cloth; (iii) white cloth.
3 (a) Explain the meaning of the term profit.
  (b) Showing all your workings, and using the revenue and cost figures already calculated, show the total profit that the Barengo textile industry would make for the production and sale of (i) purple cloth; (ii) red cloth; (iii) white cloth.
4 Should the textile industry specialise in the production of its most profitable cloth, or should it produce a wide variety of different cloths? Give reasons for your answer.

Intermediate level

1 Explain the meaning of the terms: (i) revenue; (ii) cost; (iii) profit.
2 Showing your workings, calculate the total profit made on the sale of: (i) purple cloth; (ii) red cloth; (iii) white cloth.
3 Before deciding on which cloth to produce, what information would you require? Why?
4 Why might shops stock goods that make little or no profit?

Higher level

1 Explain, with appropriate diagrams, the terms cost, revenue, and profit.
2 Assess the profitability to the producers of the three cloths.
3 What factors would you recommend that the textile producers consider before changing their production pattern?
4 Why do firms supply goods that make little or no profit for themselves or the retailer.

> **✓ Review terms**
>
> Profit; total revenue; total cost; fixed cost; variable cost; normal profit; average cost; average revenue; marginal cost; marginal revenue.

> **ACTIVITY 5**
>
> Talk to your parents and try to calculate the fixed costs for running your house. What bills would still have to be paid if you were away on holiday for a month?
>
> Find the cost of running your home for a month. What is the average total cost?
>
> Using Table 3.3, plot (a) total cost and total revenue and (b) total profit on graph paper. Mark the points of maximum profit for both graphs.

Coursework Suggestions

Idea

There are several problems in looking at this topic. The first is to find a firm that will actually allow you access to its figures.

If your family or close friends are involved in a business, then it may be possible, but most organisations do not want to make their figures available, for obvious commercial reasons.

The other problem is that there is a clear clash with accountancy. The coursework needs to be a piece of economics, and not accounts.

If you can obtain the information, and your teacher is prepared to offer careful guidelines on the work, then it would be possible to look at this subject area. Otherwise, perhaps look elsewhere.

3.4 CIRCULAR FLOW OF INCOME

The basic economic problem

The function of any economy is to solve the basic economic problem, as outlined in section 1.1 (page 1), of scarcity. Scarce resources, created by a shortage of the factors of production, labour, land, capital and enterprise, and people's unlimited demand for goods and services creates this problem. It is impossible to produce everything that people want and need and so choices have to be made. The first decision is **what to produce**, and the second is **how to produce** the goods and services that we need. Finally, **to whom to distribute** concerns how we share out those goods and services that have been produced. All economies face these problems but it is the way in which they are solved that determines what an economy is like.

Two sector economy

In order to appreciate how an economy solves the problem of scarcity it is important to understand how it works. Tracing the path of money around an economy helps to explain how it works.

To begin with we will assume a simple two sector economy of firms and households with no government and no international trade. This is a closed economy. If we start at the production stage, the manufacturing of goods and the production of services, all of the factors of production are required. In order to take part in the production process all of these factors require payment, **rewards**. Labour needs **wages**, land receives **rent**, capital receives **interest** and enterprises gain the reward of **profit**. Therefore, production creates **income** (Y) in the form of wages, rent, interest and profit (WRIP). This money income is passed on to the owners of the factors of production, the households (individuals).

The households, when they receive their income, have two choices of what to do with it. They can save it, **savings** (S), or use it to buy goods and services which is called **consumption** (C). Consumption is buying goods and services to satisfy a person's wants and needs and saving is that income which is not spent on consumer goods and services but placed in a bank or building society, or some other financial institution. The amount that is saved or used for consumption is determined by many factors such as the amount of income, trends and fashions and the **rate of interest** (the cost of borrowing money, see page 53).

Buying consumer goods and services, consumption, creates effective demand in the market. People have the ability to purchase and wish to do so. This is registered by the producers as a demand for their product and so they respond by producing what is demanded.

Some savings may be put in a box or under the bed: this is known as **intended savings**. This type of saving can mean that the money is lost to the circular flow. For the circular flow diagram it is assumed that all savings go to financial institutions: this money is known as **real savings**.

The fact that individuals put their savings into financial institutions provides a fund of money for producers to borrow. The financial institutions then lend the money that they have collected, in the form of savings, to firms who wish to improve or purchase new capital. The purchase of capital is **investment**. This creates a demand for capital goods (see pages 4 and 21).

The demand created by consumption and investment produces a total demand for all of the goods and services produced in the economy, both capital and consumer goods. The level of this total demand determines production and completes the circular flow. The total demand created is expressed as a single monetary figure, the **Aggregate Monetary Demand** (AMD). The total is arrived at by adding together the monetary demand for all the goods and services that exist (price × quantity × all the goods and services). Figure 3.14 shows the simple two sector economy.

If money flows around this economy from stage to stage then the level of AMD determines the level of output which in turn determines the level of income. Therefore AMD is equivalent to output which is equivalent to income:

AMD = Output = Income.

At the household stage income can be split into consumption (C) and Savings (S). In a shorthand style this can be written as

Y = C + S.

AMD, which is equivalent to income (Y), is made up of a demand for consumer goods and services (C) plus a demand for capital goods, which is investment (I). This can also be written in a shorthand style.

Y = C + I.

If the two equations above are combined:

Y + C + S and Y = C + I.

Then:

C + S = C + I

and, therefore:

S = I.

This identity produces what is known as an **equilibrium condition**. When the level of savings equals the level of investment the circular flow will be perfectly balanced and will not change. This equilibrium condition only applies to the two sector economy.

Injections and withdrawals

Savings put under the bed or into a box can be lost to the circular flow, but so can savings put into financial institutions. There is no reason why the financial institutions should lend out all of the money that is saved with them, except that they wish to make a profit. If firms do not wish to borrow money to invest then real savings will leave the circular flow and not return until needed. This

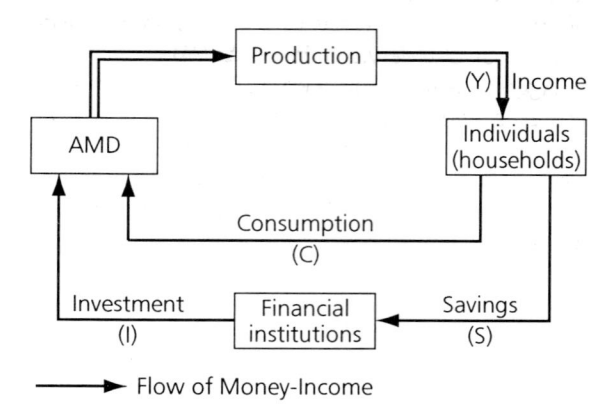

Figure 3.14 The simple two sector economy

is a leakage, or **withdrawal**, from the circular flow. The term leakage implies an accidental removal but saving is a conscious effort, therefore the preferred term is 'withdrawal'.

Investment is not a withdrawal. It is money put into the circular flow. Financial institutions have the ability to create money, and can actually lend more money than they have available through savings (see section 4). Investment is an extra amount of money put into the circular flow which increases the size of the economy. It is called an **injection**. The people investing and those saving are usually different, with different motives.

The aim of those investing is to *make* money that they do not currently have to purchase capital goods. The aim of those savings is to *put aside* an amount of money for the future, or for a special reason. To simplify the situation, in the following discussion it is assumed that all borrowing is for investment.

If savings is a withdrawal (S = W) from the circular flow and investment is an injection (I = J) into the circular flow, the equilibrium condition can now be generalised to withdrawals equal injections (W = J). The **equilibrium condition** for all of the circular flow models is:

Withdrawals (W) = Injections (J).

The three sector economy

The three sector model includes firms, households and a government sector. It is still a closed economy with no international trade.

Production still creates income, but the difference in this model is that the government takes its share of the factor incomes in the form of **direct taxation (T)**. Income is now divided into consumption, savings and taxation. The income before taxation is **gross income** and what is left after taxation is **net income**. Net income, also known as **disposable income**, is then split between consumption and savings.

At the demand stage (AMD) there is a demand for consumer goods (C), and capital goods (I), plus a demand by the government for goods and services. **Government expenditure (G)** is used to provide merit goods and public goods (see page 81), purchase capital for state run industries or consumable items such as paper for schools and medical supplies for hospitals.

The money that the government has to spend comes either from tax revenues or from borrowing (the Public Sector Borrowing Requirement – PSBR, see page 83). Government expenditure forms part of the AMD which determines production. Aggregate monetary demand is now consumption plus investment plus government expenditure.

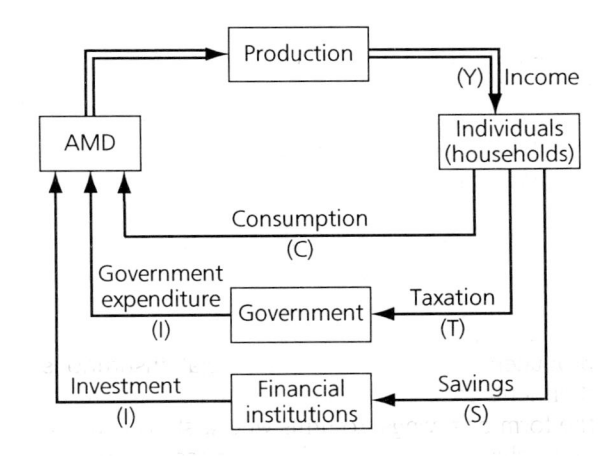

Figure 3.15 Three sector circular flow

The open economy

The simplified open model includes households, firms, the government and international trade.

Production still creates income for the owners of the factors of production, but this income is now split into four parts. Firstly the income is taxed, producing disposable income, and then the remainder is either saved, used for consumption of home produced goods or used to purchase foreign goods and services, **imports (M)**.

Aggregate monetary demand is still consumption plus investment plus government expenditure but also includes the demand by households overseas for goods and services produced in the home economy, **exports (X)**. Export demand is therefore part of AMD.

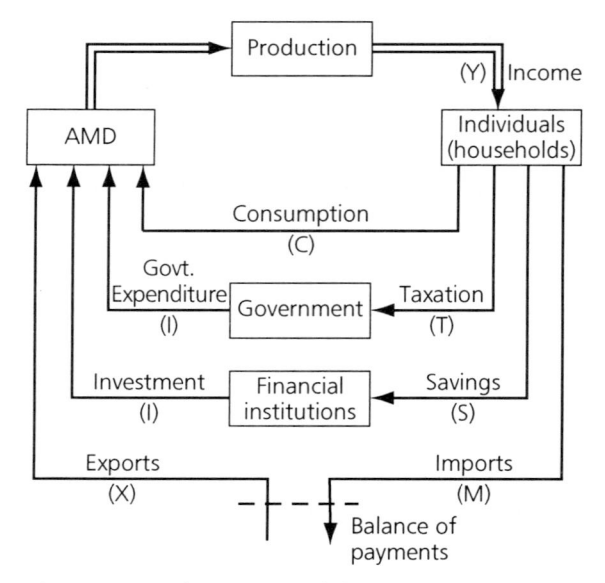

Figure 3.16 The open model

Injections and withdrawals

In the two sector model savings is a withdrawal and investment an injection. The equilibrium condition is that injections should equal withdrawals.

Government expenditure is also an injection because it is money put into the economy by the government. Although the money spent by the government is often taken from taxation, it can be money borrowed. Government regularly spend more than they collect in tax. Equally, governments may wish to tax but not to spend the resulting money; this would be a withdrawal. There is no reason why government tax and expenditure should be equal. Therefore, expenditure is an injection and taxation a withdrawal.

Money spent on imports is clearly a withdrawal. It is leaving the circular flow and entering the economy of another country. Exports are very clearly injections. This is money from other economies being injected into our circular flow creating a demand for home produced goods and services. The level of exports and imports are not necessarily connected nor are they equal, although government would like them to be.

If all of the injections are added together and all of the withdrawals are added together then a new equilibrium condition can be established:

Injections = Withdrawals:
(I + G + X) = (S + T + M).

ACTIVITY 6

Take your weekly income and calculate how much is used for consumption and how much is saved.

Use the simple two sector circular flow model and imagine that income is £100. If £80 is used for consumption how much is saved? If investment equals £40 what happens to the model? (Assume that AMD creates production which creates income and they will all be equal.)

Using government statistics or newspapers try to find the amount of any of the following injections or withdrawals; consumption, savings, government expenditure, taxation, imports and exports. Using your information, calculate whether:

- savings do equal investment or
- if government expenditure is equal to taxation or
- exports are equal to imports

Review terms

Wages; rent; interest; profit; income; savings; consumption; rate of interest; intended savings; real savings; Aggregate Monetary Demand (AMD); output; equilibrium; withdrawals; injections; direct taxation; gross income; net income; disposable income; government expenditure; imports; exports.

Data questions

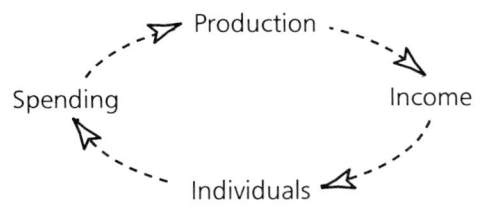

Circular flow of income in Barengo

Production → Income → Individuals → Spending → Production

The diagram above represents the most simple circular flow of income diagram for the early Barengo economy.

As the textile industry begins to develop, the circular flow becomes much more complicated, with injections and withdrawals from the circular flow.

These could include imports and exports; savings and investment; taxes and government spending.

Foundation level

1 Explain what is meant by 'the circular flow of income'.

2 What do the terms 'injection' and 'withdrawal' mean?

3 What are imports and exports; savings and investment; taxes and government spending; injections and withdrawals?

4 Draw a diagram showing the more complicated circular flow of income.

Intermediate level

1 Examine the flow of money in the closed economy model shown above.

2 Explain the meaning of the terms 'injection' and 'withdrawal', using examples.

3 Draw a circular flow diagram for the economy of Barengo, showing injections and withdrawals.

4 Explain why a government may wish to know the details of its circular flow of income.

Higher level

1 Draw a circular flow diagram for the economy of Barengo, showing injections and withdrawals.

2 Explain the flow of money within the diagram you have drawn.

3 What is the value of knowing the details of the circular flow of income?

4 What other financial information might be of value to a government, and why?

Coursework Suggestions

Idea

Investigate your own, and perhaps your family's flow of income.

- Where does the money come from?
- How is it spent?
- Draw a diagram to show the movement of money, including injections and withdrawals.
- Consider your diagram as a microcosm of the national one.

3.5 MONETARY AND FISCAL POLICY

The circular flow of income, described in section 3.4 (page 47), is rarely in equilibrium. It is usually unbalanced with decisions about savings, investment, government expenditure, taxation, exports and imports all made by different people for different reasons.

A circular flow that is not in equilibrium creates a number of problems. For example, a decrease in investment decreases the demand for capital goods which decreases the demand for workers and so creates **unemployment**. A decrease in savings will increase consumption and the demand for consumer goods will increase. The supply of these goods cannot be increased immediately and so the price increases which creates **inflation**.

When these problems occur the government needs to try to do something about them. They have a number of policy 'weapons' that they can use. These weapons, or policy instruments, can be divided into two groups: **monetary measures** (**monetary policy**) and **fiscal measures** (**fiscal policy**). Both monetary and fiscal policy are central elements of every government's economic policy.

Monetary policy

Monetary policy is the control of the supply of money within the economy. In the UK it is put into action by the **Treasury**, acting through the Bank of England, on behalf of the UK Government. An important part of the money supply has always been bank deposits and so any policy to control the money supply must be designed to control the commercial banks' ability to create credit. Thus monetary policy is a collection of methods designed to increase or decrease the number of bank deposits.

```
                    MONETARY POLICY
                   ↙              ↘
        Direct controls        Indirect controls
              ↓                       ↓
     * Quantitive and        * Open market operations
       Qualititive controls   * Special deposits
       (Bank of England       * Funding
       directives)            * Interest rate policy
```

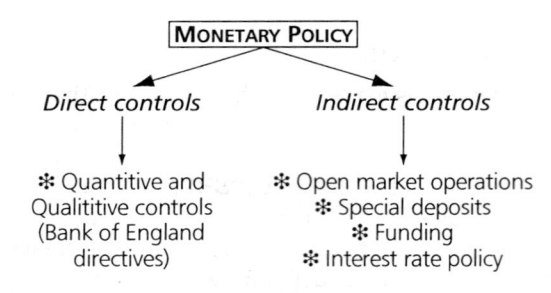

Figure 3.17 Monetary policy

Direct controls

Direct controls are either **quantitative** or **qualitative controls**. Quantitative controls would be a directive from the Bank of England on the amount that the commercial banks can lend, either as an annual or a monthly limit. This would also include strict credit limits and regulations on hire purchase terms. For example, the Bank of England could insist that the maximum loan for a new car was 60% of its purchase price and the remainder could only be borrowed over two years.

Qualitative controls are again instructions from the Bank of England, which tell the banks where they may lend the money. This can be to industry or consumers. It could be to exporters, importers, people buying UK goods or only to those investing in the purchase of capital. This would depend very much on what the UK Government wanted to decrease or increase. These direct controls are instructions that the banks cannot ignore as they are controlled by the Bank of England (see section 5.3, page 107) and so must obey their orders.

Indirect controls

Indirect controls are not instructions from the Bank of England but actions that they take which have an effect on how the commercial banks operate. Thus, their actions have an indirect influence rather than the authority of an order.

One indirect instrument is **open market operations**. This involves the Bank of England buying and selling UK Government securities on the **money market**, which affects the commercial banks' reserves and their ability to create credit. If the Bank of England sells securities it reduces the commercial banks' reserves and so decreases the money supply. If the Bank of England wishes to increase the money supply it would buy government securities to increase the reserves of the commercial banks, which would increase their credit creation.

A further instrument is using **special deposits**. Each commercial bank is required to place with the Bank of England an amount of their deposits. The Bank of England has the power to demand the commercial banks to increase their deposits with them. These deposits become **frozen assets**: they cannot be used by the commercial banks. This reduces the banks' ability to create credit and so decreases the money supply. An alternative is that the Bank of England reduces these special deposits that they hold and this increases the commercial banks' ability to create credit, increasing the money supply.

Funding is a further instrument available to the government. Funding is a process where the Bank of England replace short term treasury bills, which have a life of 91 days, with long term government bonds. This reduces the commercial banks' **liquid assets** and their ability to create credit. Liquid assets can be quickly and easily converted into cash: the more banks have the more loans they can make. If the supply of these liquid assets decreases then the banks have to decrease the amount of loans given, decreasing the money supply.

The **rate of interest** is the final indirect policy, and has always been the most popular policy option.

The rate of interest is the price of money, the cost of borrowing money. An increase in the price of money, the rate of interest, is the same as a decrease in the supply of money. The opposite is also true, a decrease in the price of money is the same as an increase in the supply of money.

The government through the Bank of England is able to control the interest rate because of its position in the financial markets. If the Bank of England increases its own interest rate (the base rate) then the commercial banks and building societies will follow. They may at some time need to borrow from the Bank of England and so cannot afford to have a lower interest rate. If the interest rate rises then less people can afford to borrow money and so less loans are made, decreasing the money supply.

All of the policies listed decrease, or increase, the supply of money within the economy. If less money exists then less goods and services can be produced; if more money exists then more goods and services can be purchased. Controlling the money supply, therefore, influences the amount of consumption and saving in the economy as well as the level of investment.

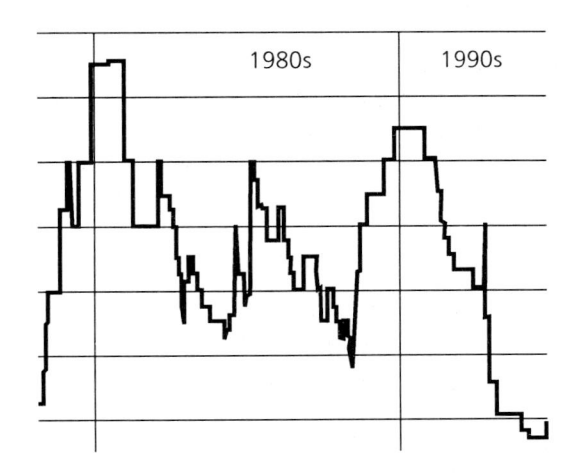

Figure 3.18 UK base rates 1980–1994

> **ACTIVITY 7**
>
> Use your local bank or building society and find the rate of interest charged for (a) loans and (b) savings
>
> Find the Bank of England's interest rate (base rate) and two different savings and borrowing rates for two banks and two building societies. Can you find a connection between them?
>
> Ask your parents, or a relative who has a mortgage, how an increase in the mortgage rate of 5% might affect them. How might it affect their general spending and what effect might it have on the economy.? What would happen if the mortgage rate decreased by 5%?

Fiscal policy

Fiscal policy is made up of three weapons that are available to the government, **taxation, government expenditure** and the **Public Sector Borrowing Requirement (PSBR)**. The third element comes from the relationship between expenditure and taxation. If expenditure is greater than taxation then a PSBR exists. If taxation is greater than expenditure then a **Public Sector Debt Repayment (PSDR)** exists.

Fiscal policy is a powerful set of weapons directly controlled by the government; there is no need of a third party to put any of these weapons into practice.

Government expenditure creates demand within the economy, therefore any change directly affects the state of the economy. Taxation alters the level of disposable income which affects an individual's consumption, saving and investment. Thus, changes in taxation indirectly affect the state of the economy. Both weapons (government expenditure and taxation) have an effect on the economy by changing the level of demand that exists.

Government expenditure is usually on **public goods** and **merit goods**. Public goods such as 'Defence' and 'Law and Order' are necessary for the economy. Merit goods such as 'Education and Health' are vital for the well being of the people. It is easy, therefore, to increase government expenditure but very difficult to decrease it.

decrease in taxation is very easy for the government. However, an increase in taxation causes many problems and is very difficult. It is also believed that changes in taxation have an effect on other factors such as workers' motivation.

Government expenditure is an injection into the circular flow and taxation is a withdrawal. The relationship between these two determines the size of the PSBR or PSDR. A PSBR is a **budget deficit** and a PSDR is a **budget surplus**. There are two schools of thought regarding the PSBR; firstly it can be thought of as a transfer of wealth within the economy; borrowing that will be repaid when a budget surplus exists. The other view is that the PSBR actually increases the money supply within the economy (PSDR decreases the money supply). The UK Conservative Government have been trying to run a **balanced budget** since 1979. This has resulted in some years showing a PSDR.

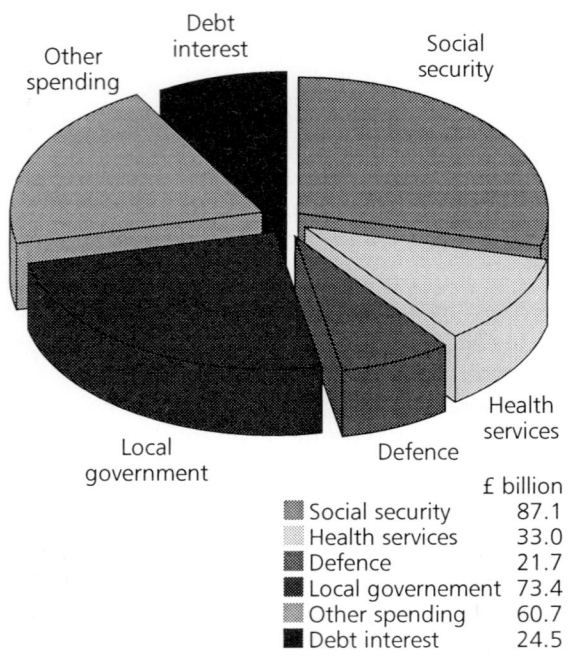

	£ billion
Social security	87.1
Health services	33.0
Defence	21.7
Local governement	73.4
Other spending	60.7
Debt interest	24.5

Figure 3.19 Public money 1995–96

Taxation in the UK comes in many forms, income tax, VAT, excise duty, etc. (see section 5.5, page 112). It is a way of taking money away from households and firms in order for the government to provide the public and merit goods that are needed. This method is not very popular and so a

> **Review terms**
>
> Monetary policy; fiscal policy; direct controls; indirect controls; quantitative and qualitative controls; open market operations; special deposits; funding; interest rate policy; government expenditure; taxation; PSBR; PSDR; public goods; merit goods; budget deficit; budget surplus; balanced budget.

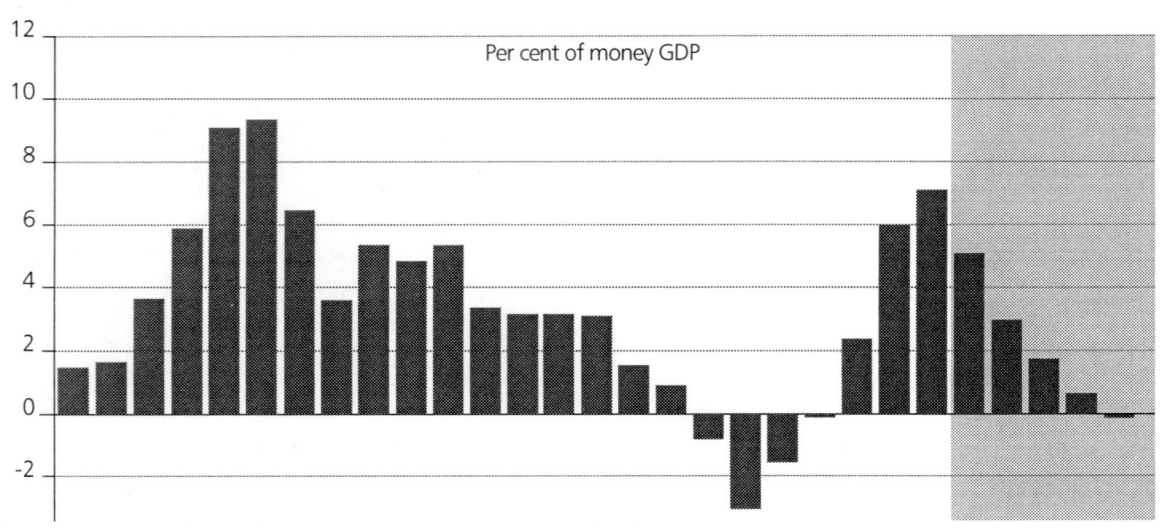

Figure 3.20 The Public Sector Borrowing Requirement in the UK

INTERNATIONAL FISCAL AND MONETARY REVIEW

Barengo and the west

Observers at the conference between representatives of the Barengo Textile Works and the UK Treasury were able to see the differences in attitude and understanding to fiscal and monetary matters between people of different cultures.

Barengo relies on import taxes – tariffs – to finance its government activities. There are rumours that some type of sales tax might be introduced in the future but, at the moment, the tariff is the sole source of income. There is no income tax, VAT, or any of the other taxes which are a feature of the western world. Moreover, budgets are expected to balance every year.

Historians would recognise that the UK enjoyed a similar system many years ago.

Trouble free economic development?

Inflation has never been a problem in Barengo because wages have always been very low, and there has never been much demand for money. No need has existed, until recently, for the type of monetary policy which can be found in western countries.

If Barengo is to develop economically, while preventing the inflationary ills that trouble the western world, then it will need to introduce an effective fiscal and monetary policy.

The problem of doing this is that it will appear to be such a great change that its unpopularity with everyone is assured.

Herein lies one of the greatest problems facing developing countries.

Data questions

Foundation level

1 List five features of the economy of Barengo that are different from that of western countries.

2 Explain the meaning of the terms 'fiscal' and 'monetary' policy.

3 How would you use fiscal and monetary policy to control inflation?

4 Why might some of the people of Barengo complain about the use of fiscal and monetary policy?

Intermediate level

1 Outline the main differences between the economies of the western world and Barengo.

2 How would you use monetary and fiscal policies to control inflation?

3 Which groups of people in Barengo would object to particular aspects of fiscal and monetary policy?

4 Why does Barengo need to control inflation?

Higher level

1 How does the economy of Barengo differ from those of the western world?

2 Why is it surprising to learn that in Barengo, budgets are expected to balance every year?

3 Outline the objections in Barengo to the introduction of fiscal and monetary policy.

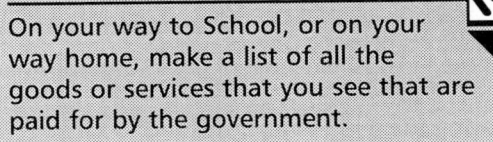

ACTIVITY 8

On your way to School, or on your way home, make a list of all the goods or services that you see that are paid for by the government.

Produce a list of the goods and services, provided by the government, that your family enjoys without paying directly.

Ask a parent, relative or friend who is earning a wage how much tax they pay per week or per month. If the amount they paid increased by 50%, how would it affect their demand for goods and services and the hours they work?

Coursework Suggestions

Here is a difficult area for coursework. To try to analyse the general movement of government policy would be too advanced for most students, and it is not good policy to attempt work which later proves to be over-demanding.

Some candidates try to analyse the Budget, but all too often the result is a copy of a few newspaper articles, so that the work lacks any form of originality.

If you want to do anything connected with monetary or fiscal policy, you should consult your teacher, and make sure that the topic is one that is within your capabilities, and that the material you will need is readily available to you.

3.6 THE GAINS FROM TRADE

International trade helps countries to obtain goods and services that they cannot produce themselves; it also builds a strong friendship between the countries trading. The spread of technology is also facilitated as countries trade. This is especially helpful to the Less Developed Countries.

Climate is very varied around the world and so different countries can produce a variety of products that other nations cannot. For example, in the UK we can produce wheat and potatoes but not oranges or bananas; in Spain the opposite is true.

A major reason for the existence of trade is that countries are thus able to obtain the resources that they need. Some countries have very few natural resources such as coal and oil while other countries have plenty of one resource; for instance, Kuwait has oil, but very little else. In this case, trade benefits everyone.

The workers in different countries have different skills, which may be the result of influences or of necessity. Some countries can therefore produce certain goods better than others.

The greatest benefit of trade is that countries are able to purchase goods and services that they would normally not be able to. This gives a greater quantity and variety of goods and services to the people of every country and increases their **standard of living**.

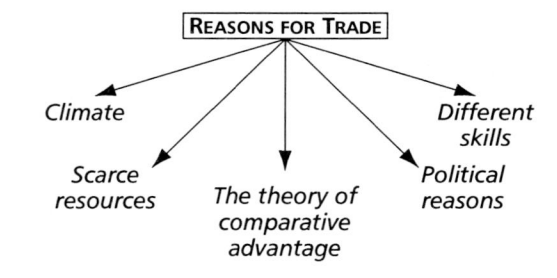

Figure 3.21 Reasons for trade

The most important reason for international trade is the **Theory of Comparative Advantage**. This theory, produced by **David Ricardo**, emphasises the benefits to be gained through specialisation and trade. If countries specialise then they may gain from economies of scale and should produce goods of a higher quality and at a lower price. Everyone should then benefit from a greater variety of goods at a cheaper price and of a better quality than if each country produced its own goods and services.

The Theory of Comparative Advantage

David Ricardo's theory states that:

> If countries specialise in the production of that good or service in which they have a comparative advantage (can produce most efficiently) then after trading every country will be better off.

This means that countries should not produce for all of their needs but should specialise and trade instead.

The theory, in simple terms, is saying that:

- First, countries decide which good or service they are most efficient at producing.
- Secondly, they should specialise in that good or service and maximise output.
- Thirdly, each country should trade freely at a fair rate of exchange (see page 89).

To show how the theory works in simple terms, assume that only two countries exist, both producing the same two products. Both have the same quality and quantity of resources and factors of production. Money and transport costs are ignored.

Table 3.5 Production possibilities for two countries

	Cars		Wheat
USA	4,000	or	24,000 tonnes
Japan	5,000	or	20,000 tonnes

In Table 3.5 the USA can produce either 4,000 cars or 24,000 tonnes of wheat but not both. Japan can produce 5,000 cars or 20,000 tonnes of wheat in the same time period, but again cannot produce both. These figures are their production possibilities which would produce a **production possibility frontier**.

If they decide to ignore Ricardo's theory and produce on their own they would have to devote half of their resources to each product and would therefore only produce half of the quantities shown in Table 3.5.

Table 3.6 Production without specialisation

	Cars		Wheat
USA	2,000	and	12,000 tonnes
Japan	2,500	and	10,000 tonnes
World Total	4,500	and	22,000 tonnes

In Table 3.6 both countries have decided to produce both goods, ignoring the Theory of Comparative Advantage, producing a world output for cars of 4,500 and world output for wheat of 22,000 tonnes. If the Theory of Comparative Advantage actually works then both countries specialising and trading should increase the world output for both products.

The first decision to be made is, in which product should each country specialise? Which product can they produce most efficiently? To make this decision the cost of producing each good in each country must be found. This will be an opportunity cost; the cost of producing cars, in terms of wheat that cannot be produced and the cost of producing wheat, in terms of cars that cannot be produced.

Table 3.7 Domestic ratios and opportunity costs

	Cars		Wheat
Step one			
USA	1	:	6
Japan	1	:	4
Step two			
USA	6 wheat		$\frac{1}{6}$ of a car
Japan	4 wheat		$\frac{1}{4}$ of a car

Step 1 in Table 3.7 is to take the lowest figure, the number of cars produced, and divide this into the higher figure, the amount of wheat produced. This produces a ratio: for every car produced in the USA 6 tonnes of wheat could be produced. In Japan for every 1 car produced 4 tonnes of wheat could be produced.

If this is put into opportunity costs then in the USA 1 car costs 6 tonnes of wheat and 1 tonne of wheat costs 1/6 of a car. In Japan 1 car cost 4 tonnes of wheat and 1 tonne of wheat costs 1/4 of a car.

In Japan a car only costs 4 tonnes of wheat but in the USA it costs 6 tonnes of wheat. Therefore cars are cheaper to produce in Japan than the USA. Japan is more efficient at producing cars: it has a comparative advantage in the production of cars. In the USA 1 tonne of wheat costs 1/6 of a car and in Japan 1/4 of a car. Wheat is cheaper to produce in the USA than in Japan. The USA is more efficient at producing wheat than Japan, it has a comparative advantage in the production of wheat.

Table 3.8 Production after specialisation

	Cars		Wheat
USA	0	+	24,000 tonnes
Japan	5,000	+	0
World Total	5,000	+	24,000 tonnes
	(+500)		(+2,000)

The lowest opportunity cost shows which good countries should specialise in. The USA should produce wheat and Japan should produce cars.

The effect of specialising, shown in Table 3.8, is that Japan can produce 5,000 cars and the USA can produce 24,000 tonnes of wheat. If this is compared to Table 3.6, when the two countries produced both goods, it can be seen that world output has increased by 500 cars and 2,000 tonnes of wheat.

If this extra output is traded freely and fairly between the two countries then both nations will enjoy more cars and wheat than if they had produced both goods themselves. This proves that the Theory of Comparative Advantage actually works: specialisation and trade benefits everyone.

Absolute advantage

The example given in Table 3.5 shows quite clearly that the USA is able to produce more wheat than Japan, and that Japan is able to produce more cars than the USA. It is easy to see in what they should specialise and it is no surprise that the Theory of Comparative Advantage actually works in this situation.

Ricardo claimed that his theory worked in all situations. If one country could produce more of both goods, it is said to have an absolute advantage. Ricardo believed that even in this situation both countries would benefit by specialising in that good in which they had a comparative advantage, and then trading freely and fairly.

Table 3.9 Production possibilities

	Cars		Wheat
UK	4,000	or	12,000 tonnes
Germany	5,000	or	20,000 tonnes

In Table 3.9 Germany is clearly better at producing both goods; it can produce more cars or more wheat than the UK. But even in this situation both countries can benefit by specialising and trading.

Using the same process as before the domestic ratios have to be worked out and then the opportunity cost of each good can be found in each country.

Table 3.10 shows the opportunity costs: it can be seen that car production is cheaper in the UK (3 tonnes of wheat) and so the UK has a comparative advantage in the production of wheat.

Wheat production is cheaper in Germany (1/4 of a car) than in the UK (1/3 of a car), so Germany has a comparative advantage in the production of

Example of an imported luxury good

wheat. Therefore, the UK should produce cars and Germany should produce wheat.

Table 3.10 Opportunity cost ratios

UK

- 1 car = 3 tonnes of wheat
- 1 tonne of wheat = $\frac{1}{3}$ of a car

Germany

- 1 car = 4 tonnes of wheat
- 1 tonne of wheat $\frac{1}{4}$ of a car

Table 3.11 shows a comparison between world output before specialisation and after specialisation. It is necessary in this case for Germany to specialise in part but it proves that the Theory of Comparative Advantage actually works, even when one country has an absolute advantage in the production of both goods.

Remember the Theory of Comparative Advantage states that:

- If countries specialise in the production of that good or service in which they have a comparative advantage (can produce most efficiently) then after trading every country will be better off.

Table 3.11 Production considering specialisation

	Cars		Wheat
Before specialisation			
UK	2,000	+	6,000 tonnes
Germany	2,500	+	10,000 tonnes
World Total	4,500	+	16,000 tonnes
After specialisation			
UK	4,000	+	0
Germany	700	+	17,200 tonnes
World Total	4,700	+	17,200 tonnes

ACTIVITY 9

Choose ten items in your house, and find out in which country they were made. Try to find out why these items were made in their particular country.

Use an atlas and try to find where the major deposits of the world's natural resources can be found. Does any country possess all of the resources?

List all those countries that are famous for a particular good, or type of good. Why do they have this reputation?

THE FINANCIAL GUARDIAN INTERNATIONAL SECTION

Trade with Barengo

The textiles produced in Barengo are different from anything made in the UK. The colours are magnificent, the cloth feels unusual.

Producers in the UK have identified the method of manufacture; they could make identical material if they wanted.

The trouble is that production would take twice as long, and cost four times as much as in Barengo, because the raw materials for the colours are to be found only in Barengo, and the cost of labour is so much cheaper there.

Trade talks

There are products made in the UK which are simply not made in Barengo, such as agricultural machinery. There are other items, especially seeds and agricultural chemicals, which can be produced in either country, but are cheaper in the UK.

Clearly, therefore, trade between the two countries is possible. Trade talks between the two countries will take place in the near future, and certain key points will be made.

Key points

Barengo is four times more efficient than the UK in the production of its famous purple cloth, three times as efficient in the production of its red cloth, and twice as efficient in the production of its white cloth.

Britain is three times as efficient as Barengo in the production of cereal seeds, and twice as efficient in the production of chemical fertilisers.

This would appear to be a sound base for specialisation and trade.

Data questions

Foundation level

1 Which items should Barengo export to the UK, and which products should the UK export to Barengo?
2 The Law of Absolute Advantage shows why one country exports and another imports. In your own words, outline the law.
3 Many countries who trade have a comparative rather than an absolute advantage. Outline the Theory of Comparative Advantage.
4 Before trade should take place, what economic, political and social factors other than production costs should be considered?

Intermediate level

1 State the Laws of Absolute Advantage and Comparative Advantage.
2 Show how trade can be worthwhile to a country that has a relative disadvantage.
3 Explain which type of advantage exists between the UK and Barengo.
4 What factors, other than just production costs, should be considered before deciding if trade is worthwhile?

Higher level

1 Distinguish between comparative and absolute advantage.
2 Explain which is evident in the text above.
3 How can an inefficient country be able to offer goods for trade?
4 Production costs are important, but other factors can influence trading decisions. Examine the economic and non-economic factors.

Review terms

The Theory of Comparative Advantage; absolute advantage; David Ricardo; standard of living; production possibility frontier; specialisation; trade; exchange

Coursework Suggestions

This is another difficult area for sound coursework.

Idea

Look at the sort of goods various groups of people have, e.g. children under ten; people of your own age; couples without children; parents; pensioners.

- examine their possessions
- list the countries where they were made
- do different groups spend more money buying goods from different countries?

It could be that, for example, children buy a lot of imported toys from China; married couples buy television sets from Korea, etc. Or, of course, it could be that there is no pattern at all!

3.7 THE PROBLEMS OF TRADE

The balance of payments account, explained in detail in section 4.6 (page 85) shows the income and expenditure of a country in its dealing with the rest of the world.

A country, just like an individual, cannot afford to spend more than it earns. If this happens in the short run then the country may use up its reserves, its savings; it may even borrow from other countries or the International Monetary Fund (IMF), see section 5.6 (page 116). However, a country cannot do this for ever: just as with an individual, loans have to be repaid. If a country continues to spend more than it earns other countries and the IMF may refuse to lend to them, and eventually their savings, reserves will disappear. It is because of this situation that countries keep a strict check on their balance of payments account and deal immediately with any problems that arise.

Balance of payments problems

If a country's expenditure is greater than its income then there is a basic problem with the balance of payments account. Income is earned from the sale of **exports** and expenditure is on the purchase of **imports**. The problem therefore is that imports are greater than exports. The country cannot afford to pay for the goods and services that it wants or needs to purchase.

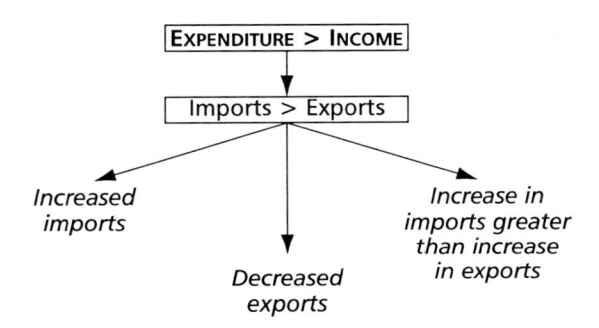

Figure 3.22 Trade problems

The balance of payments problem is due to one of three causes:

- Imports are increasing.
- Exports are decreasing.
- Imports are increasing faster than exports (exports are decreasing faster than imports).

Increasing imports

There are many reasons why imports into a country may be increasing.

If the **income** within a country is increasing then people will buy more goods and services and some of these goods and services will be imported.

When income increases people are more inclined to purchase luxury goods. If these luxury items such as television, videos and personal computers are imported, then the overall level of imports will increase.

It could be the case that the imported goods are not produced in the home country. If the people gain a taste for these goods, or if they become fashionable, then demand will increase. A good example is the many exotic fruits that can now be purchased throughout the year in the UK. Previously these were only available in selected shops at certain times of the year. Consumers have become used to the variety and demand has increased. These imported fruits have increased in quantity, increasing the level of imports.

It is sometimes the case that goods from other countries have a **reputation** for reliability, or are thought to be of better quality than home produced goods. A classic example is electrical goods. Japanese goods are thought to be the best. This reputation can be reinforced by prestigious brand names such as JVC, Sony and Panasonic. These factors increase the level of imports.

Foreign goods may be cheaper than home produced goods. This could be due to inflation in the home country, more efficient production by the foreign producer or due to the **exchange rate** (see page 89). Whatever the reason, if the foreign good is cheaper then the demand will be transferred to the imported good and the quantity demanded will increase.

Finally, if industry uses imported raw materials and increases its output as it expands, imports will also increase. Therefore a healthy growing economy will encourage an increase in imports.

Decreasing exports

Some of the reasons for increasing imports can also be used to explain why a country's exports might decrease.

If incomes within foreign countries decrease, due to unemployment for example, then their demand for other countries' exports will decrease. A general decline in the economies of overseas countries will mean that their industries will decline and the country's demand for raw materials will decrease, creating a decrease in the exports for the home country.

A country may get a bad reputation, as the UK did in the 1970s, for poor quality goods and failing to meet delivery dates. If this happens then the demand for that country's exports will decrease.

A country's exports may become expensive due to inefficient production, inflation or a change in the exchange rate. Once again exports will decrease.

Less developed countries tend to export natural resources, and as technology improves artificial substitutes are often produced. These substitutes are usually cheaper and more convenient to obtain and so the demand for the natural resources decreases, decreasing many LDCs exports. Finally it is a fact that natural resources are limited in supply and as they begin to run out the country concerned has less to export. This has been the case with the UK and North Sea oil: as the reserves have decreased the UK's exports of oil have also decreased.

Changing exports and imports

It rarely happens that the level of a country's exports *only* change or the level of its imports only. It is more likely that both will change at the same time. For example, exports could be increasing but imports could be increasing at a faster rate. Alternatively, both could be decreasing but imports at a slower rate. Both of these situations would cause a balance of payments problem for a country.

In these situations several of the factors already discussed could be happening at the same time. For example, incomes could be increasing in the home country at a faster rate than the rest of the world, thus imports would increase at a faster rate than exports. another situation might be that inflation in the home country was greater than in other trading countries, leading to a greater fall in exports than any decrease in imports.

Some solutions

If a country has a balance of payments problem then it needs to do one of two things:

- increase exports
- decrease imports.

The ideal solution would be to achieve both of these at the same time.

Increasing exports is a very difficult thing to do. A country cannot force other countries to buy their products and services, they can only encourage other nations to do so. This can be done by promoting a country's goods through **trade fairs**, producing the goods that everyone wants at a reasonable price, and trying to improve a country's reputation for reliability and quality.

Decreasing imports is relatively easier than increasing exports. **Import barriers** (see section 2.3, page 24) could be used but these invite retaliation which could start a **trade war**, with every country suffering. Import controls are also against the whole idea of the **General Agreement on Tariffs and Trade** (GATT) (see page 117) and the **European Union** (EU).

A further policy is deflation. **Deflation** means that total demand within an economy is decreased. This decreases the demand for home produced goods and imports. The economy is deflated by using fiscal policy, increasing direct taxes and/or decreasing government expenditure, and monetary policy, increasing the rate of interest to decrease demand. Deflation avoids retaliation but is less direct than import controls. The problem with deflation is that home demand is decreased which creates unemployment and bankruptcies for home producers.

A final policy option is to change the exchange rate of a country's currency. With a **fixed exchange rate** (see page 90) this would need a **devaluation**, but with a **floating exchange rate** (see page 91) a **depreciation** of the currency would be needed. A devaluation or depreciation is a decrease in the value of the currency. For example, if £1 = $2 then a depreciation/devaluation would change the exchange rate to £1 = $1.

The effect of depreciation/devaluation is clearly shown in Figure 3.23. After the depreciation/devaluation the price of the Rolls Royce exported from the UK to the USA decreased from $160,000 to £80,000 in the USA. At the same time the import

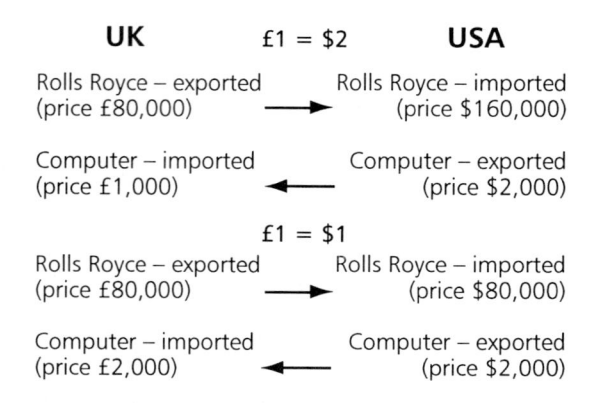

UK	£1 = $2	USA
Rolls Royce – exported (price £80,000)	→	Rolls Royce – imported (price $160,000)
Computer – imported (price £1,000)	←	Computer – exported (price $2,000)
	£1 = $1	
Rolls Royce – exported (price £80,000)	→	Rolls Royce – imported (price $80,000)
Computer – imported (price £2,000)	←	Computer – exported (price $2,000)

Figure 3.23 The effect of exchange rates on prices

from the USA, a computer, increased in price in the UK: it was £1,000 and increased to £2,000.

The total effect of a devaluation/depreciation is that the price of exports decreases and the price of imports increases.

This should decrease the demand for imports and increase the demand for exports, correcting the balance of payments.

Review terms

Exports; imports; income; reputation; exchange rate; trade fairs; trade war; import barriers; General Agreement on Tariffs and Trade; European Union; deflation; fixed exchange rate; devaluation; floating; exchange rate; depreciation.

ACTIVITY 10

Visit your local supermarket or the nearest hypermarket. Select ten items of food, some fresh and some packaged or tinned. How many of these are imported? How would your diet change without these goods?

Using the balance of payments 'Pink Book', make a note of the years since 1980 when the UK has had a balance of payments problem. Change your list so that the worst year is at the top and the best at the bottom.

Imagine income tax were to be increased; what items might people stop buying? Using the 'Pink Book', decide whether this increase in taxation would have any effect on the balance of payments.

INTERNATIONAL TRADE NEWS

Balance of payments surplus in Barengo

Barengo has continued to export its textiles to many parts of the western world. Although sales in each country are relatively small by our standards, they represent vital earnings for an area where wages are low.

Exports and imports
The total value of sales of textiles by Barengo to other countries in the year 1994–95 was £5,000,000. Imports to Barengo amounted to £4,500,000.

The imported goods are all intended to improve the agriculture of the region, and so help to eliminate the famines that have been so common.

Better wells on the way
The Barengan Regional Council has decided to bring in experts from Europe to look at the water situation. Given the increased demands of industry and agriculture, it is vital for Barengo that their wells are adequate and reliable.

Any trade balance will therefore be spent on securing these wells, as, without food and water, the region would not only cease to prosper, but be entirely uninhabitable.

Data questions

1 (a) What was the balance of exports from Barengo?
(b) What was the balance of imports into Barengo?
(c) What was the balance of trade in Barengo?
(d) How will the regional council spend the balance?
(e) Why is water so important?

2 Explain the problems experienced by a country with a balance of payments deficit.

3 What could a government do to try to solve a balance of payments deficit?

4 What could Barengo do to increase the quantity and value of its exports?

Intermediate level

1 Outline the balance of trade in Barengo.

2 What problems can be caused by a balance of payments surplus and deficit?

3 How could such problems be overcome?

4 What could Barengo do to maintain its trade position?

Higher level

1 What is Barengo's trade position with the rest of the world?

2 What problems can be caused by disequilibria in a country's balance of payments?

3 What options are open to governments to correct such positions?

4 What information would help you make such decisions?

Coursework Suggestions

Yet again, this is a difficult area to find suitable coursework topics. If you really feel that you wish to make a special study of international trade, you should consult your teacher, and find an area that is suitable, and where the material is easily and readily available. It is very easy to pick a topic, work hard, and then find that there is insufficient information to produce a decent piece of coursework.

4

Economic Terminology

Economic terms, classifications and indicators
4.1 MONEY AND THE MONEY SUPPLY IN THE UK
4.2 INCOME AND WEALTH • 4.3 EXPENDITURE PATTERNS
4.4 NATIONAL INCOME AND THE STANDARD OF LIVING
4.5 GOVERNMENT REVENUE AND EXPENDITURE
4.6 THE BALANCE OF PAYMENTS • 4.7 CURRENCY EXCHANGE
4.8 ECONOMIC ISSUES

This section should enable students to understand:
- the function and characteristics of money and its supply in the UK today
- the relevance of standard of living and cost of living and their relationship
- the structure of the balance of payments account
- the role of currency exchange
- the main economic issues at present.

4.1 MONEY AND THE MONEY SUPPLY IN THE UK

The most important part of the circular flow (see page 47) is money. It ensures that the economy functions properly. The role of the economy is to satisfy as many of the wants and needs of the people as possible. In order to do this the resources available must be used as efficiently as possible and this requires specialisation. For specialisation to work properly a good **money system** is needed. Individuals must trust the money system and be prepared to use it.

Functions of money

'What is money?' is a question that is not easy to answer. **Notes and coins** are money and CDs and apples are obviously not. In between these we have a range of items which act as money in some situations but not in others. What exists is a **spectrum of money**: at one end are notes and coins and at the other end CDs and apples. The best way to describe money is to say that anything that performs the **functions of money** is money.

The first function is as a **medium of exchange**. For anything to be used as money it must be accepted by everyone at all times. This function allows specialisation to take place. Without it economies would revert to **barter** and the progress of economies would be halted.

The second function of money is as a **unit of account** (alternatively a **unit of measurement**). If goods are to be exchanged then some method of measuring the value of these goods is needed. The method of measurement must be the same so that all goods and services can be measured in an identical way. If all goods and services have a price expressed in terms of money, then a common measurement exists and exchange becomes easier.

The third function of money is as a **store of value**. Some people may not need to spend all of their income and may want to save some to increase their consumption in the future. If the value of money is certain in the future and it can be stored and not deteriorate, then individuals will be able to purchase what they want in the future.

The fourth and final function is as a **standard of deferred payment**. A deferred payment is one made at a later date, known as credit. In a modern economy credit is used a great deal. It is very common to purchase an article and pay for it at a later date, either through a hire purchase agreement or by using a credit card. This is only possible if the seller is prepared to accept payment in the future and can be certain of the true value of the payment. Only money can perform this function.

Characteristics of money

Various items have been used as money including grain, arrow heads, religious objects, gold and silver. This has been an attempt to find something that has all the characteristics that money actually requires if it is to perform its functions.

In order for money to retain its value it must be **limited in supply**. If it can be reproduced at any time by any individual then it will lose its value.

If money is to perform its function as a medium of exchange then it will constantly be in use and be passed from person to person. Constant use means that it must be **durable**, that is, able to withstand heavy usage, and **portable**. Cattle were at one time used as money but they are difficult to transport and die after a period of time; they are neither portable nor durable and therefore were not successful as money.

Durability is important for money to function as a store of value. To return to one's savings two years later to find that their value has deteriorated or that they have died (in the case of cattle!) would be of no use.

If money is to be exchanged for goods and services it must be recognised as money and have some value that makes it **acceptable** to everyone. Without acceptability money is worthless.

Finally, a problem with early money was that it consisted of one unit only. For example, broken in half a shell loses its value and so smaller units cannot be used. However, small amounts of coins can be produced; thus money needs to be **divisible**.

Money supply in the UK

Money in the UK has developed considerably since the times when shells, grain and religious objects were the main part of the money supply.

The three main forms of money in use in the UK today are **notes**, **coins** and **bank deposits**.

Bank notes date back to the time when they were receipts for gold deposited with the

FUNCTIONS OF MONEY
Medium of exchange
Store of value
Unit of account
Standard of deferred payment

CHARACTERISTICS OF MONEY
Limited in supply
Durable
Portable
Acceptable
Divisible

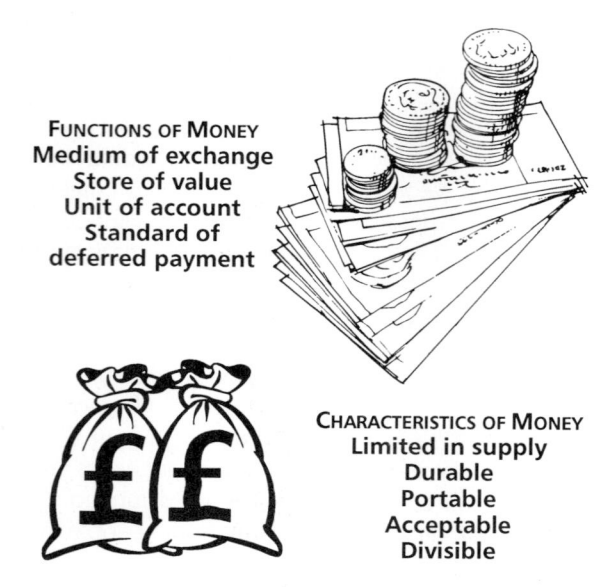

Figure 4.1 The functions and characteristics of money

Goldsmiths. The wording on today's bank notes, 'I promise to pay the bearer on demand the sum of', is from those early receipts. Today's bank notes have no value themselves: they cannot be exchanged for gold and the paper on which they are printed has little value. Modern bank notes are **fiat currency**: they are based upon trust. They are of value because everyone accepts them at all times for the purchase of goods and services.

Coins have developed from tokens to gold and silver and back again to tokens. Coins originally had a value because they were made of gold and silver. However, these metals are quite soft and so they were mixed with other harder metals in an alloy. The value remained because of the gold and silver content. It was then an easy step to remove the gold and silver and produce metal tokens, again a fiat currency based upon trust. Coins still retain a value because they are acceptable at all times by everyone as a means of exchange.

The third form of money in the UK at present is bank deposits. It is not only the most modern but also the most important in terms of the value of transactions. A bank deposit is a record kept by a commercial bank, usually on a computer, of the money held for an individual. With a **current account** this money can be moved from one account to another by using a **cheque**. A cheque is not money but an instruction to a bank to transfer funds from one account to another. This is a safe and efficient way of paying for goods and services and so is very popular. In this situation transferring money is merely a change in computer records, and does not require the physical movement of cash.

Electronic cheques such as Switch and Delta are not as yet readily acceptable as money simply because many shops and most individuals do not accept payment in this way.

The same applies to **credit cards**: some shops accept them but not all, and certainly no individual would accept payment by Visa or Mastercard.

Although electronic cheques and credit cards are increasing in use and acceptability rapidly, they will not be accepted as part of the money supply whilst they fail to fulfil all of the functions of money, the most important of which is as a medium of exchange.

ACTIVITY 1

List all of the denominations of notes and coins that are in use in the UK at present.

Ask your parents how they are paid for their job. Is it weekly, monthly, in cash, by cheques etc. Why are they paid in this particular way?

Check five local shops, five large stores and five supermarkets: how many of these accept credit cards? Why do some accept credit cards and others do not?

✓ Review terms

Notes and coins; spectrum of money; functions of money; medium of exchange; barter; unit of account; unit of measurement; store of value; standard of deferred payment; credit; limited in supply; portable; durable; acceptable; divisible; bank deposits; fiat currency; current account; cheques; credit cards.

UK Money Supply November 1994

Source: Financial Statistics

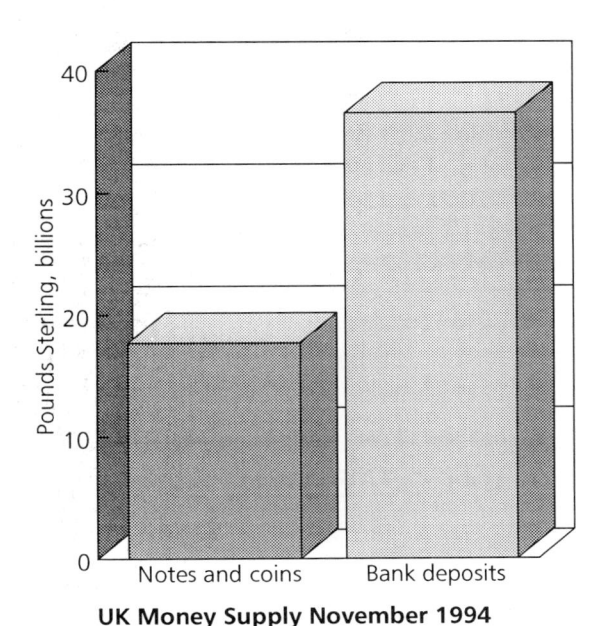

Figure 4.2 UK notes, coins and bank deposits

THE DAILY NEWS

Barengo – the old remember

Barengo is unique. It is a place which has, in living memory, moved from having no roads, few buildings and where the use of money was unknown, to a busy settlement similar to any you might find in Britain.

Life without money

Walking along the main street yesterday, surrounded by offices, shops and banks, I met a group of elderly people. For them some of the changes have been good ones. One man told me that when he was young money just did not exist. Your wealth was your possessions. 'It was very simple', he said. 'If you owned a cow you were richer than someone who had a sheep or a goat, and they were richer than someone who had a hen.'

'But things got difficult if you wanted to exchange what you had for something someone else had. The other person might not have wanted what you had to offer. Your cow might have been worth more than the thing you wanted in exchange – how could you cut off a piece of your cow? One year our cow died and we were left with nothing.'

Benefits of money

Money, they all agreed, had made life much easier. As one woman said, 'Now we must carry money around with us and whenever we want to buy something, everyone just accepts it.'

Data questions

Foundation level

1 What four advantages are given for using money as a medium of exchange rather than goods?
2 Explain what is meant by the expression 'medium of exchange'.
3 How can a bank help the money system work?
4 What problems can arise when a money system is used?

Intermediate level

1 What are the advantages of using money rather than cattle?
2 Outline and explain the functions and characteristics of money.
3 What is the role of the banks in the use of money?
4 How could the use of money cause problems to individuals and the economy as a whole?

Higher level

1 Explain the reasons why money rather than animals is used as a medium of exchange.
2 How can a piece of paper be worth anything?
3 How do banks facilitate the use of money?
4 Under what circumstances could the use of money become a problem?

Coursework Suggestions

This area is rather limited for good coursework. It may be better to consider the topic of money and wealth, thus involving sections 4.1 and 4.2.

It may well be possible to develop the Activities suggested in 4.1 (page 67) and produce a piece of coursework, but there could be a problem in the quantity of material produced proving to be too limited. If you really do want to concentrate on money, then you ought to discuss the topic carefully with your teacher.

4.2 INCOME AND WEALTH

Income and **wealth** are not the same thing. A person earning a high income is not always wealthy, and a wealthy person does not necessarily have to earn a high income.

Whilst this is true in theory, in practice income and wealth are closely linked, therefore it is usual for wealthy people to have high incomes and for those who are poor to have very low incomes or to survive on state benefits.

Income

Income is created when production takes place. Production requires the factors of production, land, labour, capital and enterprise, and these will only take part in the production process if they receive rewards. Each factor has a specific reward:

- Land receives **rent.**
- Labour receives **wages.**
- Capital receives **interest.**
- Enterprise receives **profit.**

Each of these rewards is paid to the owner of the particular factors used. Receiving these payments for the use of the factors of production is known as income. Thus:

- the *owners* of the *factors of production* receive *income* in the form of wages, rent, interest and profit, *for the use of the factors* in the *production* process.

In theory the amount of income received for each factor should be equal to their contribution to the production process, however, in practice this does not work and other factors become important in determining the amount of income received by each factor.

Wages, the payment for labour, are by far the greatest amount of income within the National Income. Rent, interest and profit added together (22·8%) do not amount to as much as wages (77·2%). Wages form the greatest part of income because everyone, with a few exceptions, has their labour to offer. However, few people own the factors of land or capital and even less have entrepreneurial skills to offer. It is because of this that for the majority of people wages form their entire income.

This provides a reason why some individuals have high incomes and others low incomes. Those receiving high incomes usually receive wages plus either interest, rent or profit, or in some cases all three. This increases total income. Other individuals rely entirely upon wages and may be unable to find a job, hence they survive on benefits.

For those who survive on wages alone income can also vary. For labour that has skills which are in demand or that possesses very special skills or talents, then wages will be very high, producing a high income. For those without any special skills and who compete with many other workers, the wage, and hence their income, will be quite low.

For a number of other individuals their income is zero, or below the minimum that the government believes is necessary to survive. These households receive **transfer payments**, which are amounts of money given by the government. These include benefits for unemployment and other reasons which enable these people to maintain a minimum **standard of living**. For many households these benefits form a major part of their income.

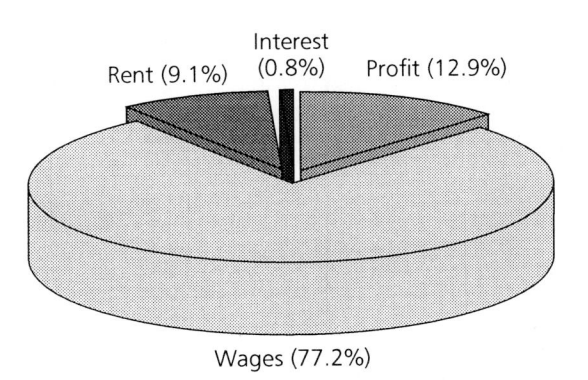

Rent (9.1%) Interest (0.8%) Profit (12.9%) Wages (77.2%)

Source: CSO Blue Book 1994

Figure 4.3 The composition of UK National Income, 1992

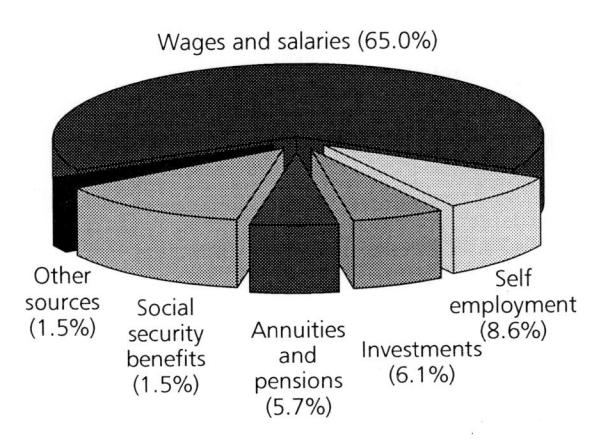

Wages and salaries (65.0%) Other sources (1.5%) Social security benefits (1.5%) Annuities and pensions (5.7%) Investments (6.1%) Self employment (8.6%)

Source: Family Expenditure Survey

Figure 4.4 The composition of UK household income, 1992

Wealth

Wealth is the ownership of **real assets**, that is, **marketable assets**. Marketable assets are real possessions that can be turned into cash if required.

The ownership of assets automatically includes the ownership of the factors of production, capital and land. Labour cannot be owned, it is merely the services of labour that are purchased. Wealth therefore inevitably creates an income in the form of interest and rent. Also because the owners of the factors organise production they receive the reward of profit for their organisational skills.

The result is that the owners of a factor usually receive a wage for their own labour, plus a reward for their factor plus an element of profit. In this case wealth creates a high income.

Although wealth and income are *not* the same thing, income can be used to purchase wealth:

- Income is a claim to wealth.
- Wealth is the ownership of assets.

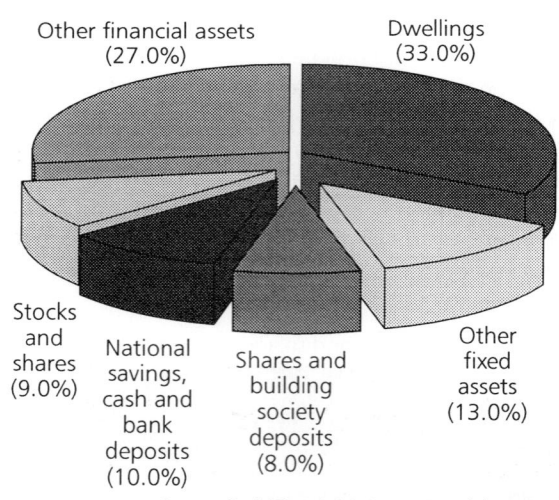

Figure 4.5 The composition of wealth – UK 1992

Other financial assets (27.0%)
Dwellings (33.0%)
Stocks and shares (9.0%)
National savings, cash and bank deposits (10.0%)
Shares and building society deposits (8.0%)
Other fixed assets (13.0%)

Source: *Social Trends 24*, Crown Copyright 1994

Figure 4.5 clearly shows that the majority of wealth held by individuals is in the **property** that they own, followed closely by **life assurance** and **pension funds** to which they have a claim. Cash and bank deposits, which can be translated into assets, form the third largest asset.

All individuals possess special skills and talents that they can use in their occupation. This is termed as personal wealth. Personal wealth can often produce high levels of income which can be converted into assets.

Wealth is often passed on within families, between generations. The ability of marketable assets to earn income and purchase yet more assets means that wealth is very often unequally distributed.

Wealth creates income which purchases yet greater wealth and even higher incomes are earned:

- The most wealthy 10% of the population own 50% of the UK's entire wealth.
- The most wealthy 50% of the population own 92% of the UK's wealth, leaving 8% of the wealth for the remaining 50% of the people.

Table 4.1 The distribution of wealth – UK 1991)

Owned by	% of wealth
Most wealthy 1% of the population	18%
Most wealthy 5% of the population	37%
Most wealthy 10% of the population	50%
Most wealthy 25% of the population	71%
Most wealthy 50% of the population	92%

ACTIVITY

Calculate your own personal income. How is it split between wages, rent, interest and profit? What is the value of your personal wealth? Do you own any assets?

Calculate the total income of your household. How much of this is in the form of wages, rent, interest and profit?

Estimate the wealth of your household and subtract any mortgage owed.

Choose either your school or your local council. List all the items that would be included if the wealth of either one were to be calculated. Can all of these assets be sold? Does it matter if some assets cannot be sold?

THE INTERNATIONAL FINANCIAL NEWS

Wealth is relative

News of the rapid development of Barengo has been much in the public eye recently.

Early stages
The economy is still very much in its early stages and, by Western standards, wages would seem very low indeed.

People content
A Barengan shopkeeper told me how he pays his assistant £5.00 per week. This is the only income the assistant has, but as the average wage in Barengo is £3.00 per week, he is happy.

The shopkeeper himself owns the land and the shop, so he has no rent to pay. He has paid for all the stock in the shop. Once his bills are paid, then, whatever money is left is his profit. What he does not spend, he saves in the bank and earns interest at 5%. He now has about £1,000 in the bank – not a large sum by our standards, but in Barengo he feels comfortably off.

Data questions

Foundation level

1 (a) How much does the shopkeeper's assistant receive for his labour?
 (b) How much rent does the shopkeeper pay for the land?
 (c) What rate of interest does the shopkeeper receive for his capital?
 (d) What profit does the shopkeeper receive?
 (e) What economic term is used to describe labour, rent, capital and enterprise?

2 List the various assets that make up the wealth of the shopkeeper.

3 What is the difference between income and wealth?

4 The article says that the shopkeeper and his assistant are more prosperous than many other people in the country. What else would you want to know before being able to comment on their standard of living?

Intermediate level

1 Explain the meaning of the term 'factors of production', and give examples from the text.

2 Show the income of the assistant and the wealth of the shopkeeper.

3 Explain the difference between income and wealth.

4 What evidence do you have and what other information would you need to decide the standard of living of the shopkeeper and his assistant?

Higher level

1 How does the shopkeeper receive his income?

2 Examine the wealth of the shopkeeper.

3 Why do some people have more wealth than others?

4 What additional information would you require to examine the standard of living of the shopkeeper and his assistant?

✓ Review terms

Wages; rent; interest; profit; income; transfer payments; standard of living; real assets; marketable assets; property; life assurance; pension funds.

Coursework Suggestions

The Activities in the chapter provide some good ideas for coursework.

Idea

Compare your personal income and wealth.

You know your income, but then look at all of your assets – savings, premium bonds, etc., your clothes, records, CDs, and anything else that you might own.

- Explain how you arrived at your valuations.
- Perhaps you could consider how you have reached that particular level of wealth on your income.

Idea

You could do the same sort of exercise for your household. This would give a better opportunity to consider income (and perhaps expenditure) in terms of the factors of production.

4.3 EXPENDITURE PATTERNS

Expenditure in the economy comes from three main sources: the government, firms and households. Government expenditure (discussed in section 4.5, page 81) accounts for approximately 19% of all expenditure but the vast majority, 61%, is household expenditure with 20% undertaken by firms.

Firms expenditure

Firms spend their money on consumables that are required in everyday production and raw materials that form the basis of production. However, by far the greatest amount of expenditure by a firm is in the form of **investment**. Investment is the purchase of **capital**.

- Capital is a person-made aid to production.

The term capital includes machinery, tools, factory and office buildings. Anything that is produced by people, (excluding natural resources, which are the factor land) in order to help the firms increase output in the future is capital.

A firm will automatically purchase capital as its machinery wears out or becomes out-dated due to new technology and this is known as **depreciation**. New capital, because it helps to increase output in the future, may also increase a firm's profits in the future. New capital is known as **net investment**.

Capital

Capital can be in many forms but it should not be confused with consumption. Three types of capital exist:

- **Fixed capital**: this includes all machinery and factory buildings. It is fixed because during the process of production it does not change its shape or form.
- **Circulating capital (working capital)**: this includes partly finished goods and finished goods that are held in stock as well as the stock of raw materials. It does not include money.
- **Social capital**: this is an indirect aid to production and includes the housing stock, hospitals and schools. All of these ensure that the work force is healthy, happy and well educated, helping to increase production.

Household expenditure

Household expenditure is usually on goods and services for immediate use, items such as food and drink. This is known as **consumption**, households are therefore known as **consumers**.

Consumers spend their money on consumption goods and services which fall into three broad categories: services, durable goods and non-durable goods.

Consumer's services are often known as non-tangible goods, that is, goods that cannot be touched. These include financial services such as banking and insurance, plus personal services such as hairdressing and entertainment.

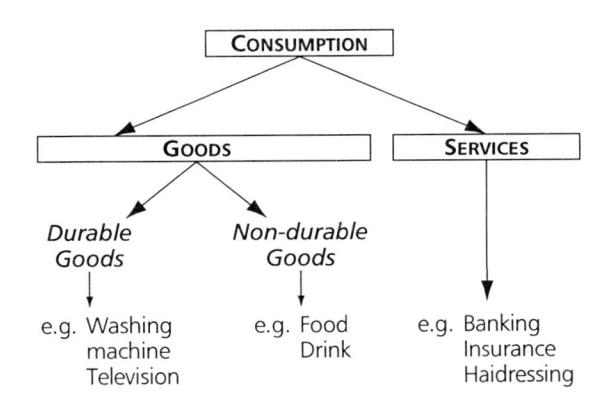

Figure 4.6 Consumer goods and services

Consumer goods can be split into two groups, **durables** and **non-durables**.

- Durable goods are those goods which are consumed over a period of time, rather than immediately. This would include televisions, video recorders, dishwashers and washing machines.
- Non-durable goods are those goods that are consumed during their use, often immediately. The best examples are food and drink. As you use these items they are destroyed.

Both durable and non-durable goods are used to satisfy consumers' immediate needs, they do nothing to aid production now or in the future.

Investment

Investment, the purchase of capital, takes place in order to increase output in the future, to decrease the cost of production or to increase the quality of production. There are various factors that influence the purchase of capital such as:

- the rate of interest
- the level of profits
- the level of demand in the economy
- the prospects of the economy

Whenever investment takes place a sacrifice has to be made. A firm cannot produce consumer goods and capital at the same time. If capital is produced, consumer goods cannot be produced, therefore this creates an **opportunity cost**:

- The *cost of producing one item* in terms of the *next best alternative* that has to be *given up*.

Consumption

A household's consumption is determined mainly by the level of their **disposable income** (their income after tax and other deductions). John Keynes produced a considerable amount of evidence to suggest that consumption increases as income increases. However, with each increase in income the increase in consumption gets smaller.

Disposable income is determined mainly by the rate of direct tax and so the rate of income tax influences the level of consumption.

Consumption can be split into two further categories, these are **necessities** and **luxuries**.

Initially income is spent on those goods and services that are necessary for the members of the household to survive, these include food and drink, heat and light and payment for the house or flat. Once these necessities have been purchased any income left is used to buy luxury items, goods and services that bring enjoyment and improve the **quality of life** for the household.

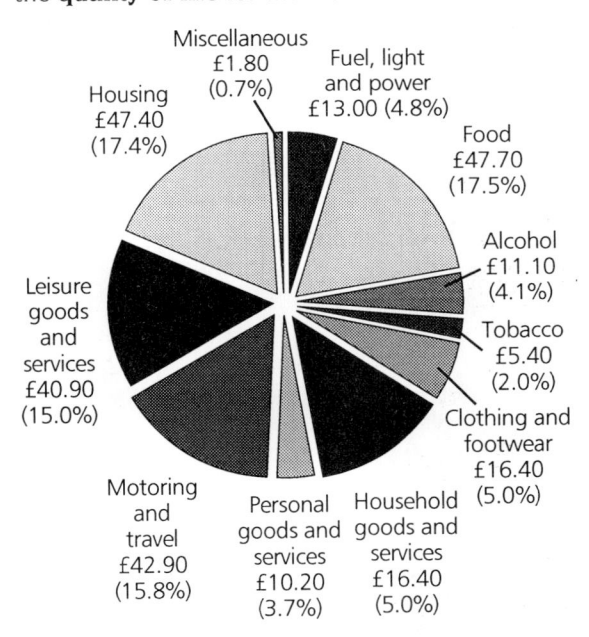

Figure 4.7 Weekly family expenditure – UK 1992

The information given in Figure 4.8 shows that out of a weekly average income of £272.10, £47.70 is spent on food which is 17·5%, £47.40 on housing (17·4%) and £13.00 (4·8%) on fuel, light and power.

If these items are added together and the total for clothing and footwear, plus half of the figure for household goods and services, a total amount for essential spending can be calculated. If these are classified as necessities, expenditure equals £140.00 or 51·5% of the average weekly income.

Not all of the goods and services bought in the categories mentioned will be necessities and some items in the other categories might be necessities, but this calculation gives an indication of how much might be spent on necessities.

The remaining 45·5% or £132.00 of income, is left to purchase luxuries such as tobacco, alcohol, cars and personal goods and services.

The pattern of spending on necessary items tends to remain quite stable, as income increases the extra money is spent on luxury items. As income decreases, maybe due to increases in direct tax, the first items that are affected are luxury items. Hence household expenditure on necessities tends to remain very stable.

The exception to this is when the cost of necessary items changes due to government policy or other circumstances. For example, an increase in the rate of interest increases mortgage repayments and therefore a household's expenditure on housing would increase.

Expenditure on luxury items is unstable. Not only does it change with changes in income, but it is also affected by the time of the year. At Christmas and Easter expenditure on luxury items increases, also during the summer with the purchase of holidays there is again an increase in expenditure. It is worth remembering that the idea of necessities and luxuries can be a very personal thing. A luxury to one person might be thought of as a necessity to another. Many people consider a television to be a necessity but survival without a television is possible. In economic terms a necessity is a **basic need for survival**.

An example of consumers' expenditure

ACTIVITY 3

List five durable and five non-durable goods that you can find in your home. List five services that your household pays for.

Take the 15 goods and services already listed and put these into two groups, one group for necessities and the other group for luxuries. Which is the biggest group? Are there any patterns, for example, do all of the durable goods go into one group or are they divided between the groups?

Use (a) your own income or (b) imagine you have an income or (c) ask your parents what their income is.

Now calculate how much is spent on necessities and luxuries. If you have imagined an income of your own you will need to think about how you would spend this before you can make any calculation.

Finally, how would you spend an increase in income and how would you cope with a decrease in income? What goods or services would be bought or no longer purchased. Classify the goods and services?

An example of firms' expenditure

THE INVESTMENT CHRONICLE

Advertisement

Investment opportunity in Barengo

The prospering textile industry of Barengo is actively seeking investment capital.

Demand
The demand for Barengon textiles is now so high that the need has arisen for investment to finance expansion.

The money is needed for the purchase of additional machinery and to fund the further expansion of the factory buildings:

- The machines required are long-lasting, depreciation will be low.
- There is adequate working capital – money is needed for expansion.
- The workforce is happy, content and hard-working.
- The industry is making high levels of profit.
- The recovery in the world economy and the high level of orders means prospects are excellent.
- The rate of return on capital investment is likely to be high.

Data questions

Foundation level

1 Explain the meaning of the terms:
   (a) investment
   (b) working capital
   (c) expansion
   (d) depreciation.

2 Why might someone want to invest money in the textile industry of Barengo?

3 What might an investor want to know, apart from the information in the text, before investing?

4 Suggest four reasons why the textile industry in Barengo might suffer from a fall in demand.

Intermediate level

1 Explain the meaning of four of the economic terms in the text.

2 Why do people invest money?

3 What additional information might a potential investor need before reaching a decision about the textile industry in Barengo?

4 Explain the factors that might cause a fall in demand for the textiles?

Higher level

1 Explain the meanings of the main economic terms used in the text.

2 What factors should be taken into consideration before making a decision about investing capital?

3 What factors could cause a fall in demand for the textiles in Barengo?

4 Is expansion always the best policy for a firm? Why?

✓ Review terms

Investment; capital; depreciation; net investment; fixed capital; circulating (working) capital; social capital; consumption; durables; non-durables; opportunity cost; disposable income; necessities; luxuries; quality of life; basic needs for survival.

Coursework Suggestions

Idea

Providing that you are sure that you can obtain enough information, you could consider the investment opportunities within a firm.

You would need to know the owner or the managing director very well. Then you could ask such questions as:

- Why do you want to expand?
- How much will it cost?
- What do you expect to gain?
- What have you done to ensure that those gains are likely?
- How do you intend to attract investment?
- Why are you using such methods?

You may even be able to assess the success of such investment.

Idea

Goods which are regarded by some people as luxuries, others regard as necessities.

- What sorts of goods are examples of this? Why is there a difference in opinion?
- Decide on a series of goods, and ask your friends and relatives into which category they would place such goods
- Does a pattern emerge, e.g. do older people have different views to younger, married to single, etc.? Analyse your results, and draw conclusions.

4.4 NATIONAL INCOME AND THE STANDARD OF LIVING

It is the aim of every economy to provide for as many wants and needs as possible. If wants and needs are always increasing then an economy must be constantly increasing its output. In order to check how successful an economy is, it is important to measure the amount that it produces.

Measurement of the National Income

The output of the economy can be measured in three ways: **National Output** (NO), **National Income** (NY) and **National Expenditure** (NE).

NO = NY = NE

These three parts of the National Income are equal because the value of any item produced is equal to its price. If the price of every item is multiplied by the number sold total expenditure is calculated. Therefore National Expenditure is equal to National Output (NE = NO).

The rewards to the factors of production are equal to the value of their input into the production process. Therefore the value of the goods and services and the rewards paid must be equal, hence National Output equals National Income (NO = NY).

Measuring the size of the economy in these three ways provides a good check on the accuracy of the calculations. If one figure is thought to be inaccurate it can be checked against the other two.

A further benefit of using all three calculations is that different elements of the economy can be analysed.

Measuring the size of the National Income by measuring the output of the economy is known as the **output method**. Measuring expenditure is called the **expenditure method**, and the measurement of income is called the **income method**.

National Output – the output method

This is the most direct method of measuring the amount produced by an economy. It simply involves adding together the output of every single firm within the economy.

The problem with this method is that **double counting** can occur. A product produced by one firm may be a component in the production of another good produced by some other firm, thus it would be counted twice. To overcome this the output method only counts **final goods and services** or uses the **value added method**.

The value added method counts the value added by the production process. If milk is purchased from a dairy, bottled and sold to shops, only the difference between the value of the milk when purchased and the value of the bottled milk is counted. This difference is the value added.

Table 4.2 The UK National Income – the output method 1993

Sector	£m
Agriculture, forestry and fishing	10,373
Mining, quarrying and oil and gas extraction	12,147
Manufacturing	118,294
Electricity, gas and water supply	13,994
Construction	29,221
Wholesale and retail trade: repair: hotels and restaurants	78,348
Transport, storage and communication	46,263
Financial and business activities	133,956
Public administration	38,199
Education, health and social work	57,457
Other services (refuse disposal)	31,292
Total	569,544
less Adjustment for financial services	23,424
Gross Domestic Product	546,120

Not only does the output method provide a total output figure it allows comparisons between sectors to be analysed. For example, which sector contributes the most, or the least, to the output of the UK? Comparisons over time are also possible, e.g. has manufacturing increased or decreased its share of output in the UK during the last five years?

National Expenditure – the expenditure method

This method adds together the expenditure of all the households and firms; government expenditure is usually divided into five categories:

- consumption (purchase of goods and services)
- investment (the purchase of capital)
- government expenditure
- expenditure on exports and imports

The prices of goods and services are usually increased due to the addition of tax; some prices are reduced, however, because governments **subsidise** (pay a part of the cost of) them. Hence expenditure has to be adjusted to get the true value of the goods and services. The adjustment is to subtract the amount of the tax and add the amount of the subsidy.

A final adjustment is to *add* expenditure on **exports** and *subtract* expenditure on **imports**. If the aim is to count expenditure on the goods and services produced in the UK, then expenditure on imports should not be counted. However, expenditure on exports which are produced in the UK should be included.

Table 4.3 The UK National Income – the expenditure method 1993

Sector	£m
Consumers' expenditure	405,639
General government final consumption	138,224
Gross domestic fixed capital formation	94,715
Value of physical increase in stocks and work in progress	–197
Total domestic expenditure	638,381
plus Exports of goods and services	157,999
Total final expenditure	796,380
less Imports of goods and services	166,266
Statistical error	–91
Gross Domestic Product at Market Prices	630,023
less Taxes	91,361
plus Subsidies	7,458
Gross Domestic Product at Factor Cost	546,120

National Income – the income method

The income method totals all of the rewards paid to the factors of production, in order to produce the nation's output. All of these incomes need to be **gross income**, which is income before tax and other stoppages are deducted.

It is income earned from the production of goods and services that needs to be counted and so **transfer payments** (see pages 69 and 83) are not included. Similarly, any increase in stocks (goods produced but not sold) is also deducted. These are not goods made available for sale.

Again, comparisons between different types of income and over a period of time, can be made. This enables government to judge the performance of the different sectors.

Table 4.4 The UK National Income – the income method 1993

Sector	£m
Income from employment	352,896
Income from self-employment	61,346
Gross trading profits of companies	73,397
Gross trading surpluses of public corporations	3,415
of general government enterprises	294
Rent	52,872
Charge for consumption of non-trading capital	3,942
Total domestic income	548,162
less Stock appreciation	2,359
Statistical error	+317
Gross Domestic Product	546,120
plus Net property income from abroad	3,062
Gross National Product	549,182
less Capital consumption	65,023
Net National Product (NN.) – National Income	484,159

GDP and GNP

When the various adjustments have been made for each of the three methods, the final figure is the **Gross Domestic Product** (GDP) at factor cost. **Factor cost** is the true cost of the good or service, counting only the value of the factors of production used.

- GDP is the *value* of the *output* of the nation in any *one year*.

GDP is an adequate measurement but there are some factors in the UK which are not owned by the UK or UK citizens. Other factors are based in overseas countries but owned by the UK or UK citizens. Other factors are based in overseas countries but owned by the UK or UK citizens. A more accurate measurement, therefore, is the **Gross National Product** (GNP):

- GNP is the *total value* of all goods and services produced by domestically owned factors of production over a period of *one year*.

In order to find the GNP figure from the GDP figure, **net property income from abroad** is added. This is the income from UK owned factors of production less any income owed to overseas factors.

The final step is to deduct an amount for **depreciation**. Depreciation includes worn out or obsolete capital that needs to be replaced. This is not an addition to the nation's stock of capital but a replacement and so is not counted. Once depreciation has been deducted, then the final figure is the **National Income** or the **Net National Product** (NNP).

Table 4.5 Deriving the National Income

	Gross Domestic Product (GDP)
plus	Net property income from abroad
equals	Gross National Product (GNP)
minus	Depreciation
equals	National Income (Net National Product)

Standard of living

Apart from acting as an indicator of how well an economy is performing, the GNP figure is useful because it gives a value for the amount of goods and services produced in any one year.

The goods and services produced are available to the people within the country and so have an influence upon their lives.

A major indication of the welfare of individuals within a country is the **standard of living**. This looks at people's welfare in terms of the goods and services available to them. Hence GNP divided by the total population is used. This provides a figure for the value of goods and services available to each individual over a period of one year (see section 6.2, page 124). The following is used to compute the standard of living indicator:

GNP ÷ total population
= GNP per head
= standard of living indicator.

Inflation

One thing that seriously disrupts National Income calculations is **inflation**. Inflation decreases the value of money and so more pounds are needed to buy the same amount of goods and services. In this situation National Income calculations might make it appear that output has increased. However, if the value of money has decreased the economy could be producing *less* but selling for a greater money value.

Inflation also has an effect upon an individual's **cost of living**. If the value of money decreases people are able to buy less with their income. This then decreases their standard of living. If the cost of living increases by 10% and incomes increase by 20% then people can buy more goods and services and their standard of living will rise. This only happens if the increase in income is greater than the increase in the cost of living.

The cost of living and the standard of living are not the same thing. However, they are linked. The cost of living influences the standard of living. If the cost of living increases by more than any increase in income then the standard of living will decrease, but if the rise in the cost of living is less than any increase in income the standard of living will increase.

THE STATISTICAL REVIEW

Shortage of figures in Barengo

Collecting accurate figures to assemble National Income figures is very difficult, even if information is easily available. When any accurate record is hard to find, the task becomes almost impossible.

Help with figures

Members of the National Statistical Society have been invited to Barengo to try to help work out their figures. However, trouble has already risen: existing methods of keeping records have proved unreliable. The statisticians tried to use the output method but discovered that, although everyone is so proud of what they make that they record their output very carefully, they are often not recording final goods.

Many goods are handed on to another firm for completion. This means goods have been recorded twice which makes it difficult to calculate the total value of outputs.

The expenditure method was tried, but it turned out that there was no accurate record of money received from charities to subsidise purchases, and goods donated to the region by other charities were sometimes regarded as imports, sometimes ignored.

Finally, the income method was used, but no stock record was available.

Mystery inflation

In fact, no-one seemed to know accurately the size of the population, and the inflation rates proved to be a total mystery.

Such are the problems of a developing nation attempting to grapple with the economic statistical requirements of an industrialised nation.

ACTIVITY 4

Use your school or local library and find the publication in which National Income figures are published. Try to find the income, expenditure and output figures for the UK.

Using the published figures for the UK's National Income, take the expenditure and output accounts.

Try to split the income account into wages, rent, interest and profit. Split the expenditure account into consumption, investment, government expenditure, exports and imports.

Find out by how much the cost of living has increased this year. By how much has your parents' income increased?

Has your family's standard of living increased or decreased?

Data questions

Foundation level

1 Explain the problems of calculating National Income in Barengo.

2 Explain how National Income should be calculated.

3 How could Barengo improve its system so that accurate records are available?

4 What use are National Income figures?

Intermediate level

1 Explain how National Income is calculated.

2 How would you solve the problems of calculating National Income in Barengo?

3 What is the problem of inflation when considering National Income figures?

4 What information can National Income figures provide for a government?

Advanced level

1 What improvements to the statistical system of Barengo would you recommend in order to allow the easy calculation of National Income figures?

2 What is the problem caused by inflation in arriving at accurate National Income figures?

3 How can a government use National Income figures to improve its economy?

4 What is the significance of the size of population to National Income?

Coursework Suggestions

This is a very difficult area for coursework, and it might well be best to avoid the topic.

Close consultation with your teacher may allow you to find a suitable title, but it could prove to be more difficult than you think.

✓ Review terms

National Output; National Income; National Expenditure; output method; expenditure method; income method; double counting; final goods and services; value added method; subsidise; exports; imports; gross income; transfer payments; Gross Domestic Product (GDP); factor cost; Gross National Product (GNP); net property income from abroad; depreciation; National Income; net national product; standard of living; inflation; cost of living.

4.5 GOVERNMENT REVENUE AND EXPENDITURE

There are a number of reasons why governments become involved in the running of an economy. If an economy was left entirely to **market forces**, the forces of demand and supply, certain goods would not be produced. Other goods might be produced but in the wrong quantities. A further possibility is that goods would be produced but consumers would be exploited.

A major failure with a **market economy** is that inequalities of income increase: the rich get richer and the poor remain poor. The distribution of income therefore becomes very unequal with the poor suffering an increasing inability to purchase the basic goods and services that they need.

Public and merit goods

If wants and needs are left to the forces of demand and supply some goods and services would not be produced. For example, defence and law and order would not exist. It is virtually impossible to charge for these services and if a method of charging was found nobody would pay. They would each wait for someone else to pay although they would hope to enjoy the benefits. These goods and services are known as **public goods**.

If the market will not provide these goods and services and if they are considered to be important, then the government must provide them.

Another form of goods are **merit goods**. These include health and education. It is believed that in a democratic society everyone should have the right to a minimum level of health care and education. However, some people would not be able to pay for these goods if their cost was left to market forces and others would not consider them to be worthwhile.

The only way to ensure that everyone has an equal share of these goods and services is to provide them at **zero price**. This is only possible if government can provide them and obtain the revenue from elsewhere.

Regulation

A major role for a government is to protect the consumer from exploitation. This involves regulation of the economy through various rules and laws. Controls over such things as monopolies, advertising, labelling of goods and health and safety laws, are all designed to protect the consumer.

Distribution of income

If it is believed that the national income should be shared more equally, this can only be achieved by government intervention.

Through its **taxation** and **expenditure** government is able to adjust the distribution of income. If the rich are taxed on their income and this money is used to help the poor, then a greater equality can be achieved. If this is taken one step further, with higher incomes being taxed more than lower incomes, and the poorest receiving more **benefits** than those who are better off, even greater equality can be achieved.

Government revenue

In order for the government to provide public and merit goods, and in order for it to protect the consumer and monitor the growth of firms, it is important that the government obtains income (revenue) as easily as possible. If at the same time this revenue can also help towards greater equality then so much the better.

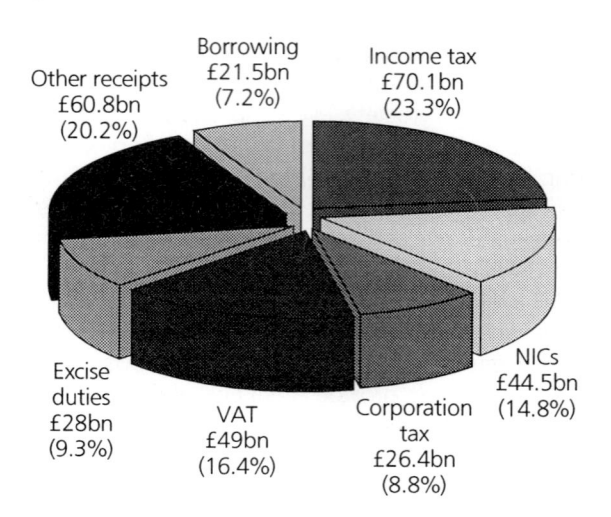

Other receipts £60.8bn (20.2%)
Borrowing £21.5bn (7.2%)
Income tax £70.1bn (23.3%)
NICs £44.5bn (14.8%)
Corporation tax £26.4bn (8.8%)
VAT £49bn (16.4%)
Excise duties £28bn (9.3%)

Figure 4.8 UK Government revenue – 1995–96

The greatest amount of revenue comes from **income tax**. In the UK this is a **progressive tax**, which means that the more you earn the more you pay. Below a set level of income no income tax is paid. Everyone that is in employment, or self employed, is liable to pay income tax. At present, in the UK, there are three rates of income tax, the lower rate at 20%, the basic rate at 25% and the higher rate at 40%.

VAT (Value Added Tax)

This is the second largest income earner for the UK Government. VAT is charged on all goods sold in the UK, at a rate of 17.5% of the purchase price, except for items such as children's clothes and food.

VAT is a **regressive tax** because it is not based upon people's ability to pay. The amount of tax paid is the same if your income is £10 per week or £1,000 per week. The more you earn the smaller the VAT is as a percentage of income, hence it is regressive. VAT increases the prices of goods and therefore increases the cost of living.

National Insurance contributions (NICs)

These contributions are the third largest provider of funds for the UK Government. NICs are paid towards unemployment benefit, sickness benefit, the NHS and the old age pension. NICs are paid as a percentage of income, therefore it is a **proportional tax**.

Excise duties

These duties are a further tax levied by the government, and are placed on special items such as petrol, tobacco and alcohol. This tax is paid as well as VAT on these items and is set by the government at each budget.

Corporation tax

This is another direct tax, this time charged on company profits. The amount earned through corporation tax depends upon the profits of the companies, hence during a prosperous time the amount will increase. During a recession the amount collected tends to decrease.

The government also receives revenue from other sources, such as profits from government-owned industries and receipts from the privatisation of nationalised industries. Income from the broadcasting licence, interest and dividends and rent and royalties from government-owned assets are also included in this section.

The amount of revenue earned by the government is often not enough to pay for everything, therefore they have to borrow from the general public. This is known as the **Public Sector Borrowing Requirement** (PSBR). The amount borrowed varies with the amount spent and received by the government.

Government expenditure

Government expenditure is usually determined by needs and as these needs change the amounts spent on the different areas also change.

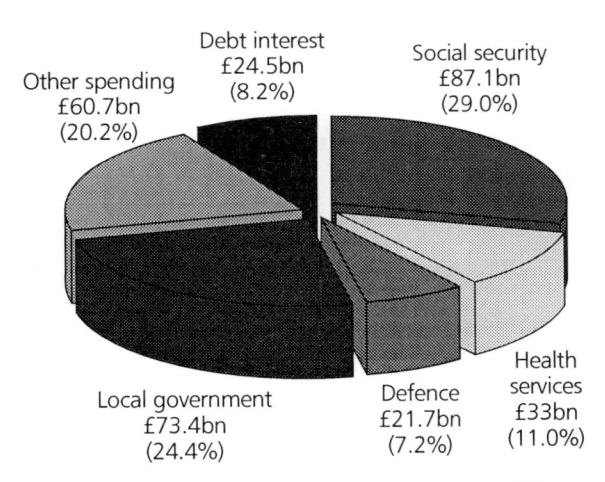

Figure 4.9 UK Government expenditure – 1995–96

- Debt interest £24.5bn (8.2%)
- Other spending £60.7bn (20.2%)
- Social security £87.1bn (29.0%)
- Local government £73.4bn (24.4%)
- Defence £21.7bn (7.2%)
- Health services £33bn (11.0%)

Social security

This includes payments for unemployment, sickness and those whose incomes are considered to be below the minimum level acceptable to maintain a reasonable standard of living.

All benefits payable, including child allowance, will be included in this area. Unemployment benefit is possibly the greatest part of this payment and as unemployment increases so will expenditure in this area.

Local government

This is the second largest expenditure item. This includes expenditure on education, housing, local roads, law and order and environmental services. Local authorities raise a great deal of their own income but they receive very large grants from central government to maintain the services listed.

Health

Expenditure on health services forms a major part of any government's expenditure. This is money spent on the entire health service: hospitals, health centres, GP practices, district nurses and all the health support agencies.

Defence

Expenditure on defence, which is a public good, pays for the Army, Airforce and Navy as well as the UK Government's contribution to any peace-keeping force.

Debt interest

This is a variable amount. If the government borrows it needs to pay interest on the amount borrowed. As borrowing increases the amount of interest payable also increases. This area of expenditure could be very large or it could be very small.

Finally expenditure under 'other' includes items such as lending to nationalised industries, money for trade and industry and employment projects.

Income and expenditure

The source of revenue for the government and the reasons for expenditure usually change very little from year to year.

However, the amounts spent do vary greatly with changes in the economy.

The government usually announces any changes in taxation in **The Budget** which takes place every November. Expenditures are also decided at this time but are not announced in the same way.

TO THE PEOPLE OF BARENGO — READ THIS

A statement from the regional council to the people of Barengo

- You can read this, because the government has started to provide education for you.
- You have water because the government makes sure that the wells always work.
- If you are ill, you will receive medicine, because the government pays for doctors.
- You work, and are paid a fair wage, because government regulations make sure that you are not exploited.
- You cannot be invaded, because the government pays for an army to protect you.
- You all know that your lives are better than ever before. You also know that if the government pays for something, it needs money itself.
- We are going to have to find ways to finance our spending, but do not worry. We will do nothing that could harm you.

We are discussing what is best at the moment. We will only act in your interests.

Regional Council

WW Johnson

Data questions

Foundation level

1 Name the services which the government supplies.

2 Using the examples in the text and your own knowledge, explain the difference between public goods and merit goods.

3 How can a government regulate to ensure that workers are not exploited?

Review terms

Market forces; public goods; merit goods; zero price; taxation; expenditure; benefits; income tax; progressive tax; Value Added Tax; regressive tax; National Insurance Contributions; proportional tax; excise duty; corporation tax; PSBR; local government expenditure; health; defence; debt interest; The Budget.

4 Why do governments provide public and merit goods, and involve themselves in regulation?

Intermediate level

1 Explain the meaning of the terms public and merit goods, and give examples of each from the text.

2 Outline the ways by which a government can regulate to prevent exploitation of the workers.

3 Why do governments intervene so as to interfere with market forces?

4 What would you expect the next Barengan budget to contain, and why?

Higher level

1 Using the information in the text, distinguish between public and merit goods.

2 Why do governments interfere with market forces?

3 What information would you require before deciding the best way for the Barengon government to raise its revenue?

4 What problems are likely to occur if a new taxation system is introduced?

ACTIVITY 5

Place the items of UK Government expenditure in order of size, putting the largest first and the smallest last.

Record your expenditure for one week. Calculate how much of your income was taken in the form of tax (VAT, excise duty, etc.).

List five items you enjoy (goods or services) that are provided by the government at zero price (you are not charged for them).

Try to estimate how much the five items would cost if you had to pay for them. Is the amount you pay in tax greater than the value of the five items on your list?

Coursework Suggestions

Idea

How does the UK Government's provision of public and merit goods affect you, or your family, or your class mates, or any other group of people?

- Make a list of the benefits that you receive.
- See if everyone is satisfied with them.
- See how much extra people would pay to improve them.

It is easy to say that you are not satisfied with something, but when it would cost money to change it, many people suddenly decide that it was not important.

Thus, you can find out about the benefits people receive, the level of satisfaction with them, and how strongly they feel that the benefits need improvement. This would allow you to draw conclusions about how a particular group of people feel about government services.

4.6 THE BALANCE OF PAYMENTS

When a country trades internationally it buys goods and services from other countries (**imports**) and sells its goods and services to foreign countries (**exports**).

A country's exports provide it with income and its imports create expenditure. Like any individual, a country cannot spend more than it earns in the long run. In the short run if expenditure is greater than income a country may use its **reserves**, a country's savings, but eventually these will run out. A country may also borrow from other countries or the **International Monetary Fund** (IMF). However, if these loans are not repaid eventually no more money will be loaned out.

It is for this reason that a country must make sure that over a long period of time its expenditure is not greater than its income.

Balance of Payments account

If the levels of income and expenditure (exports and imports) are important then they need to be watched carefully. The best way to do this is to record all exports and imports. This record is called the **Balance of Payments account**:

- a record of all external transactions between a country and the rest of the world.

The balance of payments account is split into two sections, the current account and the account that deals with transactions in UK assets and liabilities, often referred to as the capital account.

The UK current account records the money value of every good or service exported *out of* the UK or imported *into* the UK.

Table 4.6 The structure of the Balance of Payments on current account

	Exports (goods sold abroad)
minus	Imports (goods purchased from abroad
equals	Balance of Trade (visible balance)
plus	Invisible exports (services sold abroad)
minus	Invisible imports (services purchased from abroad)
equals	Current account balance (Balance of payments on current account)

The current account is split into two sections, the **visible balance** and the **invisible balance**.

The total for goods imported is subtracted from the total for the goods exported and this gives the visible balance, or the **Balance of Trade**. Services and other transactions are recorded separately, and, again, imports are subtracted from exports giving the invisible balance. The visible and invisible balances are added together to give the current account balance, the **Balance of Payments on current account**.

Visible trade

Visible trade is the export and import of goods that can be seen and touched: one of the easiest parts of the balance of payments to measure. All goods entering and leaving the UK need documents and so are easily recorded.

The export and import of goods are recorded separately to provide the balance of trade. This is important for the UK because it identifies any changes in the goods sold or purchased by the UK. This can in turn show changes in world markets, a lack of competitiveness by the UK or changes in world tastes and demand. As the UK has traditionally been a major manufacturer in the world these changes can be very important indicators of trading trends.

Visible goods are classified into six main divisions for both exports and imports, with a seventh to cover any goods not recorded in the main six.

Invisible trade

Invisible trade is split into three broad groups: **Services**; **Interest, Profits and Dividends** (IPD) and **Transfers**. These are termed 'invisibles' because unlike goods there is no visible product. The measurement of invisibles is far more difficult than for visibles. There is no common point of measurement, such as a port or airport, and documents are not required in the same way that they are for goods.

The **service** group within the invisibles category is split into five distinct services: government, sea transport, civil aviation, travel and financial services.

IPD is split between the government and the private sector. This records earnings from overseas assets and the profits from subsidiaries of UK companies. Payments to overseas citizens for the same reasons are also included.

Transfers are also split between the government and the private sector. This includes items such as the government's payment to the European Union budget and gifts by UK citizens to friends and relations overseas.

Current account

The UK's current account has constantly swung between deficit and surplus, with more deficits than surpluses. Traditionally the invisible account has always been in surplus and the visible balance

Table 4.7 UK visible trade – 1992

Category	Exports	Imports	Total
	in millions of pounds		
Food, beverages and tobacco	8,673	12,609	−3,936
Basic materials	1,946	4,613	−2,667
Oil	6,566	5,079	+1,487
Other minerals, fuels, lubricants	3304	1,555	−1,251
Semi-manufactured goods	30,354	31,157	−803
Finished manufactured goods	57,144	63,691	−6,547
Other commodities and transactions	2,060	1,749	+311
Total			= −£13,406

Source: The Pink Book, HMSO

has usually been in deficit, except when oil production was at its highest. The state of the current account often depends upon whether the invisible surplus is greater or less than the visible deficit

Table 4.8 The UK invisible account – 1992

Services	£m
General Government	–2,155
Sea transport	–397
Civil aviation	–547
Travel	–3,404
Financial and other services	+10,572
Interests, Profits and Dividends	
General Government	–560
Private sector	+6,337
Transfers	
General Government	–4,785
Private sector	–275
Invisible balance =	**£4,786**

Source: The Pink Book, HMSO

Transactions in UK assets and liabilities

The complete balance of payments account includes transactions in assets and liabilities as well as the current account. Whilst the current account deals exclusively with the sale and purchase of goods and services, the **transactions account** shows money changing hands for assets such as machinery and factories.

This account also shows how any deficits or surpluses on the current account are dealt with. If money is taken from the reserves to pay for a deficit then this is recorded in the transactions account. The same would be true if money was added to the reserves, loans repaid or money borrowed. Investment overseas by UK firms, and payments owed to foreign firms, are also placed in this account; the purchase of stocks and shares is included as well as physical assets.

Figures for the transactions account are very difficult to collect because they come from a number of different places; some are inaccurate. This means that mistakes will be made. The problem is solved by using a balancing item.

The current account plus the transactions in UK assets and liabilities account should produce a total of zero: they should balance. If they do not then errors have been made. The balance is achieved by adding the **balancing item**.

Table 4.9 The balancing item – 1992

Items	£m
Current account	–8,620
Transactions in UK assets and liabilities	8,319
Balance (which should be zero)	–301
Therefore, the balancing item	+301

The example in Table 4.9 shows an error of £301m. The current and transactions accounts should equal zero. An adjustment of +£301m is needed to achieve the balance: this is the balancing item.

The complete balance of payments account

The full balance of payments account will always equal zero: it is designed to balance, like a company's balance sheet. The importance of the account is that it records all the movements of goods, services, capital and paper assets for a country over a period of one year.

Table 4.10 The complete balance of payments account – 1992

Items	£m
Exports	107,047
Imports	120,453
A Visible balance	–13,406
B Invisible balance	4,786
C Current balance (A+B)	–8,620
D Transactions in UK assets and liabilities	8,319
E Balancing item (C-D)	301

Source: The Pink Book, HMSO

THE INTERNATIONAL TRADE REVIEW

Barengo publishes figures

The regional government of Barengo has at last produced a set of figures for its balance of payments in the year 1994–95.

A summary:

- The total value of exports of textiles to other countries was £5,000,000.
- Food to the value of £250,000 was also exported.
- Imports of goods to Barengo amounted to £4,500,000.
- Visitors to Barengo spent £250,000.
- The Barengans spent £1,000,000 abroad on loan repayments, insurance and transport costs.
- Capital exported to Barengo amounted to £500,000 and there was no capital outflow from the region. This meant that there was an addition to their reserves.

A careful and detailed analysis of these figures will be needed to assess

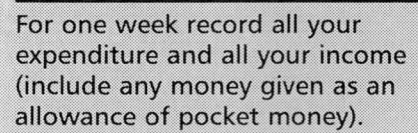

ACTIVITY 6

For one week record all your expenditure and all your income (include any money given as an allowance of pocket money).

Put your expenditure into two groups: group 1 for goods and group 2 for services.

Find the government publication in which the balance of payments account is recorded. What is the biggest export item, the largest import item and which is the best invisible earner?

Imagine that the UK was producing all its own food and North Sea oil had run out. At the same time British air travel was considered to be unsafe and nobody used any British air company.

Now construct a current account using this information and the latest current account figures that you can find.

Compare your 'imaginary current account' to the actual current account. How do these events alter the actual current account?

Review terms

Exports; imports; reserves; IMF; current account; visible balance; invisible balance; balance of trade; services; IPD; transfers; transactions in UK assets and liabilities; capital account; balancing item.

Data questions

Foundation level

1 (a) What was the total of visible exports from Barengo?
(b) What was the total of visible imports into Barengo?
(c) What was the total of invisible imports into Barengo?
(d) What was the total of invisible exports from Barengo?

2 Showing your workings, calculate:
(a) the visible trade balance
(b) the invisible trade balance
(c) the balance on the current account
(d) the balance on the capital account
(e) the balance of payments figure.

3 Explain the meaning of the terms:
   (a) visible trade
   (b) invisible trade
   (c) balance of payments
   (d) reserves.
4 What are possible problems of using reserves to finance balance of payment deficits?

Intermediate level

1 Showing your working, calculate the balance of payments position of Barengo.
2 Explain the meaning of the terms:
   (a) balance of trade
   (b) current account
   (c) capital account
   (d) reserves.
3 What are the potential problems of a country relying on its reserves when faced with a balance of payments deficit?
4 How can the balance of payments account help a government in its economic policy?

Higher level

1 Compile the balance of payments account.
2 Explain the problems which can occur to economies which experience growing and falling reserves.
3 To what uses can a government put the information given in its balance of payment account?
4 What are the difficulties of assembling an accurate balance of payments account?

Coursework Suggestions

This is a complicated area, with real difficulties in obtaining accurate information. It may well be best to avoid the topic for coursework.

4.7 CURRENCY EXCHANGE

When the UK trades internationally it buys goods and services from abroad and sells its own goods and services to other countries.

The foreign countries need some form of payment for their goods and services and so does the UK.

Barter

One way to pay for goods and services from foreign countries is to use a **barter system**. The UK could exchange wheat for bananas and oranges, or oil for Japanese televisions.

The problem with a barter system is that it needs a 'double coincidence of wants'. For example, if the Japanese wish to sell televisions, the UK must have something to exchange that the Japanese want. If the Japanese want some wheat but the UK does not want to exchange it, then the deal will not go ahead.

A further problem with barter is establishing the values of each good or service. How many tons of wheat equal one television, or how many gallons of oil equal one television, or one car? What if the oil or wheat is of poor quality?

There are so many problems with barter that it is virtually impossible to trade using this system, and so an alternative has had to be found.

Currency

An alternative to barter is to pay for the goods and services purchased with money. The UK could buy Japanese televisions and pay for them with **Pounds Sterling (£)** and the Japanese could buy North Sea oil with **Japanese Yen**.

The problem with this is that the Japanese television manufacturers could not spend Pounds in Japan and the North Sea oil producers could not spend Yen in the UK.

What is required is for each country to be paid in its own currency. When the UK exports goods, such as oil, it should receive its payment in Pounds Sterling, and when it imports goods, such as Japanese televisions, it must pay for them in the currency of the country from which the goods are purchased; in this example it would be Yen.

If this system is to work there must be a way in which currencies can be exchanged.

The **Foreign Exchange Market** is a market in which all the currencies of all of the trading nations of the world can be bought and sold. Any currency that is needed to purchase goods and services from another country can be exchanged for the home currency.

Exchange rates

If currencies are bought and sold in a market situation then exchange rates need to be established. How many pounds equal 1 US dollar, or how many US dollars equal 1 Deutschmark (DM)?

The **exchange rate** is a price, the price of a currency in terms of other currencies. This price is just like the price of any commodity but in this case it is the price of a currency:

- The exchange rate is the *price of one currency* in terms of the *value of other currencies*.

Price is established in the foreign exchange market in the same way that any price is established in any other market, by the forces of demand and supply. The demand for a currency and the supply of that same currency determine its price.

The reason for the demand for a country's currency is usually the desire to buy goods and services from that country, its exports. The supply of a country's currency exists because it is buying the exports of other countries (importing).

If the UK purchased cars from Germany it would demand Deutschmarks and supply Pounds to the market in exchange. If France purchased oil from the UK it would demand Pounds and supply French Francs (FF) in exchange. Thus:

- Demand for a *currency* = the level of a country's *exports*.
- Supply of a *currency* = the level of a country's *imports*.

There are other factors that may affect the demand and supply of a currency such as **speculation** and the flow of **hot money** – money which is deposited in whichever country has the highest interest rate.

Types of exchange rate

There are a number of different ways in which the exchange rate of a currency can be determined but these are all variations on two basic types of exchange rate, the **fixed exchange rate** and the **flexible exchange rate**.

The fixed exchange rate system is one where the rates are not determined by the market forces, the governments set the rate. The floating exchange rate system is totally the opposite: here the rate is determined entirely by the forces of demand and supply, without interference by government.

Fixed exchange rate

If a fixed exchange rate system is used the price (exchange rate of the currency) is set and guaranteed not to change. This rate, known as the **par value**, is known to everyone.

For example: £1 = $1.50 and £1 = 2DM

If for some reason the market forces did try to move the pound away from these fixed rates the UK Government would intervene.

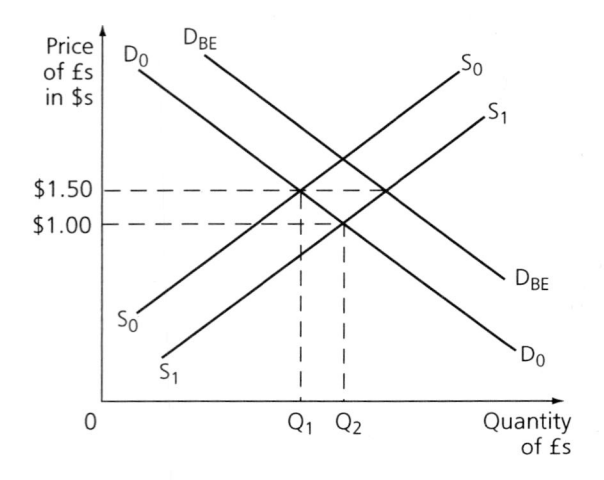

Figure 4.10 Government intervention in the foreign exchange market

In Figure 4.10 the pound has a fixed value of £1 = $1.50 where $D_0 D_0 = S_0 S_0$. If the level of imports increases then the supply of currency will also increase to $S_1 S_1$. The new equilibrium is at $D_0 D_0 = S_1 S_1$ and the value of the pound should fall to £1 = $1, but because this is a fixed exchange rate it is not allowed to do so.

In this situation the Bank of England would step in and buy up the excess supply of pounds with its reserves of foreign currency. This would increase the demand for Pounds ($D_{BE} D_{BE}$) and return the exchange rate to its previous value.

If the opposite occurred and an excess demand for pounds existed, the Bank of England would sell pounds and buy foreign currency to maintain the rate. This is **government intervention**.

The major advantage of a fixed exchange rate is stability. Every country knows the rate of exchange and unless a disaster occurs it will remain at this rate. The biggest disadvantage of this system is that it is expensive and it is difficult to keep the currency at the agreed value.

Floating exchange rate

A floating or free exchange rate means that the exchange rate of any currency is determined totally by the forces of demand and supply, the market forces. The rate can change daily or even hourly. There is no guaranteed value.

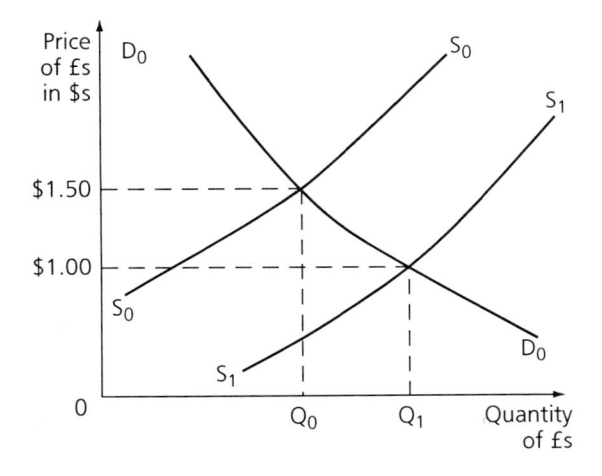

Figure 4.11 The floating exchange rate

The situation in Figure 4.11 is the same as in 4.10. The original equilibrium is at $D_0 D_0 = S_0 S_0$ and £1 = $1.50. Imports have increased and are now greater than exports, therefore the demand for £s is less than the supply of £s. Supply has moved from $S_0 S_0$ to $S_1 S_1$.

With a floating exchange rate the government does not intervene and the rate will fall from £1 = $1.50 to £1 = $1. This will make UK exports cheaper and imports into the UK more expensive.

The big advantage of a floating exchange rate is that it is automatic, therefore it is easy and cheap to operate. The disadvantage is that it creates uncertainty in the world markets and harms international trade.

Other exchange rate systems exist such as the **Exchange Rate Mechanism (ERM)**, used by the European Union countries, but these are variations of the two systems already explained.

Exchange rate problems

Exchange rates cause more problems for countries, and international trade generally, than any other factor. Should the exchange rate be fixed or floating, is it the correct rate, how can speculation be stopped? These are just a few of the questions that have to be answered.

Whatever the problems of exchange rates it is a fact that international trade would hardly exist without them.

ACTIVITY 7

Find how many Spanish Pesetas, and how many US dollars can be exchanged for £1.

If the exchange rate of the pound changed from £1 = $1.50 to £1 = $2.50, how would this affect (a) the price of holidays in Florida for UK citizens and (b) the price of holidays in London for US citizens?

If the pound fell against all of the other European currencies how might UK exports and imports be affected? List five exports and five imports that would be affected most by changes in the UK's exchange rate

Review terms

Barter; Pounds Sterling; Japanese Yen; foreign exchange; exchange rate; price; speculation; hot money; fixed exchange rate; floating exchange rate; par value; government intervention; Exchange Rate Mechanism.

THE DAILY NEWS

Barengo: a follow-up story

Several years ago, we reported a drought in the Southern Ethiopian settlement of Barengo, and, partly thanks to the contributions of our readers, the charity Faminaid has drilled a new well which supported the people, and allowed crops to be grown.

Small beginning

There, the story could have ended, but a teacher who went out there was so impressed with the quality and colours of the dress material that the villagers made that they were persuaded to make the material for export to Britain, and from this small beginning a thriving industry has developed.

Stumbling block

One of the main difficulties has been the value of the local currency, the zimba, which has varied a great deal in relation to the British pound. The solution was to agree a price in British pounds, which could be used to purchase British goods in Britain. These were then sent to Barengo.

More people are now engaged in textile making, and the money is being used to buy goods that help agriculture, so that the villagers are well on the way to becoming healthier and wealthier.

The exchange rate: £1 to zimba

1993	
January	100 zimba
April	120
July	150
October	140
1994	
January	160
April	170
July	175
October	190
1995	
January	175
April	190
July	200
October	160

Data questions

Foundation level

1 (a) When was the pound worth the smallest amount of zimba? How many zimba would you receive for £1?
(b) When was the pound worth the largest amount of zimba? How many zimba would you receive for £1?
(c) In which months was £1 worth 175 zimba?

2 (a) Explain the meaning of the term 'exchange rate'.
(b) What problems would exist if countries did not have exchange rates?

3 The exchange rate in the table above shows wide changes. This is the result of the demand for and the supply of each currency.
(a) Why might the demand for the pound rise and fall?
(b) Why might the supply of the pound rise and fall?

4 What will the people of Britain and those of Barengo gain from trade?

Intermediate level

1 Describe the changes in the exchange rate of the pound and the zimba that are shown in the chart.

2 Define the term 'exchange rate' and explain why it is important in international trade.

3 Explain why the demand for, and the supply of, currencies can vary.

4 What are the likely advantages and disadvantages of the trade in cloth between the two countries?

Higher level

1 What information does the table of exchange rates provide?

2 Explain the role of the exchange rates in international trade.

3 Why do currencies fluctuate in value?

4 Why do countries trade with each other?

Coursework Suggestions

International trade is a difficult area, and it may be better to avoid the topic for coursework. It is even possible that some Examination Boards do not allow coursework in this area. However, if you are determined, you should make careful arrangements with your teacher.

4.8 ECONOMIC ISSUES

It has generally been the aim of governments to try to solve the economic problem of **scarcity**. The way to overcome the problem is to produce as many goods and services as possible. This can be achieved by using the resources available as efficiently as possible.

Anything that interferes with this general aim needs to be controlled. **Inflation** and **unemployment** are two major causes of difficulty. Both of these cause governments great problems, and so all governments aim to keep inflation as low as possible (stable prices) and employment as high as possible (full employment).

Inflation

Inflation is a situation where prices and wages are constantly increasing. It is often defined as:

- too much money chasing too few goods

This is only one possible cause of inflation. Inflation actually means that the value of money is decreasing. It requires more pounds to buy the goods and services available.

The increase in prices can occur at different speeds: prices can rise by a few per cent per year known as **mild inflation**, or by over 100% per year, known as **hyper-inflation** or **runaway inflation**. Inflation can be created in two ways. The two processes are known as **demand–pull** inflation and **cost–push** inflation.

Demand–pull inflation

Demand–pull inflation starts with excess demand in the economy. When demand is greater than supply within a market this leads to an increase in price. If prices increase then workers will demand higher wages. If wages go up this creates extra income which creates more demand and so excess demand exists again.

This process creates a vicious circle that will go on and on if it is not stopped.

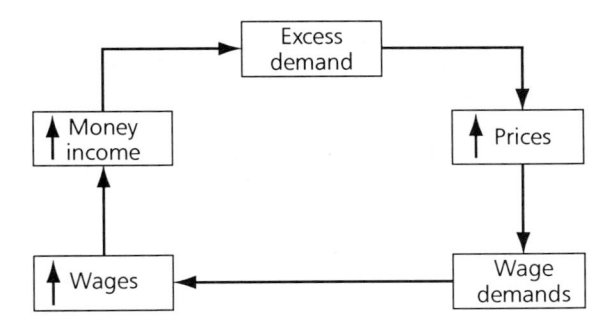

Figure 4.12 The demand–pull spiral

The causes of the excess demand within the economy can be an increase in the money supply or too much demand created by the government through fiscal or monetary policy (see page 94).

Cost–push inflation

Cost–push inflation starts with the costs of production increasing. This increased cost can be the cost of raw materials (often imported into the UK), wages or entrepreneurs demanding higher profits. Once costs increase this has to be passed on to the consumer in the form of higher prices.

Higher prices create wage demands, higher wages increase the costs of production and so the process continues unless it is stopped.

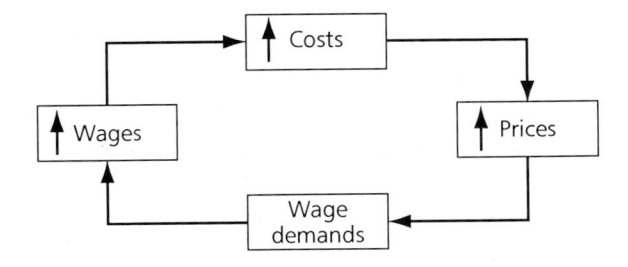

Figure 4.13 The cost–push spiral

Brazilian currency issued in August 1994 to combat inflation

Why is inflation a problem?

Inflation is a problem because it decreases the value of money. If money becomes worth less and less, nobody will want to accept it. If people refuse to accept money it loses its major function as a medium of exchange and stops being money. If the money system of an economy collapses then the economy itself will collapse; people will go back to **self-sufficiency** and **barter**. When inflation occurs there will always be winners and losers. The losers will be those people who are on fixed incomes such as pensioners, the unemployed, the sick and students surviving on grants. People lending money will also lose: what they are repaid will be worth less than the amount loaned out, in terms of the amount it will purchase. People who save and those workers in weak trade unions will also suffer during a period of inflation.

Those gaining will include anyone who owes money, such as home buyers who have a mortgage, and workers in strong trade unions who can obtain an increase in wages that is greater than the rate of inflation.

Policies to cure inflation

The policy used to cure inflation will depend upon the cause and the government's political ideals. If inflation has been caused by excess demand, demand-pull, then demand in the economy needs to be decreased.

Demand can be decreased by decreasing government expenditure or increasing taxation. Decreasing government expenditure decreases demand directly and increased taxation decreases consumers' income which would decrease consumption. This is known as **fiscal policy**.

Alternatively, demand can be reduced by using **monetary policy**: an increase in the rate of interest which decreases borrowing and causes consumers to spend less.

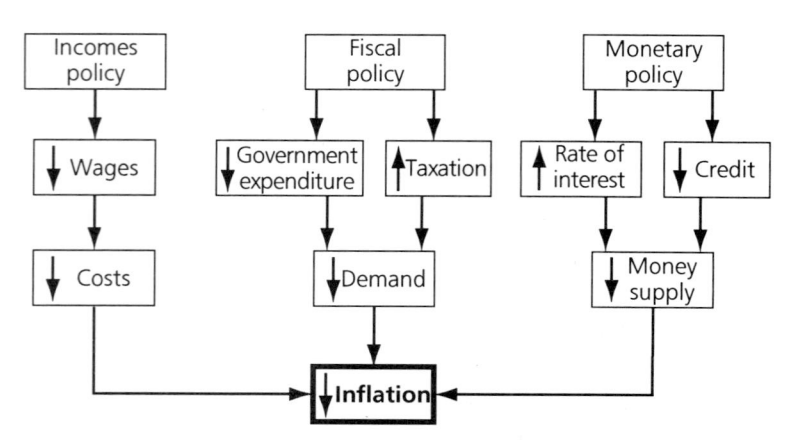

Figure 4.14 Policies to cure inflation

Some economists believe that excess demand is created because there is too much money in the economy. In this case the growth of the money supply needs to be decreased. This can be done by decreasing the PSBR or by raising the rate of interest.

If the cause of inflation is rising costs, cost–push, then these costs must be controlled. Prices are difficult to control but wages may be halted by using an **incomes policy**. This stops wages rising above a set limit.

Unemployment

Unemployment exists when:

- People are *willing* and *able to work* but *unable to find employment*.

This actually means that workers who could be helping to produce goods and services cannot find a job and so are sitting at home looking for work. They are paid unemployment benefit to help them maintain a minimum standard of living.

Unemployment can be created in a number of ways. A decrease in demand within the economy means that less goods and services are needed. With less goods and services produced less labour is needed which creates unemployment. This is known as **cyclical unemployment**.

Over time tastes change and the type of products demanded change as well. When this happens some industries will decline whilst others grow. This creates **structural unemployment**, unemployment created by a change in the structure of the economy.

Technology is another factor that changes over time. New and improved products are produced and technology replaces parts of jobs and in some cases complete jobs, making the workers unemployed. The best example is the replacement of people by computers in offices and the replacement of car workers by robots. This type of unemployment is known as **technological unemployment**.

Other causes of unemployment include people changing jobs (**frictional unemployment**) and those who do not wish to work or who are unable to do so (**residual unemployment**).

There are those who believe that many people do not want to work: the **voluntary unemployed**.

This same group believes that unemployment can never go below a certain level, known as the **natural rate of unemployment**, in the long run. Any decrease in unemployment below this level is thought to be only temporary.

Problems of unemployment

The major problem with unemployment is that it is a waste of resources. Labour is one of the most valuable and versatile factors of production. Any labour that is not employed could have been producing goods and services and increasing output to satisfy more of the wants and needs of society.

If 10% of the working population is unemployed then 10% more output could have been produced if these people had been working.

The unemployed do not earn any income and have to claim benefits to maintain a minimum standard of living. These benefits, transfer payments, are paid by the government. This increases government expenditure but at the same time these people, who used to pay tax, are no longer doing so. The government's expenditure increases and its income decreases at the same time.

Unemployment creates the greatest problems for individuals. Those workers who are unemployed lose their skills and confidence, feel unwanted and depressed and suffer hardships due to a much lower standard of living.

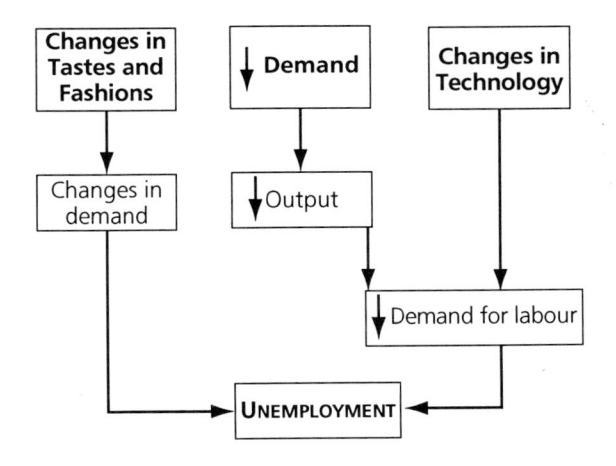

Figure 4.15 The causes of unemployment

Workers protesting at job losses

Policies to cure unemployment

The policy used to cure unemployment will depend upon the cause. Very little can be done to cure frictional or residual unemployment, and in a changing and developing economy a government would not wish to stop people changing jobs.

If unemployment is structural or technological then again the government can do very little to stop it and would not necessarily want to. In this situation the government would want to help the unemployed to find new jobs in new areas. This would involve retraining schemes and encouraging new firms to sites where the unemployment exists.

If unemployment is caused by a lack of demand the government can use fiscal policy, either increasing government expenditure to increase demand or decreasing taxation to increase people's income which will increase demand. Both could be used to increase demand and output.

Monetary policy, decreasing interest rates, could also be used to increase demand; this in turn would need more labour to increase output, cutting the level of unemployment.

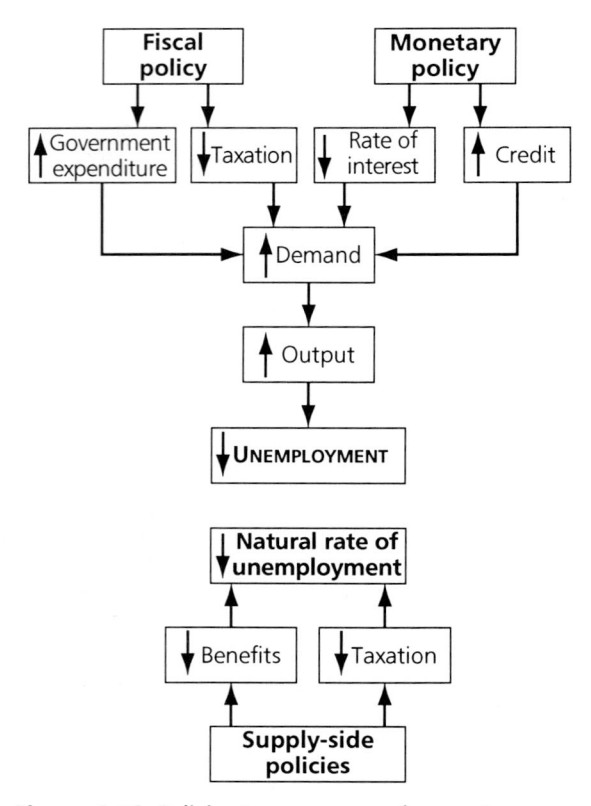

Figure 4.16 Policies to cure unemployment

If it is believed that a natural rate of unemployment exists then the government will not attempt to decrease unemployment below this level. The policies used would be to decrease the voluntary level of unemployment by using **supply-side policies.** Any policy used would be to help the markets to solve the problem naturally; examples would be to decrease benefits and income tax. This would encourage those who do not wish to work to find employment.

Other issues

Two issues of **economic growth**, explained in detail in section 6.1 (page 120), and the **balance of payments equilibrium**, explained fully in section 4.6 (page 85), concern all governments. Economic growth is needed to increase the output, the GNP, of a nation, and a balance of payments equilibrium is an important relationship with the rest of the world. Despite the importance of these two issues, inflation and unemployment have been the priority with any UK government.

ACTIVITY 8

Find the latest unemployment figure, both as a percentage and an amount, for the UK, and the latest rate of inflation.

Find the unemployment rate for your town or area. Is the rate increasing or decreasing? Do you know why? How does your unemployment rate compare with the rest of the UK?

Write down five items that you or your parents regularly buy. Over a period of time, at least one month, record the price of these items. Have they increased or decreased?

Can you calculate the rate of inflation for this basket of goods? Compare your inflation rate with the national figure.

THE DAILY FINANCIAL NEWS

World Conference of Finance Ministers

The theme of yesterday's meeting of the World Conference of Finance Ministers was 'Inflation or unemployment: which is the worse evil?'

The British Chancellor of the Exchequer gave the address, in which he explained the dangers of inflation – the rising prices, the increasing uncompetitiveness of the nation's industry, the balance of payments crisis that could result and the consequent unemployment.

He talked about the dangers of unemployment in terms of the economic costs of support and the waste of resources, together with the social effects. He emphasised the need to control these problems. The meeting then broke into small groups to allow the ministers to discuss their own experiences.

Barengo experiences

The representative from the Regional Council of Barengo explained that his economy was growing so quickly that there had not been any unemployment, and wages were still so low that inflation was not a problem. However, he was anxious to point out that he understood there could be difficulties in the future, and asked what he should look out for, so that he could spot the dangers before they became major issues.

Inflation

It was agreed that inflation would appear first. Because there was full employment, someone would need workers so badly that higher wages would be offered, and so the inflationary process would begin.

Or increased affluence would lead to a greater demand for imported consumer goods, so fewer local products would be made.

The advice given to the Barengan representative was clear – do something to stop inflation as soon as you can, or your economic development will slow down, you will then have unemployment and face potential disaster.

Data questions

Foundation level

1 Making use of the text, what are the problems of (a) inflation and (b) unemployment?

2 Explain the causes of cost–push and demand–pull inflation.

3 Outline two measures the Regional Council of Barengo could use to prevent inflation.

4 How can inflation cause unemployment?

Intermediate level

1 List the main problems caused by inflation and by unemployment, as laid out in the text.

2 What causes inflation?

3 How could the Regional Council of Barengo prevent inflation?

4 Explain the relationship between inflation and unemployment.

Higher level

1 Explain the problems of inflation and unemployment that are mentioned in the text.

2 Evaluate the measures available to Barengo Regional Council of to prevent inflation.

3 What is the relationship between inflation and unemployment?

4 Why are inflation and unemployment permanent international issues?

Review terms

Scarcity; inflation; unemployment; mild inflation; hyper-inflation; runaway inflation; demand–pull inflation; cost–push inflation; barter; self-sufficiency; fiscal policy; monetary policy; incomes policy; cyclical unemployment; structural unemployment; technological unemployment; frictional unemployment; residual unemployment; voluntary unemployed; natural rate of unemployment; supply-side policies; economic growth; balance of payments equilibrium.

Coursework Suggestions

Inflation and unemployment are major economic issues, and so they provide scope for coursework. However, the causes and cures of both can be found in the text books, and do not provide a sound basis for a piece of work.

There would be little scope for work using original material, analysis and evaluation. You would be better trying to tackle the issues on a personal basis.

Idea

How has your group's purchasing power been affected by inflation in the past six months?

- What effect has this had?
- Has it meant that you are able to buy less?
- Have you changed your spending pattern?
- Have you taken a part-time job to allow your purchasing to be maintained?

Idea

You could consider the economic and social effects of unemployment.

- How has the spending pattern of someone who has become unemployed changed?
- What effect has it had on their lives?
- What do they do with their time now?
- What are their thoughts on the future?

Or, of course, you could find someone who has become employed after a period of unemployment, and ask the same sort of questions. That would be an original approach, and so would offer some interesting results.

5

The Economic Institutions

The institutional and organisational framework within which economic behaviour takes place

5.1 BUSINESS ORGANISATIONS • 5.2 TRADE UNIONS AND EMPLOYERS' ASSOCIATIONS • 5.3 FINANCIAL INSTITUTIONS • 5.4 THE ROLE OF CENTRAL AND LOCAL GOVERNMENT • 5.5 TAXATION IN THE UK
5.6 THE EUROPEAN UNION AND OTHER INTERNATIONAL INSTITUTIONS

This section should enable students to:
- explain the types of business organisation in the public and private sectors
- understand the role and functions of trade unions and employers associations
- explain the role and functions of the main financial institutions
- understand the role, functions and basis of expenditure of local and central governments
- outline the varieties of taxation in the United Kingdom and differentiate between progressive, regressive and proportional taxation
- identify the main international trade groupings with reference to the European Community.

5.1 BUSINESS ORGANISATIONS

There are many types of business organisation, ranging from one man working on his own to very large firms, which everyone knows, to state owned industries. Together, they make up the business structure of the country.

The Public Sector
Nationalisation

Some industries have attracted particular attention from government. These include coal, gas, electricity, water, the railways, the post and telephones.

These industries are vital to the public, and so governments have tried to make sure that they do not act against the national interest.

There are two ways of making sure that this does not happen. Firstly by imposing strict rules on the way they behave or by the state actually owning and running the industries. This is known as **nationalisation**, which became a policy of the UK Government in the period 1945–50 (after the Second World War).

Before 1945, civil aviation, the post, telephones and the BBC were state owned. To these were added coal, gas, electricity, the railways and road transport.

Nationalised industries are called **public corporations**, and are run in the same way as any other business, but are responsible to specific Cabinet ministers for their activities. It was not intended that they should make a profit but charge a fair price and provide good quality goods and services for all.

Privatisation

Mrs Thatcher became Prime Minister in 1979, and her Conservative Government decided that many of the nationalised industries should be returned to the private sector, where they could be owned and controlled by shareholders rather than the state. It was believed that these industries were inefficient and wasteful and the private sector would eliminate this.

Thus, the public were offered the opportunity to purchase shares in a variety of these industries, which are now public limited companies, e.g., British Gas; British Telecom; British Airways.

This also helped to raise money which the government could use as an alternative to increasing taxation. Until 1980, the nationalised industries employed about 8% of the workforce. By 1992, as a result of **privatisation**, this had fallen to 3%.

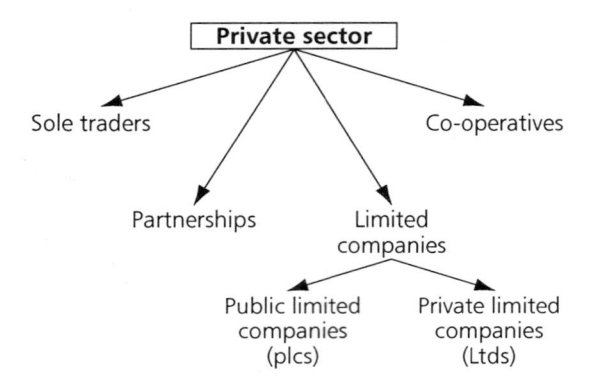

Figure 5.1 The private sector

The private sector

There are five types of business organisation in the private sector.

The sole trader

The **sole trader** owns his/her business. This does not mean that the owner needs to be the only person who does the work. The owner can employ as many people as he/she wants, and pays them wages. The profits that remain belong to the owner.

The size of the firm is limited by the amount of money that the owner can raise.

The owner is also responsible for all of the debts of the firm; this is known as **unlimited liability**. They may even be forced to sell their own personal possessions to pay the debts of the company.

It is very easy to set up as a sole trader. In Britain, four out of every ten businesses are sole traders, but they only represent 3% of the total turnover of business.

Partnerships

Instead of working on your own as a sole trader, you could form a **partnership** with other people.

For instance, a bricklayer and a plasterer may form a partnership so as to offer a wider service to customers.

The partners will each provide a share of the money needed to start the business, and each will take a share of the profits.

Like the sole trader, the partners can employ workers if they wish.

All partners are responsible for all the debts of the business, including those incurred by the other partners in the business. And again these responsibilities are unlimited, with personal possessions being at risk if the partnership gets into debt. About a quarter of all businesses are partnerships.

Limited companies

The main difference between **limited companies** and sole traders and partnerships is that the financial liability of the owners is limited to the amount of capital that each has put into the company. This is known as **limited liability**. All such companies must include the word 'limited' in their names, so that everyone is aware of their position.

The companies are legally separated from their owners. The company can sue and be sued; it can enter into contracts, and can incur debts which are not those of its owners. The company is a legal person in its own right.

There are two types of limited company – private and public.

Private limited companies are distinguished by the fact that they have the term 'Limited' or 'Ltd.' after their names. They cannot offer shares for sale to the general public. Shares are sold to family and friends. Most limited companies fall into this category. There are about half a million in the UK, but only about 3% are large enough to be **Public Limited Companies** (PLC), whose shares can be openly traded on the Stock Exchange.

In order to protect other businesses, the public, and those who want to buy shares, a series of Companies Acts has been passed. These require the publication of details regarding the financial position of the firm and its management.

Limited companies are owned by the shareholders, who, each year, can attend a meeting at which they elect a Board of Directors, who are responsible for the running of the company.

Table 5.1 The size of business in the UK – 1989

Number of employees	Number of businesses	Total employment
1–99	134,797	1,201,000
100–199	2,471	342,000
200–499	1,495	460,000
500–999	520	366,000
1,000+	587	2,506,000

Source: Annual Abstract of Statistics

Cooperatives

In a **cooperative**, the business is controlled either by the workers themselves, or by the consumers of their products.

The first consumer cooperative began in Rochdale in 1844, and rapidly spread to other parts of the UK.

The customers paid a small amount of money to buy a share in the business, and the shareholders elected a committee which decided how the business would be run, and appointed staff to do the work and ensure that their wishes were carried out. Goods were sold at normal retail prices and the profits returned to the shareholders in the form of a dividend, which varied according to how much each had spent.

Some societies continue to operate in this way, while others have reduced the actual price of the goods, so as to attract customers into their shops. The number of consumer cooperatives has declined in recent years as a result of competition from supermarkets. In 1950, they had about one eighth of retail turnover but, by the beginning of the 1990s, this had fallen to one twentieth.

Much of the produce sold by the consumer societies is bought from the Cooperative Wholesale Society, which manufactures and imports on their behalf.

Employee cooperatives also began in the nineteenth century. In these, the workers themselves share the profits. They declined throughout the twentieth century, but revived in the 1980s as workers continued to run the firms after management decided to close them.

ACTIVITY

Find five privatised industries. What were they called before and after privatisation?

What are the advantages to the consumers of nationalisation? Why did Mrs Thatcher's government support privatisation?

List five sole traders, partnerships, private and public limited companies that operate near your home. Where is your nearest cooperative?

Review terms

Nationalisation; privatisation; public sector; private sector; public corporation; sole trader; partnership; limited companies; private limited companies; public limited companies; cooperatives.

THE ECONOMIC TIMES

Barengo, an economic miracle

The activities in Barengo have been reported regularly. Years ago, it was an area threatened by famine, with misery and starvation the most likely future for its inhabitants.

Modern times
Today, it is a thriving community. The people have specialised, so that there are farmers and textile workers, shopkeepers and blacksmiths.

Workers' cooperative
The textile workers have formed a workers' cooperative. They all work, and they share the profits. There are now over fifty people involved in this activity; at least 45 of these people are spinners and weavers and dyers.

However, the need to keep records of orders, the payments made, and the money received, has given rise to a modest clerical section of five or six people.

Farmers
The farmers work for themselves and sell their produce to the shopkeepers, who buy from other parts of Ethiopia as well. Most of the shops are family-run partnerships.

The idea of limited liability is unknown in Barengo, but the area is wealthy enough for money to have become the normal method of payment. The state-owned National Bank has set up its first branch in the area.

Data questions

Foundation level

1 Name the five types of business organisation mentioned in the text.

2 Explain the advantages and disadvantages of limited and unlimited liability.

3 Outline who takes the decisions in each of the business units you have named, and who keeps the profits.

4 Outline two of the main problems that a workers' cooperative may face.

Intermediate level

1 List the types of business organisation mentioned in the text.

2 For each of these, outline the decision and profit taking process.

3 What problems might the workers' cooperative experience?

4 Would limited liability help the Barengan economy? Give reasons for your answer.

Higher level

1 What types of business organisation were mentioned in the text? Explain how each one makes decisions.

2 What problems might the workers' cooperative face?

3 Would limited liability help the Barengan economy? Give reasons for your answer.

4 How could the Ethiopian government help the area to develop further?

Coursework Suggestions

Idea

Many books suggest that firms do better when they become limited companies. Test that idea.

- Find a sole trader who is unlimited, and ask why he is unlimited.
- Find a small business that is limited, and ask why.
- Pose questions about the ease of obtaining credit, to see if being limited makes any difference.

- Find out how the owners feel about the type of business organisation that they have chosen. See if they are happy with their choice.
- Ask some wholesalers if they treat limited and unlimited companies any differently, especially over credit.
- Approach a bank, and see what the attitude is there.
- Ask a few ordinary people if they know the difference between limited and unlimited companies, and see if the status of a firm affects their use of it.

You will have started your coursework by posing a question. You will have collected evidence, and analysed it, then drawn a conclusion.

Idea

There are several types of business organisation. How much do the general public know about them? Does the knowledge influence buying habits?

Draw up a questionnaire to find this out, and interview a range of people. Analyse the results, and draw a conclusion.

5.2 TRADE UNIONS AND EMPLOYERS' ASSOCIATIONS

Trade unions

Trade unions are organisations of workers who have joined together to help each other gain better wages and conditions in the work place.

Many years ago when the wages were very low and the hours very long, the unions were much needed. Groups of workers, acting together, were far more likely to bring about changes in pay and conditions than individuals asking for improvements on their own.

In the third quarter of the nineteenth century, unions of skilled workers were formed, and towards the end of that century, unions for unskilled workers appeared.

Employers did not accept the unions automatically, and the two sides often disagreed. Employers could threaten to dismiss staff, while the unions had their own methods of trying to force their wishes on employers.

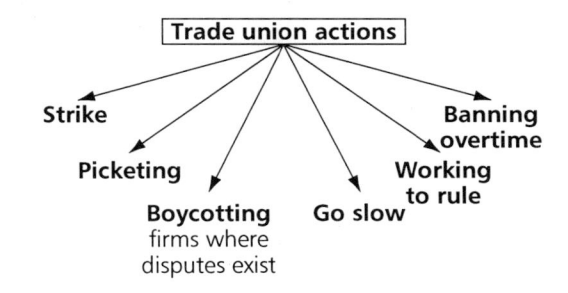

Figure 5.2 Union action

The most severe of these was the strike, which means that the union members refuse to go to work until their demands have been met. Employers cannot make any money if no-one is working, and they will still have expenses to pay (their fixed costs), so they would be faced with losing more and more money the longer the strike continued.

In the late 1970s and early 1980s, the amount of time lost through strikes grew so Mrs Thatcher's Conservative Government passed several Acts of Parliament which were intended to limit the power of the unions, and so reduce the number of strikes.

Britain had certainly gained a bad reputation for strikes, but this was not altogether justified when compared with other countries.

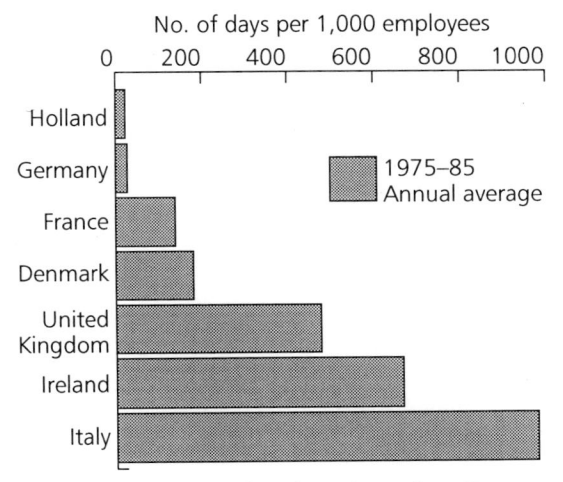

Figure 5.3 Working days lost through strikes

Number of trade unions

The number of trade unions has declined greatly in recent years, so that now there are now fewer than 300 trade unions in the UK, many of which do not have large memberships.

The biggest unions have been formed as the result of amalgamations between smaller unions, such as the Transport and General Workers' Union which has nearly 1.25 million members. This trend towards larger unions has been partly in response to changes in the law.

Most unions are affiliated to the **Trades Union Congress** (TUC), which is the central body of the trade union movement. It holds an annual conference which decides on general policy, although the individual unions can ignore the decisions if they wish.

Membership

The membership of trade unions has declined greatly in recent years, but nevertheless, about 40% of workers in the UK are members of unions. Some industries have more than this, some less. For example, most coal miners are members of a union, but the hotel and catering industry does not have high membership. It is higher among full-time than part-time workers, among men than women, and in large rather than small firms.

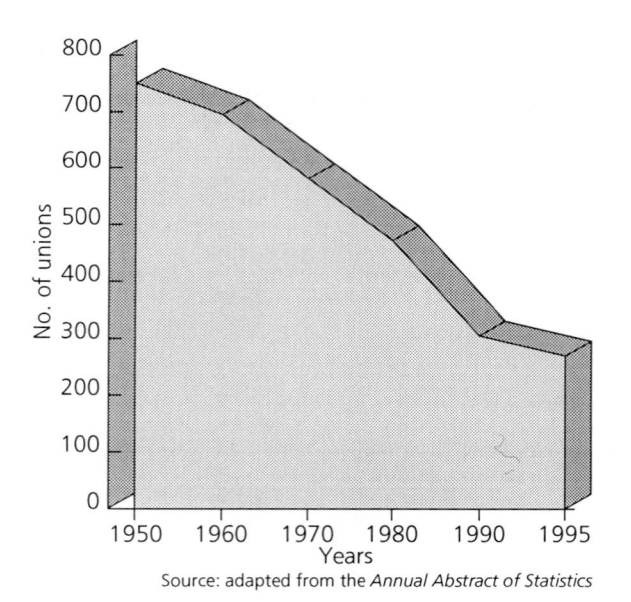

Source: adapted from the *Annual Abstract of Statistics*

Figure 5.4 Number of trade unions 1950–1995

Since the Employment Act of 1990, an employer cannot refuse to employ someone who is not a member of a trade union. This Act made the enforcement of a **closed shop** illegal. Closed shops can still exist but workers can no longer be forced to join a union against their will.

Functions of trade unions

Trade unions exist to:

- improve the wages of members
- improve the working conditions of members
- ensure the provision of educational, recreational and social amenities for members
- influence national policy making.

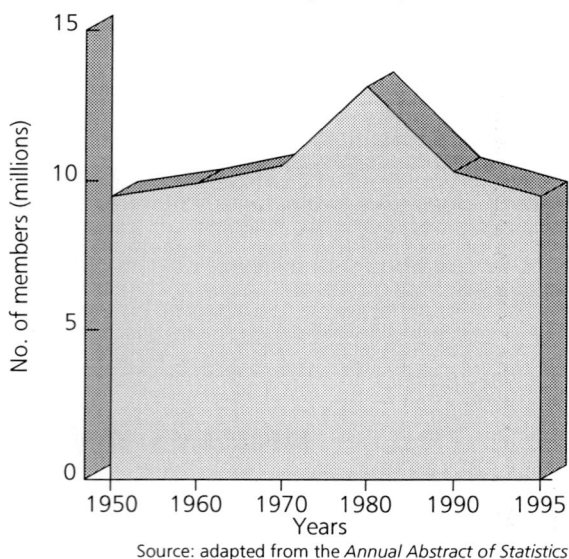

Source: adapted from the *Annual Abstract of Statistics*

Figure 5.5 Membership of trade unions 1950–1995

Employers' associations

Just as employees have associations, called trade unions, so the employers also have their own groups. The most famous is the **Confederation of British Industry** (CBI). Most large firms, and many small ones, are members. It has an annual conference, and regularly issues statements on behalf of its members, but it has little real power.

Many industries also have associations, to which firms within the industry belong. They give each other support and encouragement, but, again, they do not appear to have much real power.

✓ Review terms

Trade unions; strike; picketing; go slow; work to rule; overtime ban; Trades Union Congress; closed shop, Confederation of British Industry.

ACTIVITY

Ask friends or relatives if they belong to a trade union. Find three that do. Note the names of the unions to which they belong, and the actual jobs that they do.

Ask them why they are members, and if they can tell you one thing that the union has done or could do for them.

Find someone who is an employer, and find out what he thinks about trade unions.

Why do you think that members of trade unions and employers feel so differently about the unions?

Data questions

Foundation level

1. Identify the three groups of workers involved in the dispute. Why did each group think that it should be paid the most?
2. Which group, if any, do you think should be paid the most, and why?
3. How might trade unions be able to help workers?
4. What factors should be taken into consideration when deciding a person's wages?

Intermediate level

1. Explain the dispute in the textile industry.
2. How might unions help to sort out the dispute?
3. Why are some people, like doctors, paid more than others, like waiters?
4. Why has trade union membership fallen in the UK in the last decade?

WORKER'S NEWS

Labour trouble in Barengo

Our regular reports from the Southern Ethiopian area of Barengo have always commented on the rapid strides that the area has taken, with the development of industry and the appearance of a money-based economy.

Equal pay
The textile cooperative has now become the largest employer of labour, and includes skilled and unskilled manual workers, as well as white collar workers who look after the administration of the business.

We are told that all the workers within the cooperative receive equal pay – the profits are simply divided between the number of people working there.

Complaints
It appears that this policy has led to complaints from skilled workers who say they should receive more money than everyone else because the textiles could not be made without their skills. The unskilled workers have not been slow to reply, saying that they should be paid the most because they do the hardest and dirtiest work. The administrative staff argue that they often work longer hours than the rest, and do work that the others could not do; they have put their claim that they should receive the most money in writing to the 'Worker's News'.

Threats
There were threats from each group of workers that they would stop work unless their demands were met, so members of each group have joined together into unions; representatives from each union are now trying to solve the argument.

Higher level

1 Explain the arguments about wages in the textile industry.
2 Why are some people paid more than others?
3 How can trade unions intervene in the process of wage determination?
4 What is the future of trade unionism in the UK?

Coursework Suggestions

Idea

Select a trade union.

- Find out when it was founded and what its original aims were.
- Who has it merged with over the years?
- How has it changed in size?
- What are its current aims? How have they changed since it was founded, and why?
- What is its likely future?

Idea

Has there been a strike in your area recently? If there has, go to the library, and read the newspaper articles about it.

- Describe what happened, and give the different versions from the union, the employer, and anyone else who wrote about it.
- Why are there so many different accounts?
- Which is most likely to be true, and why?

5.3 THE FINANCIAL INSTITUTIONS

As the economy has developed, a whole range of specialist financial institutions has emerged to ensure the financial system works easily and smoothly.

The commercial banks

These are institutions that collect money from the general public, look after that money, and use it by lending to others who may need it.

Mergers have left four major commercial banks in the UK: Barclays, Lloyds, Midland and National Westminster (Natwest). There are several smaller banks, such as the Bank of Scotland, and the Trustee Savings Bank (TSB). All these are sometimes called high street banks, because you can find one in the main street of every town.

The role of a **commercial bank** is to hold money in accounts for its customers, and offer a variety of services.

These include:

- **loans and overdrafts,** provided that the bank is satisfied that you will be able to repay them.
- **cheque books,** standing orders and direct debits, to make payments easier
- **security facilities,** including night safes for businesses and strong rooms for the safe keeping of valuables
- exchanging **currency** for holiday makers and businesses dealing with foreigners
- **financial advice**
- **executor and trustee services** to handle estates after death.

Merchant banks

Originally, these were firms specialising in the export of British goods. This involved the sending of money from one country to another, and the merchants gained a reputation for trustworthiness. Their **bills of exchange** were therefore always accepted. As trade developed, other trading companies appeared, but their bills of exchange were not always so readily accepted, so the original merchants began to do this, for a commission.

In this way, the established merchants became bankers specialising in bills of exchange.

Merchant banks still deal in bills of exchange, the issue of new shares and securities, and act as advisors to large companies.

Building societies

Like the commercial banks, the number of **building societies** has fallen as a result of mergers. Three of the largest are the Halifax, Nationwide Anglia and the Woolwich.

The main function of building societies is to loan money to individuals to purchase their own homes. This accounts for about 80% of the combined funds of these societies.

The borrower obtains a mortgage from the society. This is a loan. The borrower pays interest on that loan, and repays the loan and the interest over periods as long as 25 years.

If the borrower fails to pay, the society can take over the house and sell it to someone else so as to recover the money owed.

Building societies obtain the money that they loan out by encouraging people to save with them. They pay interest on these savings but charge a greater rate of interest on the mortgages they give. This creates a profit for the building society.

Building societies are now able to do more than just loan money for house purchase; they offer personal loans, cheque books and credit cards, and in many ways act like commercial banks. Indeed, there is increasing competition between commercial banks and building societies, and the distinction between them is starting to disappear. The second largest building society, the Abbey National, became a bank in 1989 and in 1994 the Halifax and Leeds Permanent building societies announced that they were to merge in 1995. It is expected that they will also become a bank.

ACTIVITY 3

Find someone who has an account at a commercial bank and someone who has a building society account.

List the services that they both offer, and those that are different.

What is the difference between the two?

Insurance companies

Insurance companies accept payments, known as premiums, from individuals or companies, and in return agree to pay any financial loss from particular risks, such as fire or theft.

The premium is based upon the chance of the risk actually happening, and so is based upon very precise statistical evidence.

Some risks may never happen. You may not have an accident whilst driving your car, but it is possible to insure your life, and it is certain that you will eventually die.

Life insurance allows an individual to make sure that, on their death, the relatives will have enough money. Life insurance companies have data on all types of people, and their likely life expectancy, and so can fix a suitable premium.

The Bank of England

The Bank of England was founded in 1694 to lend money to the government. It is now the central bank of the UK, and was nationalised in 1946. It has three key activities: banker, market operator and policy maker.

As a banker

It acts as the government's bank. The income of the state is held in the public accounts section of the Bank of England. The government uses this to pay for its expenditure. It acts as a bank to the commercial banks, all of which have accounts at the Bank of England.

- It acts as a bank to foreign central banks.
- It acts as a bank to a few wealthy private customers.
- It manages the currency of the country, issuing notes and coins.
- It is the registrar of government stocks.
- It serves the national debt.

As a market operator

- It controls the market for short-term loans.
- It controls interest rates.
- It influences lending policies of the commercial banks by open market operations.

It manages the nation's foreign exchange controls, which are held in the exchange equalisation account. It can buy and sell currency on the foreign exchange markets of the world to maintain the value of sterling.

As a policy maker

- It advises the Treasury on the economic state of the country
- It has an international role with the IMF, etc.

```
                    BANK OF ENGLAND
                   ↙       ↓       ↘
           Banker              Policy maker
       e.g. Banker's bank    e.g. Advises the
            Issues notes          treasury
            and coins             Liaises with
                                  the IMF
                    Market operator
                    e.g. Controls
                         interest rates
                         Manages the
                         value of
                         sterling
```

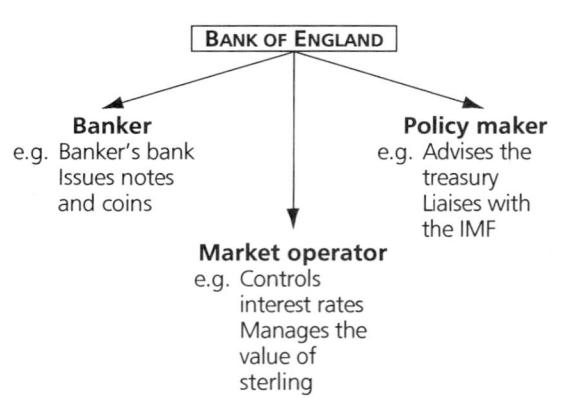

Figure 5.6 The role of the Bank of England

The Stock Exchange

The **Stock Exchange** deals with the buying and selling of existing shares in **public limited companies** and **securities** issued by the British and foreign governments. It is important to remember that the money coming from the sale of a share that has already been issued goes to the owner of the share, and not to the company.

The value of the share reflects what buyers think about a company. If the price of a share is rising, then buyers think that the company is doing well. If it is falling, then buyers have less confidence in the state of the company.

ACTIVITY 4

If you were to start an insurance company, what factors would you take into account in order to calculate the premium to insure a house in your area against theft.

Make a comprehensive list of the factors that would affect the premium, and explain why each is important.

✓ Review terms

Commercial banks; merchant banks; bills of exchange; loans; overdrafts; cheque books; security facilities; currency; financial advice; executor and trustee services; building societies; insurance companies; the Bank of England; the Stock Exchange; securities.

The Bank of England

THE INTERNATIONAL FINANCIAL NEWS

A loan to Barengo?

The Textile Works of Barengo has approached the Royal British Bank with proposals for a loan to develop their flourishing factories in Southern Ethiopia.

The management of the Textile Works has approached a British financial institution as the National Bank of Ethiopia is not in a position to offer a loan itself.

The laws of the country say that foreign capital can only be imported with the approval of the National Bank, however. We understand that this approval has in fact already been given, although we have not had it confirmed.

Reports of labour troubles

The Royal British Bank is said to be concerned about reports of labour troubles at the Textile Works; it will need to be reassured that the reorganisation has been successful.

There may also be questions about the types of security that can be offered.

However, the Textile Works will be able to show years of quite spectacular growth, a profitable range of products, and full order books, all of which should influence the Royal British towards a favourable decision.

Land and labour are cheap in Barengo, so the key questions remain the state of the labour market and the quality of the management team.

The successful future of the area could depend on the result of this important loan application.

Data questions

Foundation level

1 **(a)** Give two reasons why the Royal British Bank may not give the loan.
  (b) Give three reasons that might persuade the bank to give the loan.

2 Explain why banks want security for a loan.

3 Why might the National Bank want to keep foreign money out of the country?

4 Outline two factors not mentioned in the text that might influence a bank's decision to loan someone money.

Intermediate level

1 Outline the reasons why the loan may be granted, and the reasons why it might not.

2 Explain five factors that a bank may take into consideration before giving a loan.

3 Why might the National Bank want to control the import of foreign capital?

4 How else could a central bank influence the development of an industry?

Higher level

1 Give the case for and against the granting of the loan.

2 What sorts of security do banks want for loans, and why?

3 What would a central bank hope to achieve by restricting the amount of money imported into its country?

4 Explain any methods that might be available to a central bank to encourage the growth of an industry.

Coursework Suggestions

Idea

Do building societies and banks differ in the services that they offer?

■ Find out what building societies and banks do.

Of course, on its own, that will not be a very good piece of coursework, so follow it up by seeing what people think about the quality of the service they both offer. Use the Consumers

Association reports (see page 141), and newspaper articles.

Ask people who have accounts at banks and building societies how they feel about the differences. Prepare your questions first.

Idea

You have been left £1,000 in a will, and wish to invest it.

- What factors would you take into account in deciding how to invest the money?
- What options are available to you?
- Where would you invest it, and why?

5.4 THE ROLE OF CENTRAL AND LOCAL GOVERNMENT

It seems an obvious statement but the role of government is to govern, and no matter what type of society is being considered, the statement remains true.

In the UK, the role of the government changed quite considerably over the years: a greater and greater responsibility for the well being of the population has been accepted by the government.

There have always been rules, so the need for some type of agency to uphold these rules has existed (the Police); there has always been a need to protect the society from outside attack, so some form of security system has been needed (the Army, Airforce and Navy). People are required to organise all of this, so an administration has existed. People need to be paid for such activities, so there has always been some form of taxation.

The role of central government

The development of the government's responsibilities is a matter of history and is well documented. These responsibilities fall into four distinct areas:

The provision of essential **public services**. This is the most basic government function, and cannot be performed by anyone else. It involves the maintenance of the head of state, the legislative system and provision for law and order and external security.

The control of sectors of the **economy** for economic, social or strategic reasons. This may mean that some industries receive financial support, or they may be state owned, such as the postal service. The amount of government control is a political matter, and different parties have different views on the extent of government involvement.

The pursuit of **social policies**. This can involve the amount and nature of expenditure on social services, such as education and health.

The control of the economy as a whole. This includes the maintenance of employment, economic growth, and the balance of payments (see section 4.8, page 93).

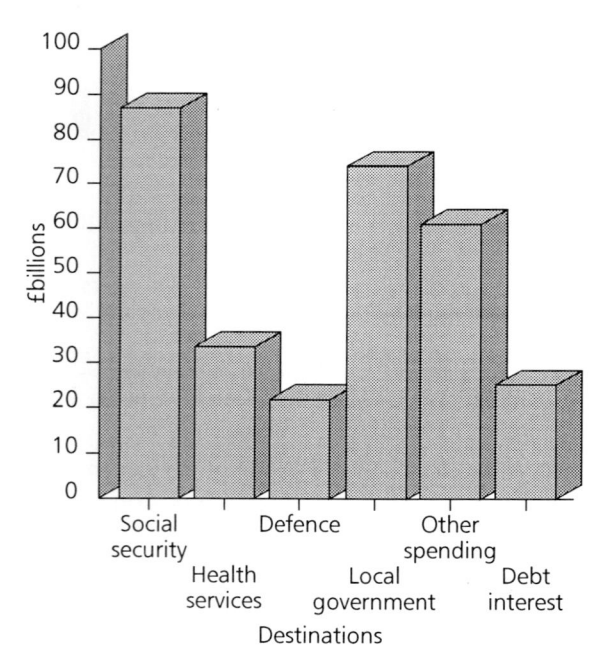

Figure 5.7 UK Government expenditure

Source: *The Budget in Brief* HM Treasury, HMSO

The role of local government

Local government is responsible for activities that are local rather than national.

However, local authorities have to act within a framework of rules laid down by central government.

The main areas of concern to local authorities include:

- **consumer protection**, which means ensuring that all the consumer laws and trading standards are obeyed
- **education**, which means the operation of a system created by central government, and largely involves the building and maintenance of the schools, the payment of staff and the provision of equipment
- **environmental health services** (pest control, waste disposal, etc.)
- **leisure facilities**, which will include the running and maintenance of parks and leisure centres
- **libraries** and **museums**
- personal **social services** for the elderly, infirm and handicapped
- **planning permission** for new buildings, or the change of use of existing ones
- **police** and **fire services**
- the maintenance, but not construction of **roads**
- the provision of **housing.**

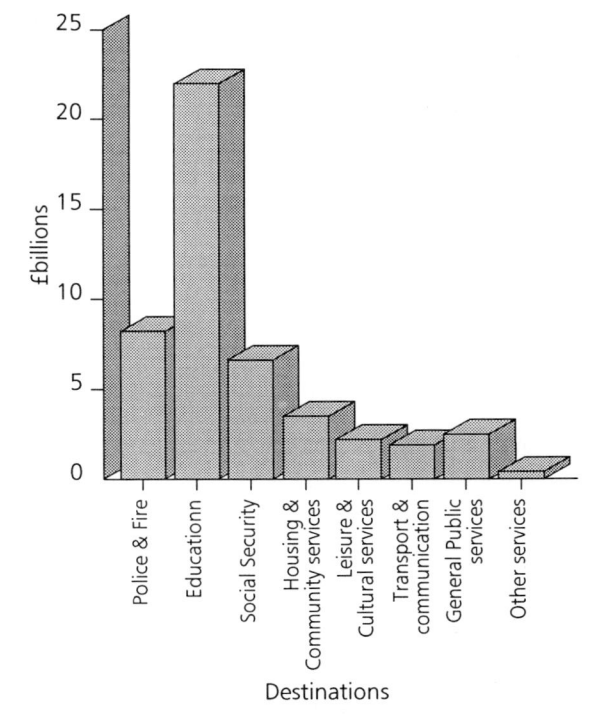

Figure 5.8 Local government expenditure

POLITICS TODAY

Developments in Barengo

In years gone by, Barengo was a region which had no settled population. There were a few tribes, who moved around the area as they wished, and each of these tribes had their own rules.

There was no need for anything else, as the tribes did not mix with each other, and no-one stayed in any one place for long.

Change in the region
Now, however, everything has changed. The community initially grew up around the new Faminaid well, but there is now an established town, with a factory, shops, and a service industry.

It is in need of rules and regulations – a government.

Regional Council set up
A Regional Council has been appointed, and the old tribal laws have been adopted to ensure that society remains regulated.

Now the Council is trying to establish its role with the citizenry. In most countries, the level of government activity has evolved over the years, but in Barengo it will take only a few months. The pace of economic change in the area means that decisions will need to be taken very soon.

Important questions
The important questions relate to the amount of social responsibility the Council should have for unemployment, illness, education, etc., and the amount of control which should be exercised over the economy.

The decisions that are made now will affect Barengo for many years.

Data questions

Foundation level

1 (a) Why was there no need for proper government in Barengo in years until recently?
(b) What has the Regional Council already done?
(c) What decisions have yet to be made?
(d) Why will these decisions have to be made soon?

2 Explain the different ways in which the Central Council could control the economy.

3 How much control do you think a government should have, and why?

4 Explain the problems that could result from not taking the decisions quickly.

Intermediate level

1 What progress has been made in establishing the role of government in Barengo?

2 Outline the arguments for and against government control of the economy.

3 What factors should the Central Council consider before deciding on its level of social responsibility?

4 Why is speed so important in Barengo?

Higher level

1 Consider the progress towards a government in Barengo.

2 What factors should the Regional Council take into account before deciding upon the level of social and economic responsibilities it would accept?

3 Why do some governments own particular industries?

4 What methods of control are available apart from state ownership?

Coursework Suggestions

Idea

Everyone has different ideas about the role of government, and the amount of government control.

- List some of the main things that central (or local) government does, and conduct a survey to see how well people think they are doing.
- Find out how much each government service costs, so that you can tell those who are critical.
- Find out how those who are critical believe the government should operate.

Government can do whatever they are required to do, but everything costs money. Your survey gives opinions; they need to be considered in conjunction with costs. You could ask the following questions:

- Would people pay 5p in the £1 more for better hospital provision? The easy answer is yes or no, but it is not sufficiently exact.
- How much better would the hospital provision need to be?
- Do people fully realise what 5p in the £1 means to them?

This is an area rich in possibilities, but the direction of the work needs to be carefully considered before surveys are begun. Talk to your teacher, and decide what you are trying to achieve. Then write your questions down and talk them through. This should enable you to collect data that will produce sensible results, and allow you to make effective evaluations.

5.5 TAXATION IN THE UK

Central government revenue

In order to pay for its activities, the government has to obtain money from somewhere. The income of the government is called revenue and comes from the general public in the form of taxation. There are two types of taxation: direct, and indirect.

Direct taxation

This is so called because the individual pays the money directly to the revenue authorities.

Income Tax

This is a tax on the income of individuals and firms, and provides the UK Government with about one third of its income.

Every individual is given a **non-taxable allowance**, which varies according to factors such as marital status. This is subtracted from a person's earnings to leave a **taxable income**.

The first part of earnings are taxed at 20%. The next is taxed at 25%, and any earnings over that are taxed at 40%.

This means that the more a person earns, the higher proportion of income is paid in tax. This is known as **progressive taxation**.

If everyone paid at exactly the same rate, and there were no personal allowances, everyone would pay the same proportion of their income as taxation. This is known as **proportional taxation**.

Regressive taxation is the term applied when the more a person earns, the smaller the proportion of taxation is paid.

National Insurance contributions

These are intended to help pay for social security benefits. They are earnings related and are charged as a percentage of income.

ACTIVITY 5

How much income tax would you pay if you were single, and earned per year: (i) £10,000; (ii) £20,000; (iii) £50,000; (iv) 100,000; and (v) £250,000?

For each bracket, calculate the proportion of income that would need to be paid.

Is the system of progressive taxation, where the more you earn, the more you pay, fair? Justify your answer.

Capital Gains Tax

This is a tax on the profit that a person makes from selling their assets. Not all assets are included – the sale of a private house, for example, would not be considered for tax purposes, and gains below a limit are ignored. The gain is added to a person's income, and taxed at the appropriate rate.

Inheritance Tax

This is the taxation of the wealth of someone who has died. It is charged at the rate of 40% on estates over a particular value – at the moment about £150,000.

Corporation Tax

This is a tax on the profits made by companies. In the same way as income tax, the rate is fixed in the Budget.

Indirect taxation

These are taxes on expenditure and so are paid by the individual to the provider of the good or service, who then passes the revenue on to the revenue authority.

It may be possible to avoid paying these taxes by refraining from buying goods and services that are taxed but, as most items are taxed, this is not likely.

Such taxes tend to be regressive, as they take a higher proportion of the income of the poor than the rich.

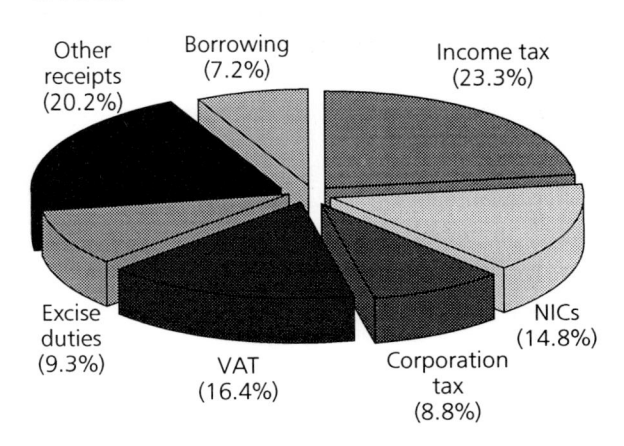

Other receipts (20.2%)
Borrowing (7.2%)
Income tax (23.3%)
NICs (14.8%)
Corporation tax (8.8%)
VAT (16.4%)
Excise duties (9.3%)

Figure 5.9 UK Central Government revenue

Customs duty

This is imposed on goods imported from outside the European Union.

Excise duty

This is imposed on goods such as petrol, tobacco and alcohol as a separate tax and produces about one third of total revenue from indirect taxation.

Value Added Tax (VAT)

This is a general expenditure tax imposed on most goods, except food, and many services. The UK was obliged to introduce this system of taxation as part of its membership of the European Union.

As far as the consumer is concerned, VAT is a percentage, currently 17.5%, which is added to the cost price of a good or service. However, the process is rather more complicated, as VAT is charged at every part of the manufacturing process, as in the following example:

Suppose a sculptor buys a lump of rock from a quarry:

- The quarry charges the sculptor £1,000 plus 17.5% VAT = £1,175.
- The sculptor works on the rock and creates a sculpture of Mrs Thatcher.
- He sells it to a museum for £10,000 plus 17.5% VAT = £11,750.
- The quarry has produced a piece of rock which cost nothing, and was sold for £1,000; £1,000 was therefore added to the value of the rock, and so the quarry must pay £175 in VAT.
- The sculptor bought the rock for £1,000 (+ VAT) and sold it, after work, for £10,000 (+ VAT); he has added £9,000 to the value of the rock, and so he must pay £1,575 in VAT.
- If the museum were to sell the sculpture to a grateful nation for £20,000 (+ VAT), then the museum would have added £10,000 to its value, and so would have to pay £1,750.

Other forms of income

These include income from loans that the government may have made, rent from Crown lands, and charges for goods and services such as medical prescriptions and dental treatment.

ACTIVITY 6

Some goods, like petrol, have an excise duty and VAT to pay as well.

List these goods, and find out the cost price, the amount of duty, and the amount of VAT.

How much tax is there on the same products in other countries within the European Union?

Why are there such differences?

On the other hand, the government may itself have to borrow money; this is known as the public sector borrowing requirement (see page 83).

Local government revenue

Central government provides about three quarters of the money needed by local government in the form of grants and also imposes spending limits. The rest of the money is raised by the local authorities themselves.

Council Tax

Domestic properties are valued and placed into one of eight categories, according to their value, and the same amount of council tax is paid by the owner of each property in a band. Single occupants pay 25% less, and people on low incomes also pay reduced amounts.

The Uniform Business Rate

Business property is valued, and the central government charges a proportion of that value each year. This is distributed to the local authorities according to their populations.

ACTIVITY 7

What are the value bands for the Council Tax in your area? Find out how much money is raised in each band.

Can you suggest a better way of raising local government revenue?

Central government grants

Council tax

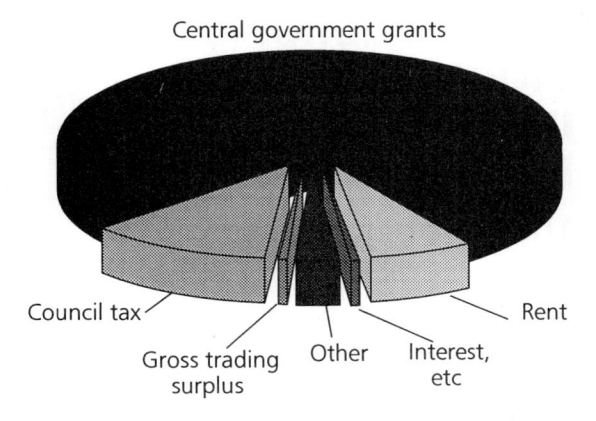

Gross trading surplus

Other

Interest, etc

Rent

Figure 5.10 Local government revenue

> ### ✓ Review terms
> Direct taxation; Income Tax; non-taxable allowance; taxable income; progressive taxation; proportional taxation; regressive taxation; National Insurance contributions; Capital Gains Tax; Inheritance Tax; Corporation Tax; indirect taxation; Customs Duty; Excise Duty; Value Added Tax; PSBR; Council Tax; Uniform Business Rate.

THE DAILY NEWS

New taxes cause trouble

We in Britain are used to paying income tax, VAT, and excise duties. We complain, but we have to pay. The people of Barengo, South Eastern Ethiopia, do not see why they should pay a newly proposed sales tax, however, and they intend to complain to some effect.

Tariffs or sales tax?
The regional government in Barengo used to raise its money by imposing tariffs – taxes – on imported goods. Now that the economy is growing, and the government finds that it has to provide more services such as better roads, different ways of raising revenue have to be found.

The government has said that it will impose a sales tax on all goods and services sold in shops. This would be only 5%, and would be paid only by the purchaser, but it has caused an outcry.

It has been popularly condemned as a tax that will hurt the poor rather than the rich, and there are great fears that it will damage the retail industry of the area.

The government replies that its services have to be paid for, and that the new sales tax is the easiest way of raising the money.

Meanwhile, the chief adviser on taxation at the World Council for Equality has condemned the tax as regressive, and is trying to persuade world leaders to join in the opposition, hoping that this will help to prevent the introduction of the tax.

Data questions

Foundation level

1 (a) How did the Barengan government finance its activities in the past?
(b) Why does the government say that it needs more money?
(c) How does it intend to raise the money?
(d) Why do some people think the tax is unfair?
(e) What damage might it do to the economy?

2 Explain the meaning of the term 'regressive taxation' and outline why it is regarded as unfair to poor people.

3 Outline two other ways in which revenue could be raised, explaining the advantages and disadvantages of both.

4 Governments can increase or decrease taxes on particular goods, so as to influence what we buy. Select a good and explain what a government might gain by trying to stop us buying it.

Intermediate level

1 List five of the main points raised in the article.

2 Explain the difference between progressive and regressive taxation.

3 Governments can increase or decrease taxes on particular goods, so as to influence what we buy. Why might this be done?

4 How can taxation be used to influence the level of economic activity in a country?

Higher level

1 Summarise the article.

2 Explain the differences between progressive and regressive taxation, and how they can be used to alter the distribution of income.

3 How can taxation be used to pursue social policies?

4 Apart from simply raising revenue and pursuing social policies, show the other uses to a government of taxation.

Coursework Suggestions

Idea

It is commonly thought that the less money you have, the more likely you are to support progressive taxation, while the more wealthy you are, the more you are likely to favour regressive taxation.

Test that hypothesis by designing a series of questions, and using them to interview people who earn different amounts of money. It would be interesting also to take into consideration which political party they support.

You might find it difficult to find people willing to answer your questions, but it is a valid topic, if you can. The information collected should be analysed, and a proper conclusion drawn.

5.6 THE EUROPEAN UNION AND OTHER INTERNATIONAL INSTITUTIONS

The European Union

Origins

The Second World War left the countries of Europe needing to rebuild the homes and industrial buildings that had been destroyed. The production of industry also had to be changed, from the needs of war-time to those of peace.

This was made more difficult by the fact that the war had been expensive, so that no country had enough money to make all the changes as quickly as they would have liked.

Some of the countries of Europe decided to help each other, in order to speed up the process of recovery.

In 1948, Belgium, Holland and Luxembourg established economic links, and these three joined with France, Italy and (West) Germany in 1952 to form the **European Coal and Steel Community**. This established a unified market in coal and steel for the six countries.

In 1956, the same six countries signed the **Treaty of Rome** to found the **European Economic Community**, which is now called the **European Union**. The aim was to move towards the elimination of **tariffs** among the members, together with identical import duties for other countries.

The UK did not want to join at this stage, partly because of a desire to maintain independence from other countries, and partly through ties with the Commonwealth.

Instead, the UK became involved in the establishment in 1960 of the **European Free Trade Association**, with Austria, Denmark, Norway, Sweden, Portugal and Switzerland. Finland joined later. The aim of this group was the abolition of tariffs between member countries, but without the aim of a common import duty. This satisfied the desire of the UK to offer preference to Commonwealth goods.

However, trade with the Commonwealth declined, and the economies of the members of the European Community prospered, so the UK applied for membership in 1962, but was rejected. Denmark, Ireland and the UK joined in 1973. Greece, Spain and Portugal joined later.

The structure of the European Union

The European Commission

This body consists of 17 Commissioners appointed by the member governments: one from each of the smallest countries, and two from the five largest. It administers European Union policy, including the finances.

The European Council of Ministers

The Council of Ministers decides the policy of the European Union. One representative from each country attends. The representative will vary according to the subject under discussion, so as to ensure that those attending have a grasp of the issues. The heads of states will attend if the issue is of great importance.

The European Parliament

Each country elects members. It does not make major decisions, but it does have to pass the budget of the European Union, and so it does have some power. In 1979, the European Parliament delayed the budget, and it could use this as a bargaining tool once again.

The European Court of Justice

This deals with matters of European Union Law.

The European Union as a trade group

The **Treaty of Maastricht** was signed in 1992. Its aim was to move the members towards full economic union, with a single currency. This did not prove to be popular with the people of many of the member countries. In fact, the Danes rejected the Treaty in a Referendum, and so it is uncertain if the measures will be implemented.

The Single European Act

This was introduced in 1992, and aimed to create a single market within the European Union by ensuring the free movement of people and goods within the Union.

The General Agreement on Tariffs and Trade (GATT)

Most of the countries of the world, including the UK, are members of **GATT**. The aim is to lower tariffs between members, so as to encourage trade. This is done by protracted bouts of negotiation known as 'rounds', and has proved to be very successful.

The International Monetary Fund (IMF)

This was formed in 1945, and membership was open to all countries in the world. Most are now members. The aims were to encourage world trade and international monetary cooperation by keeping foreign exchange rates stable. To this end, each member made a financial contribution, which could be loaned to any member that needed to borrow in order to avoid currency movements.

The International Bank for Reconstruction and Development (IBRD)

This is sometimes called the **World Bank.** It has funds provided by the developed nations, and makes loans, especially to less developed countries, for particular projects intended to improve economic and living standards.

ACTIVITY 8

What is the difference between the UK Parliament and the European Parliament in terms of power and the politics of the members?

THE DAILY NEWS

European Union ministers to visit Barengo

A surprise announcement from Brussels yesterday was the forthcoming visit to Barengo by trade representatives of the European Council of Ministers.

It appears that the Barengans have approached the European Union asking for a reduction in tariffs on textile goods exported from Barengo to several countries in the European Union. The Barengans have recently secured a loan from the UK, through the Royal National Bank.

Barengo's thriving textile industry is set to expand even more, but high tariffs imposed by the European Union could cause this new initiative to sputter.

Trade treaty

In return for a trade treaty, the Barengans are prepared to buy all their new machinery from Europe, a valuable concession. Barengan ministers declare that they are ready to sign a trade treaty with the European Union immediately.

Developing

Our sources comment that the Council of Ministers will find it difficult to refuse such a treaty, especially with Barengo, which has done so much to develop its economy in recent years.

Data questions

Foundation level

1 What does Barengo want from Europe, and what is it prepared to offer in return?

2 Explain the role of the Council of Ministers in this process.

3 Why could high tariffs in Europe harm the textile industry of Barengo?

4 Outline the help that any other two international organisations could give to Barengo.

Intermediate level

1 Explain the problem faced by the Barengan textile industry.

2 How could the European Council of Ministers help to solve this problem?

3 Which other international organisations could Barengo approach, and what help could they expect?

4 If you were a European Minister, what information would you expect to receive in order to help you make a decision, and why?

Higher level

1 How could the European Council of Ministers help to solve the problem faced by the Barengan textile industry?

2 Outline the process by which such help could be given.

3 Explain the sort of assistance other international organisations could give Barengo.

4 What sort of trade treaty could be made between the European Union and Barengo?

Review terms

European Coal and Steel Community; Treaty of Rome; European Economic Community; European Union; tariffs; European Free Trade Association; European Commission; European Council of Ministers; European Parliament; European Court of Justice; Single European Act; GATT: IMF; World Bank

Coursework Suggestions

Idea

How much do the people of Britain know about the European Union? How much do they know about the effect on the UK economy of membership? Try to find out.

Devise a series of questions, such as the names of the member countries, the aims of the Union, etc., and ask twenty people of different ages and occupations. Analyse your answers so as to show how aware they were of the European Union.

Idea

The UK trades a great deal with the other members of the European Union.

- Find a company near where you live that exports to Europe.
- Find out how the quantity and value of these exports has changed since we joined.
- Is it easier to export to Europe than anywhere else?
- What are the differences?
- Has 1992 made any difference?
- What is the likely future?

6

The Assessment of Economic Behaviour

The criteria against which economic behaviour might be assessed

6.1 ECONOMIC GROWTH • 6.2 THE STANDARD OF LIVING AND THE QUALITY OF LIFE • 6.3 ECONOMIC PERFORMANCE

At the end of this section students should be able to understand:
- the need for economic prosperity
- the effect of external or social costs
- the difference between the standard of living and the quality of life
- how to use economic indicators to measure economic performance.

6.1 ECONOMIC GROWTH

Economic growth is usually seen as the way to improve the living standards of the people within a country. Economic growth is the increase in an economy's level of real output over a period of time. Gross National Product (GNP) (see section 4.4, page 77) is the most commonly used measure of an economy's level of output per year.

The definition of growth is actually:

- the percentage *rate of change* in *real* GNP *per capita* over *one year*.

This means the annual percentage increase in the number of goods and services made available to each person within the country during the year.

The advantages of growth

Economic growth is generally considered to be important because it creates many benefits which everyone can enjoy.

A higher level of output (economic growth) provides more goods and services for the people to enjoy providing a higher standard of living.

If an economy is growing, that is, it has an increasing GNP, more goods and services are produced. This requires more workers. The level of unemployment is thus reduced and provides more tax revenue for the government. An increase in revenue allows the government either to decrease the tax rate or increase expenditure on schools, hospitals, roads or other public goods. Whatever choice is made the people benefit.

The extra goods and services produced through economic growth allow a country to support an increased population without the people of the country suffering. If the increase in output is greater than the increase in population, everyone benefits.

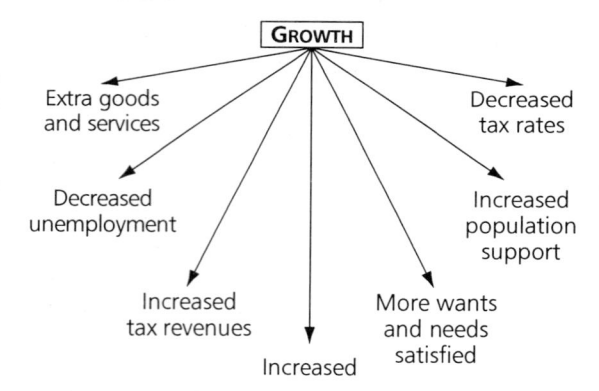

Figure 6.1 The benefits of growth

Growth →
- Extra goods and services
- Decreased unemployment
- Increased tax revenues
- Increased (...)
- More wants and needs satisfied
- Increased population support
- Decreased tax rates

Benefits of growth: supply of jobs exceeding demand

The problems of growth

Economic growth is always assumed to be a good thing, but this is not necessarily the case. The way that the growth is achieved is very important. In many cases the cost of the growth is greater than the benefits it provides, especially if it produces pollution and waste.

Growth within an economy is not always enjoyed by all of the people equally. Some regions, such as the South East of England, may benefit more than other regions. This produces an unfair balance in the country and the regions that grow suffer **external costs** such as **pollution**.

Growth provides more goods and services but if the distribution of income is unequal then not everyone can afford the extra produced. Again this produces an unfair situation where the rich gain a great deal and the poor gain very little.

The increase in output created by growth requires more raw materials and capital. This uses the scarce natural resources even more quickly than before. Many of these resources cannot be replaced.

An increase in output requires more factors of production, the increase in demand for these factors increases their price and hence the cost of living. The extra capital required for growth initially demands more labour but eventually labour is replaced by capital. This creates **unemployment** which is a **social cost**.

Finally, it has been found that in countries that have a very high rate of growth they have also developed a faster lifestyle. This has produced its own social difficulties such as health problems and a higher crime rate.

Social and external costs

One of the problems of economic growth is that it creates social and external costs, known as **externalities**. Social costs are those costs suffered by society as a whole due to the actions of one party. This is not a money cost but an opportunity cost. If a chemical factory pumps waste into a river then

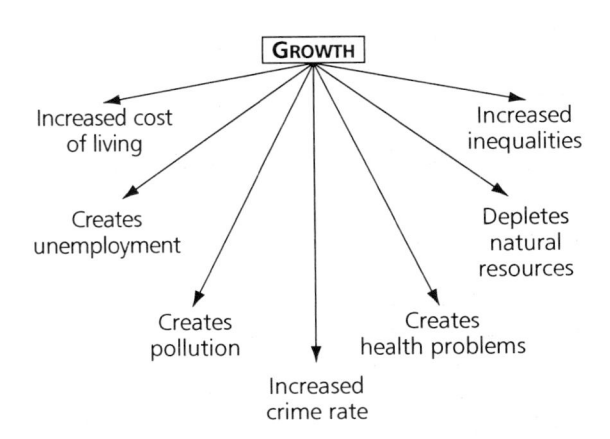

Figure 6.2 The costs of growth

GROWTH
- Increased cost of living
- Creates unemployment
- Creates pollution
- Increased crime rate
- Creates health problems
- Depletes natural resources
- Increased inequalities

Cost of growth: traffic congestion

society suffers. The river is dirty and the fish cannot survive. This is a cost to society as a whole. They have a dirty river instead of a clean one.

An external cost is also a social cost, but is described as the result of an action in a market. Externalities can provide benefits as well as costs.

Unbalanced growth that benefits one area leads to an increase in the number of people and firms within an area. This creates a number of external costs such as **overcrowding** and pollution, all incurring social costs for society.

The fact that growth increases the income of many people usually leads to the purchase of more luxury items. One such item is the motor car. Growth usually produces more cars and these pollute the atmosphere (external cost) and create more accidents, which not only produces a money cost for police and hospitals, but a social cost for society to bear.

The **depletion of resources** may not create a social cost now but in the future there will be less resources and so future generations will suffer. Growth now is creating social costs in the future.

The result of a greater use of capital, usually associated with growth, is that less labour is needed. People are either made redundant or need to retrain in order to find other employment. Those made unemployed or who need to retrain incur disruptions and hardships not felt by everyone. To such individuals these are social costs.

Growth creates a faster lifestyle which has been shown to produce other problems such as heart disease, cancer, stress related illnesses, a higher suicide rate and a higher crime rate. These are all social costs that result from economic growth.

ACTIVITY 1

List ten ways in which your life has changed in the last five years. Are any of these changes due to economic growth within the UK? Can you think of any way in which growth has affected you?

Look at your local area. Are there any examples of growth (new industrial estates or shopping areas)? Why have these been built?

Are there any examples of social costs within your local area? Can you list five social costs that affect you directly?

✓ Review terms

External costs; social costs; pollution; unemployment; externalities; unbalanced growth; overcrowding; depletion of resources.

THE INTERNATIONAL HEALTH JOURNAL

The problems of growth

The western world has discovered that economic growth brings both benefits and costs. The benefits centre around increased prosperity; the costs are often environmental.

The rapid economic growth of some of the developing parts of the world is demonstrating both the welcome benefits and the unwelcome costs at a far greater rate than that experienced by the western world.

A good example of this is Barengo, which is rapidly gaining a reputation as a textile producer.

Benefits

The benefits of increased prosperity to the region are obvious.

Once it was the centre of regular droughts and the charity Faminaid was involved in rescue operations; wells had to be sunk to provide water. Those days would appear to be in the past. The increased wealth produced by the textiles has meant that more wells have been sunk by the Barengans themselves and a regular water supply is ensured. This has allowed agriculture to flourish, and the region now produces all its food.

There is no unemployment as work is available in agriculture, in the factory, in shops and transport. People have earned enough money to buy food and, increasingly, they are able to purchase other consumer goods. These are the benefits of growth.

Cost

However, there are potential dangers. The most obvious is the pollution that can be caused by the dyeing processes of the textile industry.

Here, Barengo has been very fortunate. The textile industry began to develop under the guidance of experienced textile workers, and they were able to show the people responsible for washing and dyeing the textiles the dangers of allowing waste to accumulate in the rivers.

Having been short of water for many years, the Barengans understood the need to ensure that there was no pollution, and they have made sure that this has not been a problem.

The change in the style of life they lead has affected some people. They are not used to working set hours, and many of the jobs are very different from those they did before. This has caused possibly stress-related health problems, but no-one seems to feel this is significant.

Some people are clearly wealthier than others but, again, this does not appear to be a problem to the community. At the moment, the advantages of economic growth far outweigh the disadvantages. The people are far healthier, far wealthier, and the environment is undamaged. Let us hope that this continues.

Data questions

Foundation level

1 (a) Give three advantages of economic growth.
 (b) Give two disadvantages.

2 Explain the meaning of the terms
 (a) economic growth
 (b) social costs
 (c) external costs.

3 The text says that everything in Barengo seems fine. Give five pieces of information you would want before making such a statement.

4 What future problems could occur in Barengo?

Intermediate level

1 Using the text, outline the advantages and disadvantages of economic growth.

2 Explain, with examples, the meaning of the terms 'social costs' and 'external costs'.

3 The text draws a conclusion about life in Barengo. What information would you require to reach such a decision?

4 What are the most likely problems Barengo may face in the medium term?

Higher level

1 List the advantages and disadvantages of economic growth.

2 Explain the difference between social and external costs.

3 What detailed information would you require before drawing a conclusion on the state of Barengo?

4 What different problems may Barengo face in the short, medium and long term?

Coursework Suggestions

Economic growth does present opportunities for coursework, but the great problem is gaining accurate information.

It may be better to consider the question at a local rather than national level, so that you can collect the information yourself.

Idea

Over the years, there has been considerable economic change within this country. Take a period of time – 10 years, 20 years, 30 years – whatever you want.

- Find out what you can about the changes in the national economy over that period.

Find a group of people who have lived through the changes that you have outlined, and question them to find out about the changes they believe have happened.

Then you can compare the realities of economic growth with the gains and costs that they have experienced from that growth.

Idea

Find a firm – probably a small, local one, as this is more likely to give you the information that you need.

- Assess its growth over a period of time
- Look at the benefits to the owner and his staff, e.g. more money, more people employed, etc.
- Consider also the costs that they perceive, e.g. longer hours, more stress, etc.
- Then you could pose the question: is it worth the extra effort?

6.2 THE STANDARD OF LIVING AND THE QUALITY OF LIFE

Economic growth is important because it provides more goods and services for the people. The fact that each individual has the chance to enjoy these extra goods and services should improve their lives, their **standard of living**.

The major reason why governments try to achieve economic growth is to make extra goods and services available to satisfy more of the wants and needs of individuals, and so improve everyone's standard of living.

The standard of living, also known as the level of **economic welfare** or real income is best defined as:

- the level of material well being of an individual or household.

Hence the more goods and services produced the better an individual's or household's standard of living. This is why economic growth and standard of living are so closely linked.

Measurement of the standard of living

If the standard of living is the material well being of individuals and households, the only way to measure it is to calculate the amount of goods and services that are available to each person.

Firstly the amount of goods and services produced by an economy is needed. This is the **Gross National Product (GNP)**. This is the monetary value of all of those goods and services produced by domestically owned factors of production in one year. In the case of the UK it would be those goods and services produced by factors of production owned by the UK or UK citizens.

If the GNP, output of the nation, is then divided by the total number of people in the country, **GNP per head** is found. This is also known as **GNP per capita**.

This provides a money value for the amount of goods and services that are available to each individual in one year. This is the accepted measurement for the standard of living.

This is only a money figure which measures the amount of goods and services per person, nothing else. It relies heavily upon the GNP figure being accurate and the value of money remaining constant. If **inflation** exists and the value of money changes, other calculations have to be made.

Use the following to measure the standard of living

$$\frac{GNP}{Total\ population} = GNP\ per\ head\ (per\ capita).$$

The quality of life

The standard of living does not measure the **quality of life** of individuals within an economy because it is only a measure of the material well being of those people.

The quality of a person's life includes far more factors than the number of goods and services they have available to purchase.

Leisure time is very important to most people. An increase in leisure time should increase the quality of an individual's life. The more leisure time they have the less they work. However, if this increase in leisure was due to unemployment or a shorter working week with less money, it would not improve their quality of life.

Merit goods, such as health and education, and **public goods**, such as defence and law and order, are a very important indicator of the quality of life. The more zero priced merit and public goods, and the better the quality of these, the better the quality of life for the people within an economy. A person who knows that if they fall ill they will be treated in a hospital without charge must have less worries than one who would have to pay for such treatment and may not be able to afford it.

Those people that live away from congestion, pollution and the fear of earthquakes and floods, must also have a better quality of life than those who suffer from these external costs. In this case organisations such as Greenpeace, who fight against pollution and other external costs, have an important influence on the quality of life for many people.

For a large number of people discrimination greatly reduces the quality of their life. Ethnic minority groups and women in the UK have the law on their side and if the laws on **equal opportunities** are strictly enforced it should reduce discrimination and so improve the quality of life for many people.

The standard of living has an effect upon a person's life but they are not the same thing. The quality of life is a far wider concept than the standard of living, and it does not have a single measurement. An attempt to measure the quality of life would involve a number of factors: some of these factors, such as peace of mind, cannot be measured.

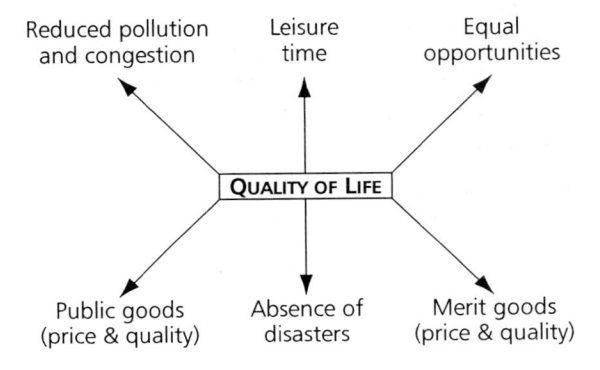

Figure 6.3 Factors affecting the quality of life

Social costs

Section 6.1 shows clearly that one of the costs of economic growth is an increase in social costs. Social costs, such as pollution and congestion, have an adverse effect on people's quality of life. However, economic growth increases output and provides more goods and services per person; this increases the standard of living.

A very important conflict is therefore created: an increased standard of living should improve everyone's quality of life, but the process of increasing the standard of living actually harms people's quality of life.

Economic prosperity

It is the function of an economy to produce as many goods and services as possible (**economic prosperity**). This should satisfy as many of the people's wants and needs as possible. However, as stated in section 1 (page 1), people's wants and needs are never ending, therefore an economy

Contrasting qualities of life

constantly needs to be increasing its output. If more goods and services are produced GNP increases and GNP per capita also increases. Not only are more goods and services produced, but production creates income and higher incomes are enjoyed. This is a definite improvement in the standard of living.

Higher incomes, more goods and services and a better range of goods are more easily recognised by individuals than the social costs that may be created. As economies are run by governments who wish to be elected the greater output becomes more important than lower social costs.

- Private wealth outweighs social costs.

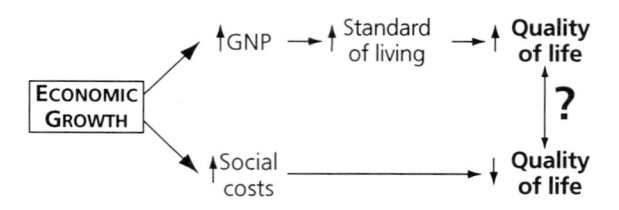

Figure 6.4 Economic growth and quality of life

With the population in most countries increasing, due to a reduced death rate, the need for more goods and services becomes even greater.

It is for this reason that economic prosperity is important. It also explains why the standard of living is often considered to be more important than the quality of life.

ACTIVITY

Calculate your household income and find your income per capita (income per head in your house).

Name two social costs that affect your life. What five changes to your life could you make that would improve the quality of your life?

Using the GNP per capita for the UK compare this to the income per capita in your household.

Is the figure different to the national figure? If it is try out find out why.

Is the national figure accurate?

Contrasting qualities of life

THE STATISTICAL NEWS

An international comparison

The figures in the table opposite have been extracted from a recent survey of the state of the economy in Barengo and UK statistical tables.

Figures reveal relative standards of living

These figures appear to suggest that there is a great difference between UK and Barengan standards of living.

Strikingly, those who are enjoying the greater material benefits are less content with their lifestyle than those with the fewer possessions.

	UK	Barengo
GNP per capita per week	£280	£5
Average number of hours worked per week	40	55
% of households with television	98%	4%
% of households with videos	65%	1%
% of households with washing machines	99%	2%
% of households with cars	75%	1%
Recreational facilities	many	few
Public's level of satisfaction with their quality of life	low	high
Merit goods available	full welfare facilities	limited facilities

Data questions

Foundation level

1 Explain the meaning of the terms:
   (a) Standard of living
   (b) Quality of life
2 Give five examples of the higher standard of living in the UK than in Barengo.
3 How can people believe that they are enjoying a high quality of life when their standard of living is so low? Equally, how can people who appear to have such a high standard of living believe that they have a low quality of life?
4 What can a government do to improve the quality of life for its citizens?

Intermediate level

1 What evidence is provided to demonstrate the better standard of living in the UK?
2 How can the citizens of the UK believe that their quality of life is so low, and the Barengans think theirs to be so high?
3 What is the difference between standard of living and quality of life?
4 How could the UK Government improve the quality of life for its citizens?

Higher level

1 What evidence is available, and what else would be required to consider fully the standards of living of the two countries?
2 Compare the terms 'standard of living' and 'quality of life'.
3 How could you explain the disparity between the apparent differences in the standard of living and perceptions of quality of life?
4 What problems face the Barengan government in improving the quality of life for its citizens?

Coursework Suggestions

Idea

The data material provides an idea for coursework.

People earn different amounts of money, and have different standards of living. However, this does not equate to the quality of life. Quality of life is clearly a more personal feeling. It may depend on your age, where you live, how much you earn – or just how you feel at the time.

Select a group of people who have different standards of living, and are of a variety of ages, etc., and find out about their possessions and what they think of their quality of life.

Analyse the results, so as to see if there is a relationship between standard of living and quality of life.

The results also tell you why people have different perceptions of their quality of life, or even the problems of life in the UK.

Review terms

Standard of living; economic welfare; Gross National Product (GNP); GNP/head; GNP/capita; inflation; quality of life; leisure time; merit goods; public goods; equal opportunities; economic prosperity

6.3 ECONOMIC PERFORMANCE

Traditionally all governments pursue four aims. These are:

- **full employment** (zero unemployment)
- **stable prices** (zero inflation)
- **a balance of payments equilibrium**
- **economic growth.**

A fifth aim, of **greater equality**, has been added to this list by many governments but there has been a great deal of argument about this.

A problem with these aims is that they are not all achievable at the same time. Policies to cure **inflation** often create **unemployment** and hinder growth. Policies to cure unemployment tend to create inflation and harm the balance of payments but create growth.

It is because of this that governments tend to choose one or two of these aims as their priority, and then try to keep the other aims at a respectable level.

The major aim of any government is usually political and not economic. It is because of this fact that those aims which most affect the people of the country have usually been the priority.

The major aim of every government until 1980 was the achievement of full employment. In 1980 this changed, and from then onwards the maintenance of stable prices has been the main aim followed in the UK.

Stable prices

Stable prices means that there is no inflation. In reality, however, this is very difficult to achieve and so inflation in single figures and as close to zero as possible has been the aim.

Looking at the UK between 1985 and 1994 it can be seen that the rate of inflation has constantly been in single figures and never rises above 10%. The lowest level was in 1993 with 1·6% and the highest was in 1990 with 9·5%.

Between 1986 and 1990 inflation was increasing, except for 1988, and so this was not a successful period. However, between 1990 and 1993 it was decreasing every year and so this was a successful period. From 1993 the trend has been increasing which is less encouraging.

If asked to describe the trends for inflation it could be described in two ways.

Firstly, the difference between 1985 and 1994 shows a downward trend, 5·3% to 3·3%, a fall of 37·7%.

Secondly, there are four basic trends during this period; decreasing between 1985 and 1986; increasing between 1986 and 1990; decreasing between 1990 and 1993 and increasing between 1993 and 1994. For all four trends a rate of change could be calculated.

Whether the pattern is thought of as successful or not depends upon how low a government wishes to keep inflation, but it would seem that 1990 to 1993 was successful.

Full employment

The term full employment suggests that everyone has a job, that is everyone who is willing and able to work has a job. This is not possible for many reasons (see section 4.8); hence, the aim of governments has always been to keep unemployment as low as possible.

Figure 6.6 on the next page shows unemployment in the UK, as a percentage of the **working population**, between 1985 and 1994.

In 1985 unemployment was at 11·6% and rose to 11·8% in 1986. From 1986 to 1990 there was a continuous fall to 5·9%, a fall of 50%. 1990 to 1993 shows an increase to over 10%, when it began to fall again into 1994.

As with inflation, unemployment shows two major trends, 1986 to 1990 and 1990 to 1993, with two minor trends from 1985 to 1986 and 1993 to 1994.

Overall the general trend has been a decrease, 11·6% in 1985 to 10·4% in 1994.

It is interesting to note that the trends for unemployment are almost the opposite to the trends for inflation.

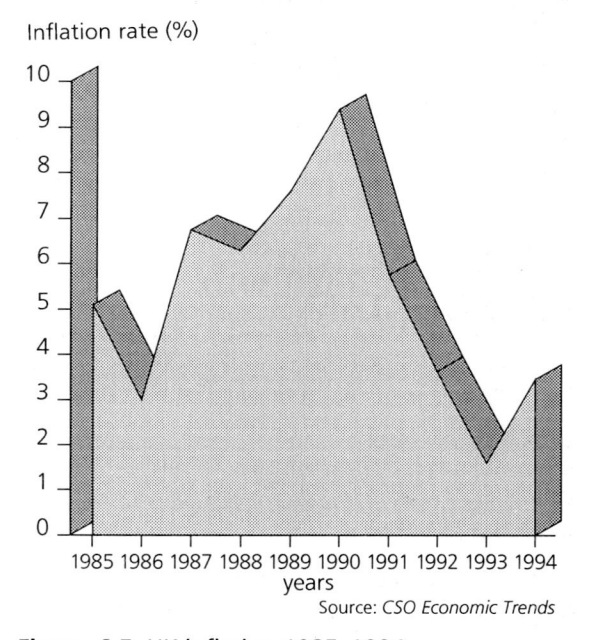

Figure 6.5 UK inflation 1985–1994

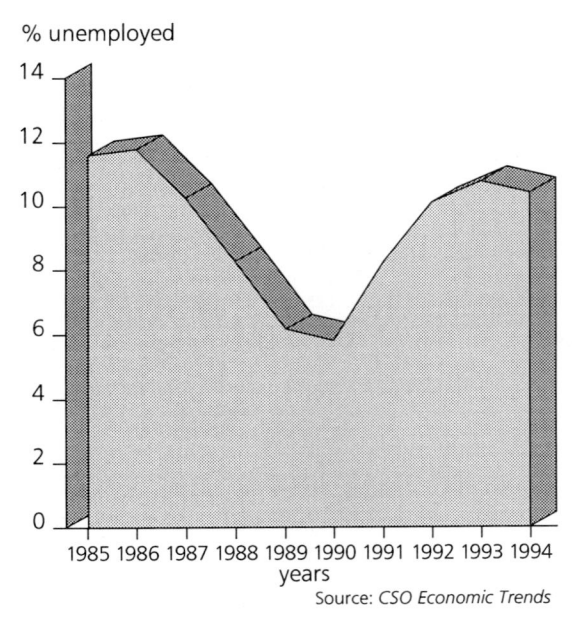

Figure 6.6 Unemployment in the UK 1985–1994

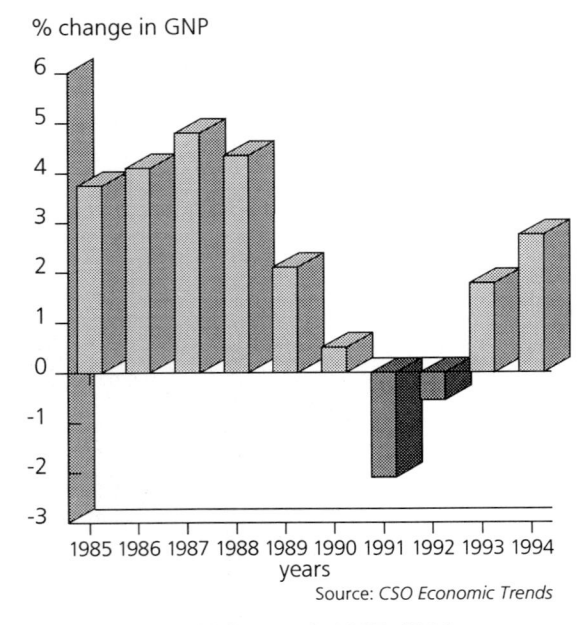

Figure 6.7 UK GNP growth 1985–1994

Whatever is regarded as an acceptable level of unemployment, if there is one, it is certainly not 10% or above. Even 5% unemployment means that one person in every 20 people who wish to work is unable to do so. 10% represents one person in every 10 people.

In only four years out of the last ten has unemployment been below 10% and never below 5%. This shows a waste of resources: labour is available for work but is not being used.

If this indicator is used the UK has not performed well. On average 10% of the working population has remained unemployed and so the economy has only produced to 90% of its capacity. The economy is not providing for as many of the peoples' wants and needs as it could have done.

Economic growth

Economic growth produces an increase in the output of the economy and enables it to provide for more of the wants and needs of the people.

There are three distinct trends for **GNP growth** in the UK between 1985 and 1994. A three year increase from 1985 to 1987 and then a decrease from 1987 to 1991. From 1991 to 1994 the trend is upwards again.

Growth never exceeds 5% for the whole period and on two out of the ten years it is negative. This shows that during these two years the economy was actually producing less than the year before. This is totally opposite to what the economy is trying to do.

It is more difficult for a **developed economy** like the UK to continue to grow and increase its output at an increasing rate. In this context a steady rate of growth would be satisfactory.

The evidence shows that the UK has not been successful at achieving economic growth. For only three years does growth exceed 4%; for only four years is it greater than 3%.

Balance of payments equilibrium

When discussing the balance of payments it is the **current account** that is important. Equilibrium in the current account means that a country is trying to balance its payments and receipts. A current account deficit for the UK, where imports are greater than exports, would mean that it owes money to other countries. A current account surplus, where exports are greater than imports, would mean that other countries would owe the UK money and they would have a deficit. It is because of this that all countries try to balance their current account, to achieve an equilibrium.

In reality it is very difficult to achieve a balance and so most countries accept a small deficit or surplus. The ideal situation is where a small deficit is followed by a small surplus.

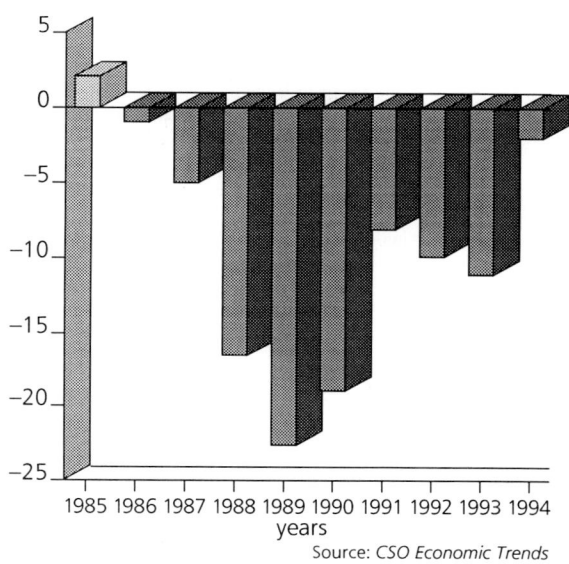

Pounds, billions

Figure 6.8 UK balance of payments account 1985–1994

Figure 6.8 clearly shows that the UK's balance of payments on current account has not performed well. For only one year out of the ten years shown has a surplus been achieved. For the remaining nine years there has been a deficit.

The overall trend for the ten year period is of a movement from surplus to deficit. Between 1985 and 1989 the trend is of a worsening current account balance with the deficit increasing each year. Between 1989 and 1991 the account is still in deficit but the amount of the deficit is decreasing. Between 1991 and 1993 the trend is reversed again and the deficit exceeds £10 billion. After 1993 the account improves and the deficit is reduced.

The general picture is of a country that is very unsuccessful at balancing its balance of payments current account. It is constantly spending more than it is earning which uses up any reserves the country may have.

Other indicators

There are a number of other indicators that can be used to assess the performance of an economy.

- **GNP per capita** is one possible measurement. This would look at an individual's material standard of living.
- **Interest rates** often indicate how well an economy is performing: high rates of interest often indicate potential problems.
- The **exchange rate** can also be an indicator; a weak pound (the pound buys less foreign currency) may indicate that other countries do not wish to buy UK goods for whatever reason.
- **Manufacturing output** is often used to assess the economy's performance. If manufacturing output increases this shows a better use of the resources available and greater output.

Whatever indicator is used, trends *over time* give a clearer picture of performance and should always be used. Some idea of the changes either as amounts or percentage changes gives a picture of the rate at which these indicators are changing. The amount of any change is usually important.

Finally, different indicators may give a different view of how well the economy is performing. This may make general conclusions difficult.

ACTIVITY 3

Use a piece of graph paper and plot *unemployment rates* and *inflation rates* for the last five years on the same graph. Plot percentage unemployed on the left hand side and percentage inflation on the right hand side, with the years along the horizontal.

Using your graph paper, try to see if there are any patterns between the rate of unemployment and the rate of inflation.

Try plotting *GNP growth* and *unemployment* and GNP growth and *inflation*. Can you see any relationship between these three?

Can you think of any reason why relationships may exist?

THE DAILY NEWS

Visitor at the Treasury

Representatives from the country of Barengo are paying a one week visit to the Treasury here in London.

Here for help
They are trying to gain some knowledge of the help an economy can receive from the collection and interpretation of statistical information – the economic indicators that are so familiar to us.

Inaccurate data
Barengo does not have a problem with unemployment at the moment, and it is careful to ensure that the balance of payments is in equilibrium. There is economic growth, but the measurement of its rate may not be accurate.

There may be inflation, but again, the figures are not necessarily correct. The officials are aware of the major aims of economic policy, and they are seeking to develop systems of record keeping that will ensure their data is accurate and up to date.

Assessment
The ways in which other indicators can be used to assess the performance of the economy, and to flag potential problems in advance, really interest the Barengans: their presence here in the UK demonstrates their desire to maintain an improving economy.

Data questions

Foundation level

1 Explain the meaning of the term 'economic indicators'.

2 Identify the four economic indicators mentioned in the text and define the meaning of each of them.

3 Why is it difficult to achieve all of the aims of economic policy at the same time?

4 What advice would you give to the Barengan officials to help them in their attempts to keep close control of their economy?

Intermediate level

1 Explain, using examples not in the text, the meaning of the term 'economic indicators'.

2 Which four indicators are mentioned in the text? Why do governments find it difficult to achieve the best results from each of them at the same time?

3 Which indicators would be of most value to the Barengans in seeking to maintain long-term improvements to their economy?

4 What problems could occur if Barengo decided that economic growth was the greatest priority?

Higher level

1 Explain the value of economic indicators.

2 The four major aims of economic policy are outlined in the text. Why do governments find it difficult to achieve all four simultaneously?

3 Outline the most valuable indicators in seeking to achieve short term and long term economic stability.

4 Why is inflation a major danger to any economy, but particularly to a developing country such as Barengo?

✓ Review terms

Full employment; stable prices; balance of payments equilibrium; economic growth; inflation; unemployment; working population; GNP growth; developed economy; current account; GNP per capita; standard of living; interest rates; exchange rate; manufacturing output.

Coursework Suggestions

To study this area at the national level may be very difficult, but the material may be more easily available locally.

Idea

What are the unemployment figures for your area?

- Look at them over a few years.
- What is the trend?
- Compare them to the national trend.
- Repeat this exercise for economic growth and inflation.

Are there any other indicators that you could use?

- What is the mood of the area?
- Do business people believe that the local economy is improving, or becoming worse?
- Does it seem easier to find a job?
- Are new businesses opening?

You can use the indicators to predict what should happen in your area, and you may have some evidence of the accuracy of the indicators that you have used.

7

Coursework

> **Simple guidelines and advice on how to complete coursework**
>
> 7.1 COURSEWORK TITLES • 7.2 PRESENTATION, EVALUATION AND ANALYSIS OF DATA • 7.3 COURSEWORK SOURCES AND GENERAL GUIDELINES
>
> This section should enable students to:
> - choose a coursework title that they find interesting and manageable
> - collect data efficiently and present it clearly
> - relate economic theory to real situations
> - produce a report that fulfils the original coursework objectives.

7.1 COURSEWORK TITLES

Almost every subject at GCSE requires both coursework and an examination. Economics is no different. It is important that you complete your coursework, but it may be possible to make it easier if you follow a few simple guidelines and read the advice given in this section.

Some teachers and parents believe that it is necessary to spend a great deal of time on coursework, but this is not true. Coursework represents only 20% of your total mark. In other words, the examination is worth 80% of the total mark, and so is far more important in determining your final grade.

This does not mean that coursework is not important, and can be ignored. The marks gained from your coursework assignment can have a real effect on your final grade. The important point is that you must plan your time correctly. Do not spend more time on your coursework than you do studying the rest of the course. If you ignore parts of the syllabus you will not cope with the examination and even if your coursework is excellent you may not gain the grade you require.

- Do not neglect the rest of your work to concentrate on your coursework.

The various examination boards make different demands for coursework. They may ask for one, two or even three items, each from a different part of the syllabus. Some examination boards state the areas of the syllabus that must be used for coursework but all of them state the maximum number of words that can be used. It is important that before you start you know all of these facts.

Each examination board publishes a **marking criteria**. These marking schemes are not secret and you should be given a copy. These will tell you how many marks are available for the different skills that are being tested, and how the marks are awarded. If you know the different areas and skills being tested and how the marks are given you should be able to produce a piece of work that is more likely to score high marks.

- Check the number of items of coursework required.
- Check which areas of the syllabus the coursework can be chosen from.
- Note the maximum number of words to be used.
- Ask for a copy of the marking criteria.
- Read the marking criteria, make sure you understand it, if not ask your teacher for help.

Starting coursework

All coursework has to be completed by the candidate, and this can cause teachers some problems. The amount of assistance which a teacher can give is limited by the regulations of the examination board. If too much help is given the candidate may be penalised. This has led to many teachers setting the *same* coursework for every student. In this situation every student will receive the same help and guidance and the regulations can be closely watched.

This approach is also thought to be easier for those students who are happier being told what to do. If this is the approach of your centre then the rest of this section can still be of some use: it will help you to understand how and why your title has been set, and how it should be answered.

In those schools and colleges that allow a free choice of topic, after negotiation, students have both an easier and a harder task. A free choice allows students to choose something that really interests them and will be enjoyable to complete. The problem is that the choices are so wide that they are endless and trying to find a good topic with plenty of economic content can be difficult.

Remember that the subject content is economics and so whatever topic is chosen the economic ideas must be strong and clear. Many students produce work that could be used for Geography, or Business Studies or a careers lesson. These items of coursework do not score as many marks as they should.

- Try to avoid work from other subject areas.
- Remember the economic content is very important.

Choosing a topic

A first step when deciding upon a coursework title is to look at those areas of the course that you find most enjoyable or seem to be easier for you to deal with. These larger topic areas can then be broken down to produce a more specific and specialised area. Remember coursework has been designed to allow candidates to show how well they understand the theory of economics and how it works in the real world.

Figure 7.1 gives an example of how the topic of price can be broken down into small topic areas.

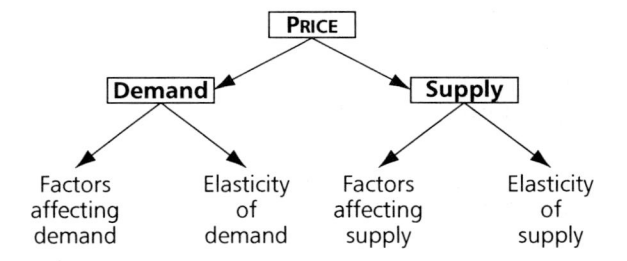

Figure 7.1 Factors affecting price

If one part of this simplified example is chosen then this too can be broken down even further. For example, you might have noticed that petrol prices have changed or that different stations tend to charge slightly different prices for their petrol. This could be an area that you would like to investigate. Demand and the factors affecting it could be a reason. Figure 7.2 breaks this down into smaller sections.

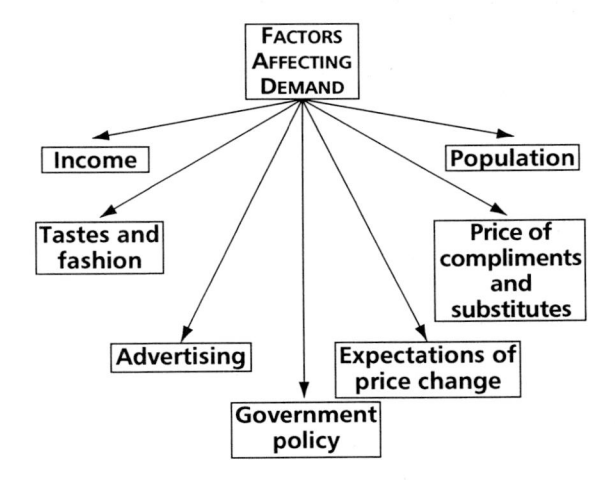

Figure 7.2 Factors affecting demand

The result of this is that you could investigate people's incomes within particular areas to see if they influence the price of petrol locally. You may or may not find a connection but you will have collected information, analysed it and drawn conclusions using the correct economic theories.

An alternative method of selecting a topic for coursework is to look at local, or national, issues. Is something happening in your local area that has economic implications? For example, is there a new road, bypass or motorway? Is a new shopping centre or leisure centre going to be built, or is one needed? Is the local authority trying to encourage industry into your area? If so why, and how are they trying to do this? If it is a local issue, there will be information available, so this could be worth considering when you make your decision.

A personal issue may be the most appropriate topic for coursework. All individuals at some time have to make economic decisions. Section 1 explains how every decision involves an opportunity cost. For example, staying on at school after the age of 16 involves a loss of potential earnings, money that the 16 year old could earn if at work. This is an opportunity cost.

What are your hobbies or interests? The local football club is a business and your youth club could not exist without money from somewhere. Both these clubs could provide subjects worth investigating.

Is there nothing for young people of your age to do at night? You could look at the possibility of providing entertainment that your friends and peers actually want. Investigate both what they want and whether it makes economic sense to provide it.

Remember the key to choosing a suitable topic is finding something that interests you, because if you enjoy doing it, then it will not be such hard work. Discuss your ideas with your teacher, to make sure that you are not attempting something that is too large or too difficult.

Whatever method is used to select a coursework topic it is important that the subject material is economic and that information is available. If possible the information should be primary rather than secondary. For example, if the topic chosen is the Bank of England all of the information will be from books and leaflets, that is, secondary information, and there is little scope for an original approach. It is far better to collect information from your own surveys and questionnaires and draw your own conclusions.

You should consider:

- local issues; personal issues; hobbies and interests.

You should always remember:

- Is the topic economic?
- Is data available (primary or secondary)?

Choosing a title

Many students believe that coursework is just an essay, so they set themselves a task such as *The cures for inflation*. Not only is this title too broad it allows little scope for originality and leads to a purely descriptive piece of work.

Choosing a title is the second step you must take before starting your coursework, and is probably one of the most important steps. The wrong title can cause you a great number of difficulties, as already shown.

One approach is for your title to ask a question or set a problem to be solved, for example:

- Why do large firms locate in the High Street?
- What factors influence the price of secondhand cars?
- How do banks decide to whom to lend money?

This sort of title creates a problem which has to be solved by you. The question needs an answer, proved by evidence that *you* have collected and analysed. This will give your coursework an aim. If you begin to *describe* rather than *analyse* and evaluate, then you will not answer the question set. The most common problem with coursework is that candidates simply describe a situation or repeat theories and fail to analyse and evaluate.

An alternative approach is to make a statement that has to be proved or disproved. Again it will force you to work towards a statement based on evidence collected and analysed, for example:

- Unemployment in my area (name of town or city) is greater than the national average.
- Competition between petrol stations is based upon facilities and not prices.

These statements have to be proved or disproved. It does not matter whether the statement is correct, simply that you work towards an answer and can prove it right or wrong. The statement forces you to produce an answer and if you begin to describe you will not achieve your objective.

This type of approach can be contrasted with titles such as *inflation* or *unemployment*. It can be seen that these are too general and too vague. *What* about inflation or unemployment? There is no aim to these titles, nothing to prove and no question to answer. The result is a long essay, or piece of work, on everything connected with inflation or unemployment. This sort of title produces coursework that scores very few marks. It is descriptive and lacks analysis and evaluation, where the majority of marks are gained.

When you decide upon a title you should at the same time have some ideas of your own about a solution. This solution can be in the form of an answer to the question or an explanation of the problem. This solution is known as an **hypothesis**. The statement discussed in the last paragraph is in fact an hypothesis, but it is also helpful to have such a statement even when you are asking a question or setting a problem. It gives your work an aim: you are trying to prove your hypothesis. Whilst doing this you will solve your problem or answer your question.

Forming an hypothesis is not an easy task. An hypothesis turns problems and questions into a form that can be tested. It requires a certain knowledge of the syllabus area being investigated backed by a sound grounding in economic theory.

You should remember:

- Coursework *is not* an essay.
- Your coursework title should *ask a question* or *set a problem* to be solved.
- Alternatively, your coursework should formulate an hypothesis (a statement to be tested).
- It is best to avoid: titles such as *inflation* or *unemployment*.
- You must ask for help if you need it!!

7.2 PRESENTATION, EVALUATION AND ANALYSIS OF DATA

It is worth repeating that coursework is not an essay; you should not produce a continuous piece of written work. This is an area where many candidates fail. As we have noted before, they believe than an item of coursework is just a long essay and lose many marks because of this. Try to produce a report. This means that you should split your work into sections which should contain the following:

- the background to the report
- the findings of the report
- the conclusions.

If your coursework is to look like a report then it should include charts, maps, diagrams and photographs if they are appropriate. This makes your work appear more interesting and also shows that you can communicate in other ways than writing. However, do not put in pictures or diagrams if you do not refer to them or they are not needed. Again this is a common mistake and is just a waste of your time.

There is no need to type or word-process your work; you will receive no extra marks if you do so. However, the general impression of a well presented, neat and tidy report is far better than something scrawled on a few sheets of tatty paper. Think about the impression you are giving to others of yourself and your work. An added advantage of using a word processor is that you can change your work easily if you wish to. You would not have to rewrite the whole piece but simply change the work at whatever place you wish and print out a complete copy again. This saves time and effort and allows you to continue to improve your work up to the deadline date.

If you are pleased with your work, which you should be, take the time and the trouble to show it at its best. Are your diagrams and charts neat and accurate? Are the pages numbered? Is what you are saying clear?

You should remember:

- to write a report
- to use a variety of presentation methods, e.g. maps, charts, diagrams
- to be as neat and clear as possible – be proud of your work.

Organisation

Your work should be organised so as to obtain the maximum marks possible. You can only do this by looking at the marking criteria, which are fairly similar for each examining board. Make sure that you have seen these criteria, and if you do not understand them, ask your teacher to explain them to you. You cannot play any game properly unless you know the rules: the marking criteria are the rules and this examination is far more important than a game. It is part of your future, so make sure that you know exactly what is expected of you.

All the boards have four assessment objectives:

- knowledge/use of information
- application
- select/organise/interpret
- evaluation/judgement.

This tells you something about what is required, but not enough. Each board has split these areas further, saying how many marks can be awarded for the level of skills demonstrated in each. The Southern Examining Group, for example, adds the following information:

- *Knowledge/use of information*: is the ability to use knowledge in relation to an economic context. This is worth a maximum of 10 marks.
- *Application*: is the ability to apply concepts, theories, terms and knowledge to resolve problems and issues. This is worth a maximum of 10 marks.
- *Select/organise/interpret*: is the ability to organise and analyse the information in order to use it to resolve the problems or issues. This, also, is worth a maximum of 10 marks.
- *Evaluation/judgement*: is the ability to draw reasoned conclusions, distinguish between evidence and opinion and present it in a precise and logical manner as a solution to problems or issues. This also is worth a maximum 10 marks.

This is very much more helpful, as it gives the maximum number of marks available for each assessment objective, and it tells you in general terms what each objective requires.

The marking criteria set out four points that need to be remembered. They should be the guidelines on which all of your coursework is based.

- You need to present information relevant to the subject of economics.
- You need to use your knowledge of economics to the topic.
- The work should be well organised, and the materials analysed.
- You need to draw a realistic conclusion based on the evidence.

Each of the areas carries the same number of marks, so they should be thought of and treated with equal importance.

There are many different ways actually to organise your work, but one possible approach is given in Figure 7.3 below.

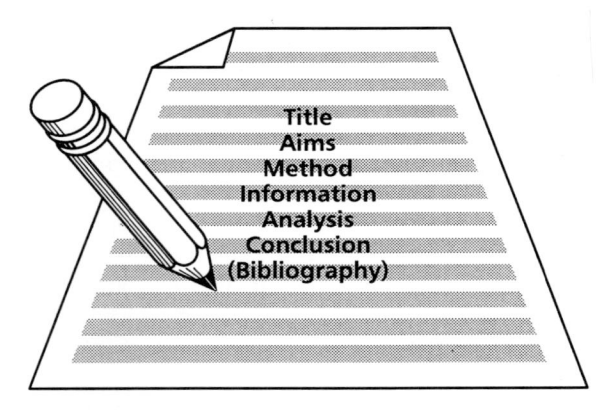

Figure 7.3 Organising your work

Title
Aims
Method
Information
Analysis
Conclusion
(Bibliography)

The necessary elements can be outlined:

- The **title** should pose a problem or ask a question, alternatively set an hypothesis to be tested.
- The **aims** are not strictly necessary, but it is useful to say what you intend to do.
- **Method** is, again, not vital, but it is useful to say how you went about your study.
- **Information** is self explanatory, but you must make sure that you do collect some information.
- **Analysis** of the information is vital, using economic terminology and methods.
- A **conclusion** finishes the assignment and allows you to answer the question set or prove the hypothesis correct or incorrect.

Finally, a **bibliography**, which is a list of the books you used, or a **list of sources**, completes your work. A list of sources allows you to show how much work you have done and thank those people that have helped you. This list can include interviews as well as books and magazines or journals that you have used.

Presentation of data

The presentation of data is very important in a coursework assignment. The third area in the mark scheme given earlier is 'select/organise/interpret'. This requires that information is selected and then presented in an appropriate format so that it can be used to solve the problem set in the question. Presenting data in the right way is therefore very important.

There are a number of different ways in which data or information can be presented:

- tables
- line graphs
- pie charts
- pictograms
- bar charts
- maps.

The secret is to make sure that the best method is used. For example, if comparing inflation over a period of time a line graph or a bar chart would be the best; a pie chart would be totally wrong. If you wished to look at unemployment around the UK then a map would be useful, unless you only wish to compare the rates in which case a bar chart could be used. Pie charts are often useful to look at *shares* of things, e.g. out of 100 people how many shop locally, how many at Sainsbury's, how many at the Co-op, etc.

When you are presenting data always think:

- What am I trying to show?
- Is this the best possible way to show it?

Do not use the same data to produce different charts or tables, it simply wastes your time. Also, never put any information into your assignment that you are not going to use. Too many assignments have leaflets and pictures that are of no help in supporting the hypothesis and never mentioned. The rule is, if you do not use it do not put it in. It will not gain you any extra marks.

Analysis of data

Once your data has been collected and presented the next stage is to make some sense of the results.

Look at Figure 7.4. This information is from an imaginary survey conducted by a group of GCSE students aged 16. It is the prices of four different products that they use, in four different shops.

They chose shower gel, a pad of A4 writing paper, a can of Pepsi Max and a king size Mars bar. The shops they chose were Boots, Asda, Woolworth's and Safeway. The hypothesis is that 'shopping at a superstore is cheaper than shopping at a chain store'.

Analysis of the data collected should present a clear picture of what the information is saying. The data shows clearly that the most expensive item is shower gel, and the cheapest item is a can of Pepsi Max. Asda is the cheapest for shower gel, king size Mars bars and Pepsi Max. Safeway is the cheapest for paper and Pepsi Max, along with Asda. Boots is the most expensive for everything except king size Mars bars. In general the prices of paper, Pepsi Max and king size Mars bars are all very similar with a difference in price of 2p for paper, 3p for Pepsi Max and 5p for king size Mars bars. The biggest difference is found with the shower gel. The price range is 51p which is a 33% difference using the cheapest price, and a 25% difference using the most expensive price.

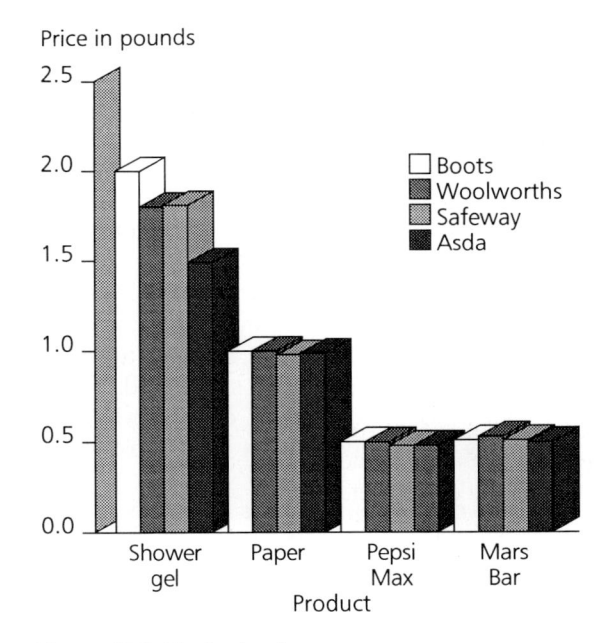

Figure 7.4 Student price survey

If all four items are purchased, Asda works out the cheapest at £3.45, followed by Safeway at £3.77, Woolworth's at £3.84 and then Boots at £4.02. It is noticeable, however, that no single store is cheaper for all four items, but the two superstores do work out cheaper overall.

Whilst this is a very simplified example it does give some idea of how simple data presented clearly can be analysed to highlight the main points of an hypothesis. The next stage would be to draw some conclusions but you must always remember that any conclusions you draw are only as good as the information collected. The next logical step is, therefore, to evaluate your information.

Evaluation

Evaluation of the information collected is something that the majority of students fail to do. It is not an easy exercise and because of this gains high marks when it is carried out.

In the simple example in Figure 7.4 the information seems to be supporting our hypothesis. It would be easy to conclude that 'shopping at a superstore is cheaper than shopping at a chain store'. But is the information really saying that? On three of the items the price difference is very small; it is only the large price difference on the shower gel that actually makes Asda that much cheaper. If the shower gel is removed then the total expenditure for the three items is very close together: a difference of 9p between the most and least expensive. In this case then, the information does still support the hypothesis even though the difference is small.

Another stage in the evaluation of your data is to ask 'how accurate is the information collected?'. Four stores have been chosen: are they representative? Why not more stores and shops? Only four products have been chosen, why? Are these really the products that a 16 year old would buy?

The use of only four stores is a weakness; more should have been used, including corner shops, mini-markets, other superstores, the Co-op, etc. However, if you live in a small village or near to a small town these might be the only shops that you could visit. In this case you are limited by your situation and should say so. If you had the chance to visit other stores you could list those you would have liked to have visited and why. Do not be afraid to admit that your research has limitations and weaknesses. In this situation it might be the best you could do and so your information is acceptable.

The products chosen are also a problem. Most young people would not buy their own shower gel, if they use it, or their own writing paper. These two products are not really *representative*. This is an error but it is too late to change it. Again do not be afraid to admit your mistake. You can discuss what products you should have chosen, or how you could have got a better sample of products for a 16 year old. You must then decide whether you are going to continue and formulate some conclusions or simply state that the information is not good enough to draw any conclusions. In this simple case the information is not good enough to test the hypothesis.

If the situation is different and it is decided to formulate a conclusion then it should be stated that it is based upon information or data that is not totally accurate.

The main point of this chapter is to advise you to go through the process of collecting information, presenting it in a visual format, analysing the information to explain what it is telling you, evaluating the information to see if it is accurate and unbiased and drawing conclusions. Even if the conclusion is 'my information is inaccurate and proves nothing' you have still completed the process and used your skills. Therefore you will gain credit for all your efforts. It does not really matter that you cannot answer the question set or test the original hypothesis.

You should remember:

- Your work needs a structure: title, aims, method, information, analysis and conclusion.
- You need to present your data clearly.
- Do not include leaflets, pictures or newspaper clippings *unless* you are going to use them.
- Analyse your data: what does it tell you? What are the main points?
- Evaluate your data: is it accurate; how could it be improved; is it biased?
- Draw some conclusions: test the hypothesis or answer the question or state that your information/data is too inaccurate to draw any conclusions.

7.3 COURSEWORK SOURCES AND GENERAL GUIDELINES

The subject that you have chosen for your coursework and the question that you have asked, or the hypothesis you wish to test, will determine the sort of information or data that you need. This in turn will determine the sources that are best for you to use.

It is not possible in this chapter to list all the sources that you might need for your work. The following list is an attempt to set out at least some of the possible approaches that you may take when collecting your information.

Notes and books

You will receive little or no credit if you simply copy out your notes, or even parts of books. This does not mean that you cannot use them. In fact, the notes and books that you have are likely to be full of useful information, which may well include the correct economic terminology that you should use, as well as the economic concepts and theories that you will be using. They may well also contain facts and figures that you want to use. One problem with any book is that the figures may not be up to date, so do not rely on them.

Newspapers and periodicals

These, of course, will comment on what is happening at the time, so you can collect up to date facts and opinions by referring to them. Editorials often comment on events, and the letters pages contain the views of people who wish to express their opinions. The normal news pages deal with what is happening, and often quote the statement of others as well.

Specialist publications

There are so many of these that it would be impossible to list them. Of particular note are the publications of the Central Statistical Office. If you want accurate figures on just about anything to do with the economy, this is where to look.

The library

Your school or college library will have a selection of books and newspapers. The papers are often kept for a long period of time, so you may be able to refer back to specific events if you know when they happened. Your local library may have material which is not kept at your school. Some libraries keep press cuttings of important events, so these may be available to you.

Librarians are there to help you, so if you do not know where to look for the information that you need, ask for assistance. They will tell you what is available on the topic, and where it is in the library.

Prominent people

Local dignitaries often like to be approached for help. If you think that, for example, your MP can help you, then write and introduce yourself, your work, and ask politely for the help that you need. Keep a copy of your letter. You may want to include it and the reply in your work. If someone refused to provide information, or even ignores your letter, do not be afraid to point this out. Suppose your title was 'What the government is doing to solve unemployment where I live', then the view of your MP would be important. If you did not receive a reply, then it would be entirely appropriate to say that your study would have been improved by a contribution from the MP, but he failed to reply to your letter. This means that you cannot be criticised for failing to gain the views of someone at the heart of the problem.

Firms

Small shopkeepers may be fed up with students asking them questions, especially when a lot of the questions refer to how much they sell and how much profit they make. They also do not have a great deal of time to spare to help you. This is understanable.

However, many larger firms have information officers who will provide answers and some of the largest companies employ people just to answer queries, so it is worth your while writing to the head office with your questions. Always keep a copy of your letter, and, once again, if you are refused information, make sure that you point out that it was refused. In this case, offer a comment on why you wanted it and what you would have done with it.

People

You may wish to interview someone because they have a particular knowledge of the subject that you have chosen. Make sure that you have prepared your questions in advance. This means that you must have worked out what you expect to learn in your interview. Take notes as the meeting progresses. You may think that you will remember everything that was said, but you will not.

You may wish to find out the views of a group of people. This can be done by constructing a questionnaire, a list of questions. When you compile your list of questions, make sure that you are clear about your objectives. Ask yourself what you intend to discover. Having decided that, then consider each question and ensure that it will make a contribution to your main objective. The phrasing of the questions is important. The language should be clear, so that the people you are asking can understand. You can have yes/no answers, or a rating scale, e.g.

1 = not at all satisfied
2 = somewhat dissatisfied
3 = just about satisfied
4 = satisfied
5 = very satisfied.

You can also ask people to offer comments, but these do not always produce good results, and can be difficult to analyse.

Surveys often take a great deal of time, but they can produce some excellent material, although the analysis of the results can be time consuming. It is important that you ask a representative sample of people. If you want to know what people in your area think about the building of a new motorway, then just asking questions of your school friends would not tell you what other groups of people think. You need to have men and women, young and old, married and single, employed and unemployed, etc., in order to ensure that you have a representative sample.

General Guidelines
Choose a topic that interests you.
Do not neglect the rest of the course.
Pose a question/Set a hypothesis.
Present your information clearly.
Use visual materials.
Do not include leaflets/pictures that are not relevant.
Analyse your information – what does it tell you, what are the main points?
Evaluate your information – is it accurate, is it biased? How could it be improved?
Answer your questions/Test your hypothesis.
Draw your conclusions
List your sources or use a bibliography.

Wordprocess if you can.
Do not spend time on a detailed artistic cover.
Put it in a simple folder or a single plastic wallet.

Good luck!

Figure 7.5 General guidelines for your report

Visits

It may be appropriate to make a visit to a site or an area to help your work. Indeed, it may not be possible to undertake the study if you do not. It may be possible to take photographs to illustrate your work. Certainly you should make some comments on your visit in your work, so that your efforts can be appreciated.

Your teacher

Your teacher is there to help you. There are rules about the amount of help that you can be given, but your teacher is able to help you to select a topic, and what sources you should use. When you are doing the work, you can approach your teacher if you have run into problems, or if you find it difficult to keep to the agreed topic. If you do find such problems, do not hesitate to go to your teacher. You will have wasted a great deal of time and effort, and not scored the marks you deserve if you do not. The teacher will make a record of such assistance, and will inform the examining board, but there is not likely to be much of a penalty, and it is better than simply not finishing the work.

Useful addresses

Bank Education Service
10 Lombard Street
London EC3

Barclays Bank Review
54 Lombard Street
London EC3

Central Statistical Office
St George Street
London
SW1P 3AQ

Economic Briefing
Information Division
HM Treasury
Parliament Street
London
SW1P 3AG

Economic Briefing
Promotions Unit
Central Office of Information
Hercules Road
London
SE1 7DU

Economic Review
Philip Allan Publishers Ltd
Market Place
Deddington
Oxford
OX5 4SE

The Economics and Business Education Association
1a Keymer Road
Hassocks
West Sussex
BN6 8AD

The Economist
54 St James Street
London
SW1 1JT

HMSO Publications Centre
PO Box 276
London
SW8 5DT

Lloyds Bank Review
71 Lombard Street
London EC3

National Westminster Bank Review
41 Lothbury
London
EC2P 2BP

If you have read this chapter and follow its advice throughout your project then your finished work should be both of a high standard and something that you can be proud of. Hopefully you will also have enjoyed completing it and you certainly will have learned something about economics.

The guidelines in Figure 7.5 form a checklist that you can follow but you should also refer back to the more detailed notes in the chapter if you need help.

✓ Review terms

Notes and books; newspapers and periodicals; specialist publications; the library, prominent people; firms; people; visits; teaching staff.

8

The Examination

> A concise guide on approaching examinations
>
> 8.1 THE EXAMINATION PAPER • 8.2 SAMPLE QUESTIONS (WITH OUTLINE ANSWERS AND ADVICE)
>
> This section should enable students to:
> - understand the examinations' rules and instructions
> - plan their time effectively
> - choose the right questions to answer
> - understand exactly what each question is asking them to do.

8.1 THE EXAMINATION PAPER

All the examination boards make their GCSE awards as a result of candidates undertaking pieces of coursework and a written examination. Thus, if you want to pass your GCSE, you have to take an exam. Some people are better at exams than others, but everyone can improve their performance by following a few simple rules.

Read the instructions

First of all, make sure that you know how many questions to answer, and whether there are any compulsory questions or not.

That may appear to be obvious, but every year some candidates do not conform to the rules, and so lose marks.

Make sure that your teacher has shown you the past papers, or, in the case of a new syllabus, has checked to see the question requirements.

Look at the instructions on the front cover of the examination paper, just to be sure that you have remembered the instructions.

It will say something similar to the instructions shown in Figure 8.1:

Now you are sure about what is expected of you. There is no point in attempting more than two questions in Section II, as you will receive no credit for more than two answers, and you must attempt all the questions in Section I.

General Certificate of Secondary Education

ECONOMICS
Time Allowed: 2 Hours

This paper is divided into two parts: SECTION I and SECTION II.

In Section I you must answer all of the questions.
In Section II you may select any TWO questions.

INFORMATION
Mark allocations are shown in brackets.

Figure 8.1 Sample examination paper instructions

Allocate your time

There is little point in devoting an hour to a section that is worth only ten marks, and five minutes to a section that could score 50.

You need to look at the questions, and then allocate your time so that you can match the time that you spend on each part of the paper with the number of marks that can be gained.

Take as an example the SEG paper. Look at it closely. The information on the front cover will tell you about mark allocations. They are to be shown in brackets after each question.

Section 1 consists of four questions, each of which is worth 20 marks in total. There may be sub-divisions, and these will be considered later.

Section 11 contains about five questions, each of which follows the same lines. Each question is split into four parts, and there are ten marks for each part. You have to answer only two questions.

Your questions and marks look like Figure 8.2.

Section I
Question 1 – 20 marks
Question 2 – 20 marks
Question 3 – 20 marks
Question 4 – 20 marks

Section II
Any Question
    a – 10 marks
    b – 10 marks
    c – 10 marks
    d – 10 marks

Any Question
    a – 10 marks
    b – 10 marks
    c – 10 marks
    d – 10 marks

Total marks 160 and time available 2 hours or 120 minutes.

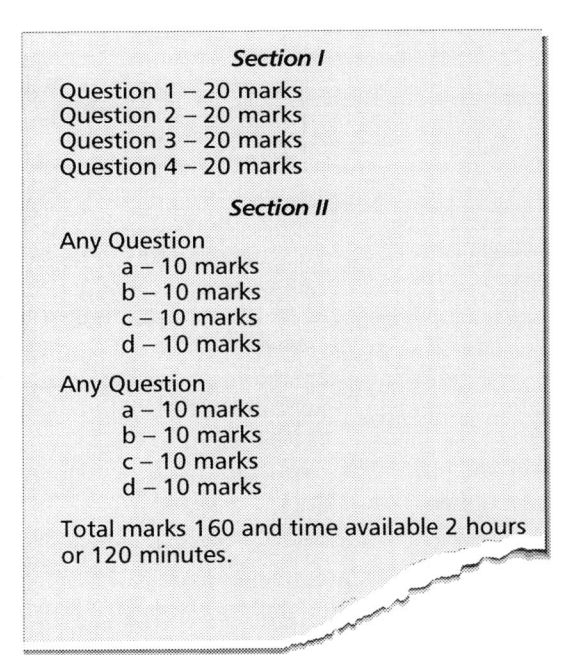

Figure 8.2 Allocation of marks on an examination paper

Half of the total marks can be obtained from Section 1 and the other half from Section 11.

This would suggest that you should spend half of your time in each Section.

In Section 1 there are four questions and you have an hour to complete that section: you should therefore allow 15 minutes for each question.

In Section 11 there are two questions, so you should allow 30 minutes per question. However, each question has four parts, so you should allow about 7 minutes for each part.

Now your questions and marks can include a time allocation as shown in Figure 8.3.

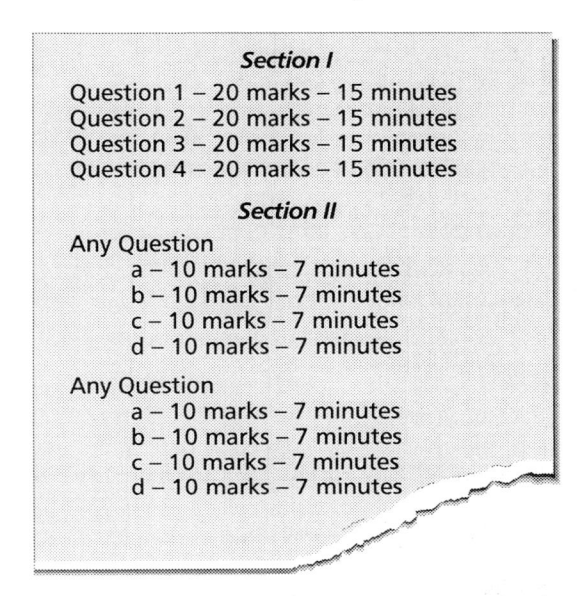

Section I
Question 1 – 20 marks – 15 minutes
Question 2 – 20 marks – 15 minutes
Question 3 – 20 marks – 15 minutes
Question 4 – 20 marks – 15 minutes

Section II
Any Question
    a – 10 marks – 7 minutes
    b – 10 marks – 7 minutes
    c – 10 marks – 7 minutes
    d – 10 marks – 7 minutes

Any Question
    a – 10 marks – 7 minutes
    b – 10 marks – 7 minutes
    c – 10 marks – 7 minutes
    d – 10 marks – 7 minutes

Figure 8.3 Allocation of time on an examination paper

You now have a clear idea of the best way of scoring marks in the time allowed.

Whichever examining board you are studying, and whatever examination you are taking, you can perform a similar analysis so that you are in a position to score the maximum marks possible and to use the time available to your best advantage.

You should always remember:

- Work out how long to spend on each part of the questions.
- Use your watch to make sure that you keep to the time scale that you have allocated.
- Practise answering questions within time limits to make this easier.

Select your questions

Many candidates like to have sorted out what to answer before starting the paper. This is not a bad idea, as it means that you can devote all your time to writing after making your decisions.

On the other hand, some candidates like to finish the compulsory questions before making their choices, as they feel that they can concentrate better on one area and do not have to worry about the others while writing.

Either way, you are going to have to make some choices eventually.

The worst mistake that can be made is if you like a particular topic, and see that it is on the paper, and so decide to do it without reading the questions properly. No matter how much you think you know, you need to be sure that you can actually answer the questions set.

You should always remember:

- to read the paper carefully
- to be sure that you can actually answer all of the parts to a question before putting pen to paper.

It is often a good idea to read all the questions once, and then go through each part again, ticking those you could do, and putting a cross where you could not answer a part.

This may leave you with a paper that shows you what to answer.

If it does not, go through it again, indicating, again with ticks and crosses, those you would feel most and least happy to attempt. The questions with the most ticks — or the least crosses — are the ones that you should select.

Look at the exact requirement of the question

When the paper was set, there would have been long discussions about what was wanted from every part of every question, and the wording would have been adjusted accordingly. Thus, the instruction in the question tells you how to respond.

Looking at a typical examination paper reveals such instructions as:

- give
- select
- name
- list
- identify
- summarise
- describe
- discuss
- calculate.
- outline
- what
- explain
- why
- how
- assess
- comment on
- evaluate

All these words have a meaning. Some are preceded by the word briefly. This is another instruction.

It is vital that you respond adequately to such instructions, otherwise you may not produce the answer which is required. Some of the words are similar in meaning, and expect a particular type of response.

They can be split into three categories:

1 Those that seek to discover what you know, or whether you can extract information from data that is given to you. These will usually include words such as give, name, list, identify, select, what and which.
2 Those that seek to discover if you have understood a subject area or some data. These include calculate, summarise, describe, outline, and explain.
3 Those that seek a judgement from you. These include discuss, why, how, assess, comment on, examine and evaluate.

Moreover, most, if not all, examination papers involve the use of material on which some of the questions are based. This is known as data response. The data response questions are preceded by information, which can include graphs, charts, and diagrams as well as the written word.

You are usually required to show that you can select particular points from this information. After that you may well be asked to demonstrate that you have understood the text. Then you may be required to evaluate the material.

- Check which examination you are sitting.
- Ask for a past or specimen paper.
- Read the instructions; do you understand them?
- Check with your teacher that you understand exactly what you have to do in the exam.
- Use a dictionary to find the correct meanings of the words used in the questions, e.g. summarise, assess, evaluate, etc.
- Practise some past questions under timed conditions.
- Ask for a copy of the mark schemes provided by the exam board.

8.2 SAMPLE QUESTIONS (WITH ANSWERS AND ADVICE)

The next few examples are intended to provide a variety of data response questions that require you to extract information from the text. These questions are developed in later pages.

Example 1

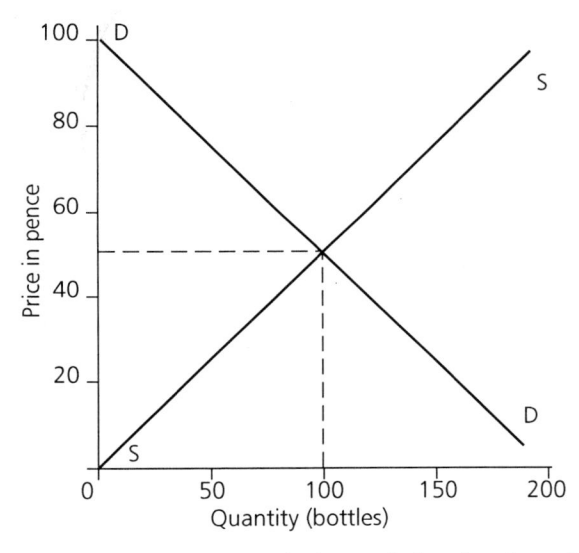

Figure 8.4 Supply and demand for bottles of lemonade per day in a school shop

Question

Give the equilibrium price and quantity.

or

What is the equilibrium price and quantity?

Advice

Just give the information requested. In either case, the answer to this is straightforward.

Answer

Equilibrium price is 50p.
Equilibrium quantity is 100 bottles.

Example 2

Inflation rates in the United Kingdom

Year	% Rise
1967	1·5
1970	6·4
1973	9·2
1976	16·6
1979	13·4
1982	8·6
1985	6·1
1988	4·9
1991	5·9
1993	1·7

You could be faced with simple questions which seek to ensure that you can interpret the figures.

Question

Which year had the greatest rise in inflation?

Advice

Another straightforward question. You have been asked for a single piece of information, so that is all you should provide.

Answer

1976.

Question

In what year and by how much did inflation rise the most?

Advice

Again, this is straightforward. You have been asked for two pieces of information so to offer anything else is unnecessary and time wasting.

Answer

In 1976 by 16·6%.

Question

Identify the two years in which inflation was at its lowest.

Answer

1967 and 1993.

Example 3

UK public expenditure 1989-90 in £millions

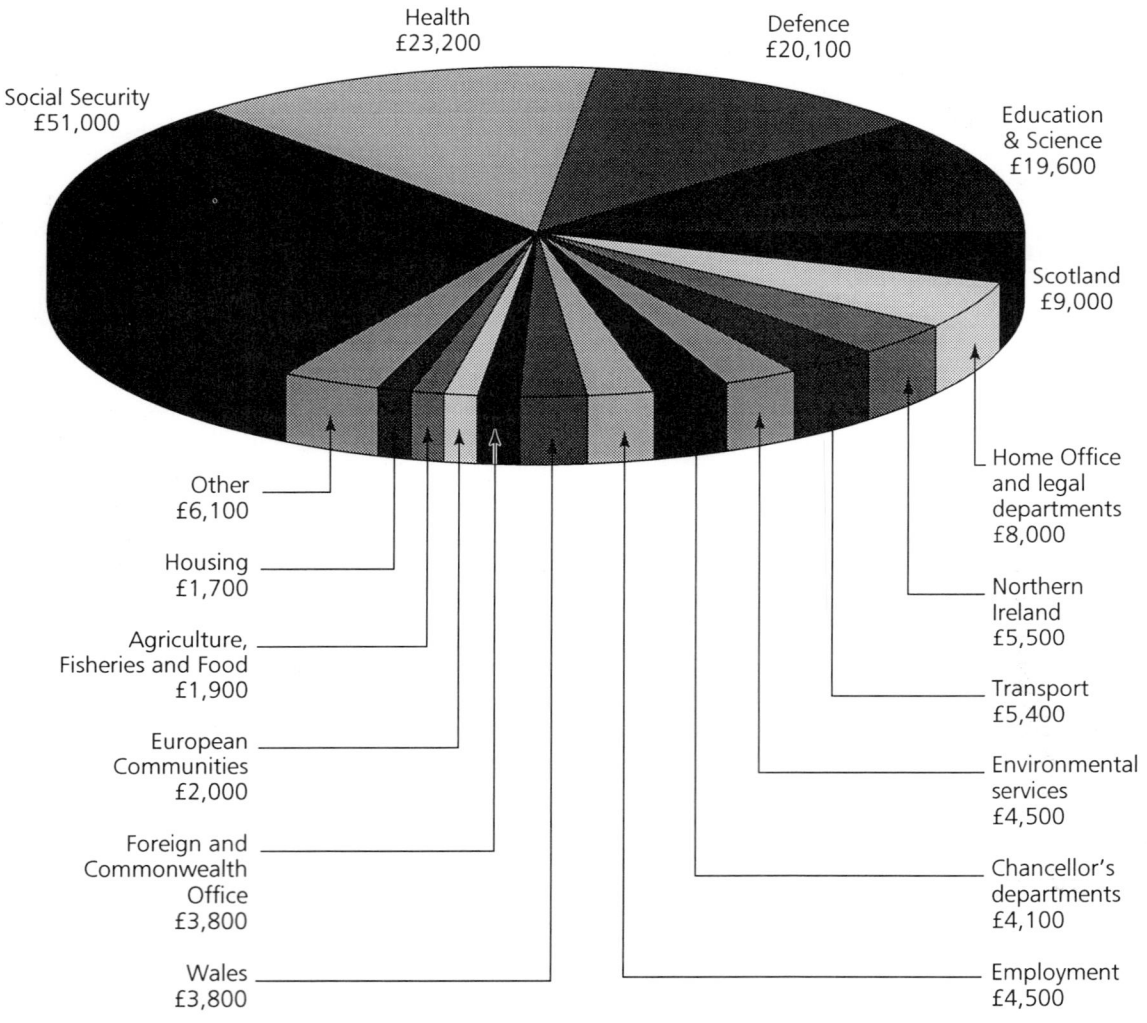

- Health £23,200
- Defence £20,100
- Social Security £51,000
- Education & Science £19,600
- Scotland £9,000
- Other £6,100
- Housing £1,700
- Agriculture, Fisheries and Food £1,900
- European Communities £2,000
- Foreign and Commonwealth Office £3,800
- Wales £3,800
- Home Office and legal departments £8,000
- Northern Ireland £5,500
- Transport £5,400
- Environmental services £4,500
- Chancellor's departments £4,100
- Employment £4,500

Question
List the five major items of government expenditure.

Advice
Just do what is asked.

Answer
Social Security, Health, Defence, Education and Science, Scotland.

Question
Name the largest single area of public expenditure.

Advice
Again, there is only one possible answer, so give it.

Answer
Social Security.

Example 4

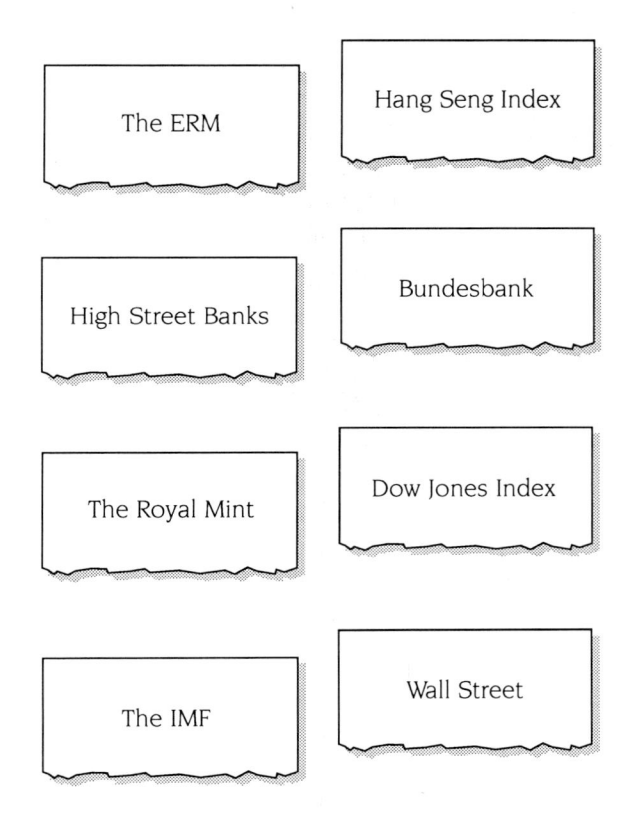

- The ERM
- Hang Seng Index
- High Street Banks
- Bundesbank
- The Royal Mint
- Dow Jones Index
- The IMF
- Wall Street

Question
Select from the above institutions two which can be found in the United Kingdom.

Advice
This is, perhaps, slightly more demanding than extracting information. You are required to demonstrate some knowledge. However, there are clues to assist you. You have been asked for two institutions, so there must be at least two included. You must give no more than two, or you have not answered the question properly. Look at the possibilities, and it becomes easy to eliminate some, even if you do not know the answer.

Answer
The Royal Mint and high street banks.

Example 5

The Budget
The Chancellor of the Exchequer is responsible for the Budget. He looks at how the economy has performed in the previous year, and decides what he wants to happen in the coming year and what he is going to do in order to make sure that it does happen.

In the Budget, he is concerned with fiscal matters. That means public expenditure and revenue. He needs the revenue, which is all the money that the government collects from businesses and individuals, so that he can pay for the activities of the government, which is known as public expenditure.

He can influence the level of economic activity in the country by his decisions. If he increases taxation, then people will have less money to spend, and so they will buy fewer goods, and so less people need to be employed. If he reduces taxation, people will have more money to spend, so more goods will be sold, which means more people will have to be employed to make them.

Question
Which major economic policy is described in the text?

Advice
You are not asked for any form of explanation, merely the name of the policy, so that is what you should give.

Answer
Fiscal policy.

Inference

All of the questions so far can be answered by reference to the material presented. You may be asked for information which is not provided.

Using example 4
Question
Select from the above two institutions which can be found in the United Kingdom and from your own knowledge name two other major UK financial institutions.

Advice

This is a more demanding question as you are required to demonstrate additional knowledge.

However, once you have extracted the two institutions from the material, look at what you have, and others are bound to come to mind. Any two suitable examples will suffice. Again, you must give no more than two, or you have not answered the question properly.

Answer

The Royal Mint and high street banks are given in the material. Any other two could include the Bank of England, the Treasury, the Stock Exchange, Lloyds of London, etc..

You should always remember:

- to make sure that you know what is required. Does the answer ask for information from the text, or from your own knowledge, or both?
- to offer only as many answers as you are asked to give
- to look at the wording carefully, so that you follow the instructions.

Generally

The next questions that you are likely to face may follow on from these data responses. They may continue to be on the data, or may move away from it and ask more general questions.

The wording of these questions is more demanding, showing that more is required than simple knowledge.

These types of questions will continue to use the kind of material in the examples above.

Example 1, page 147

Question

Calculate the value of sales at the equilibrium price and quantity.

Advice

Show your workings, but again, the answer is not complicated.

It is important to show how you have arrived at the answer, because if you make a mistake in your arithmetic, but it is clear that you knew how to go about giving the answer, you will receive some marks, but if you just write down an answer and it is wrong, you will score nothing.

Answer

Value of sales = Number sold × selling price
$$= 100 \times 50p$$
$$= 5{,}000p \text{ or } £50$$

Example 2, page 147

Question

Outline the trends in UK inflation in the period 1967–1993.

Advice

This does not invite you to repeat the figures and offer nothing else. To do so would be to fail to answer the question properly. You have been asked to outline the trends. This means that you should say what has happened to inflation over the period.

The length of your answer should depend on the number of marks available. If there are 5 marks out of a total of 100, it would be pointless to spend half your time on this section. Judge your answer in accordance with the amount of time that you have allocated to it.

Answer

Inflation was low in 1967, at 1.5% and rose steadily to 9.2% in 1973. There was then a rapid rise to 16.6% in 1976, followed by a series of falls to 4.9% in 1988. Inflation then rose to 5.9% in 1991, and fell in 1993 to a figure similar to that of 1967.

This includes some figures, and it informs the examiner that you understand what has happened over the years in question.

It would be necessary to have the data in order to answer this question, but it could be that a more general question on inflation could be asked.

Question

Explain the main causes of inflation.

Advice

Here the question has actually moved away from

the material, and could be answered without reference to it.

The length of the question depends, as ever, on the mark allocation.

However, it would not be possible to tackle this question without reference to both cost-push and demand-pull inflation. If you are not happy that you fully understand the causes of both of these, do not attempt the question unless it is compulsory. Think carefully before putting pen to paper, and try to explain the causes in as simple a way as possible.

Answer

Inflation occurs when prices and wages rise faster than the level of production.

There are two main views on the causes of inflation. One deals with increases in costs, and the other with increases in demand.

Cost-push inflation occurs if, for example, increases in world commodity prices led to price increases. Workers would find that their wages did not buy as much, so they would ask for wage increases. Wages form a large part of the price of most goods and services, so employers would increase prices to pay for the wage increases. This would lead to further demands for higher wages. This is known as the wage-price spiral, where prices and wages rise, but production remains static. This is seen to be a cause of inflation. *They should then include a simple explanation of Demand-pull inflation.*

Example 3, page 148

Question

Discuss how governments try to raise the revenue to pay for their expenditure.

Advice

Again, you are faced with a question that is not directly connected to the material.

If the question had asked, simply, 'how do governments raise the revenue to pay for their expenditure?', then you would be able to offer a list of the sources of government revenue. However, the word discuss is used. This means that you are required to make some sort of comment on the methods. This could centre around the most effective, or the fairest.

There can be no such thing as a 'right' answer to this question. There will be many answers that satisfy the examiners. This will include some form of explanation of how governments raise revenue, and some discussion.

One possible approach could involve a list of methods of raising revenue, followed by some discussion. Many candidates will be able to offer much more than this – it is not a 'model answer', but rather an acceptable line of approach.

Answer

The government can raise money by taxation. This falls into two categories, direct and indirect. Direct taxation includes such items as income tax, and is paid according to how much an individual earns, or how large are a company's profits. Indirect taxation, which includes VAT and excise duties, are taxes on goods, so that everyone who buys the goods pays the same tax.

Governments also raise money by charging National Insurance contributions. Wage earners pay these according to how much they earn.

The government charges for some services, such as making up prescriptions.

It makes money through the sale of nationalised industries, but it can only do this once per industry. Law breakers pay fines that go to the government.

There are many ways that governments can raise money, but no-one really likes paying. It might seem fairest that those who earn the most pay the most, but they might feel that is unfair if they think that they work harder than everyone else. It is up to each government to produce a method of raising money that everyone understands and thinks is reasonable.

Example 5, page 148

Question

Summarise the main points in the article.

Advice

This is more difficult than the previous questions, which have simply required a single and simple piece of information. However, it is not really difficult if you approach it correctly.

Summarise does not mean 'rewrite' the article. One of the common mistakes is to try to repeat everything in the article. The question asks you to summarise – in other words, to tell the examiner what the article is saying, but using fewer words.

Look carefully at the text. What does it say?

- the first paragraph says that the Chancellor is responsible for the Budget, in which he looks at what has happened to the economy, what he wants to happen, and how he can make it happen
- the second paragraph explains that the Chancellor has to collect money – revenue – to pay for government spending – expenditure
- in the final paragraph, it is argued that increase in taxation can cause unemployment, while reductions in taxation can create employment

It does not matter what words you use, but this is the type of information that is required.

Answer

The Chancellor is responsible for the Budget, in which he considers what has happened to the economy, what he would like to happen to it, and how he can achieve what he wants.

The Chancellor needs money – revenue – to finance government spending – expenditure.

His decisions can affect the economy, because higher taxes can cause unemployment, and lower taxes can create jobs.

Question

Using your knowledge and the information in the article, describe the role of the Chancellor of the Exchequer.

Advice

The instructions are quite clear. You are to use both the text and anything else that you know about what the Chancellor does.

The article tells you that he prepares the Budget, and operates fiscal policy. Moreover, you are told the meaning of the term fiscal policy. You are also told how his decisions can influence the economy. This is about enough to tackle the question adequately, but think about other information.

Who is the Chancellor of the Exchequer? It would help if you knew his name. He is in charge of the Treasury, and the Treasury carries out the major economic decisions that the government takes. This includes monetary policy – how much money there is in the economy, interest rates and the amount of credit available.

Does the Chancellor act on his own? He must make some decisions himself, and he will listen to his officials and make recommendations, but, like any other minister, he is a member of the Cabinet, and so his major decisions must be approved by the Prime Minister and the rest of the Cabinet.

Answer

The Chancellor of the Exchequer is in charge of the Treasury, so he is the minister who is in charge of the major economic decisions taken by the government. With the support of the Prime Minister and the Cabinet, the Chancellor directs economic policy.

He does this in several ways. Fiscal policy is the collection of government revenue and its spending. The Chancellor decides how the money is to be collected, after agreeing with other government departments how much should be spent. Thus, the Chancellor decides on the types and extent of taxation.

He also directs monetary policy, which is the amount of money in circulation. The Chancellor can influence interest rates, and by open market operations can make loan capital more or less easily available.

The economic activity of the country depends on the level of demand, and the Chancellor is crucial to this, as he can determine the amount of money people have after taxation, the price of goods after tax has been imposed, and the price and availability of credit.

Comprehension

All of these questions seek to establish what you know and how well you understand it. The next type of question attempts to extract your views, and judge the merit of your arguments. These questions require a different type of skill, and it is essential that you are able to tackle them, as they will appear throughout the examination paper.

Example 1, page 147

Question

Examine the information that a shopkeeper would need in order to increase sales of lemonade.

Advice

Read the question carefully, and try to discover what is required:

- 'Examine the information' means that you have to look at the possibilities critically.
- '... a shopkeeper would need'. It is vital that the information is applied to a shopkeeper.
- '... to increase sales of lemonade' tells you what the area under consideration should be.

What does a shopkeeper need to know? Think first of all about the factors affecting demand and supply. What could cause demand to change? Price, substitutes, complements, changes in taste.

Now apply the above to the question.

- the price that the shopkeeper charges and the price in rival shops
- the price and availability of substitute goods, such as orange juice
- that complements may be a little difficult – so perhaps they could be ignored
- changes in taste – advertising both by the shopkeeper and the manufacturer
- the cause of a change to supply
- changes in the aims of the supplier, changes in the price of components, changes in the methods of production

Now apply the above to the question.

Think about the aims of the supplier. If the shopkeeper is seeking to increase sales, then he may buy more, and the maker of the lemonade may reduce his price. The shopkeeper may also be prepared to reduce his price to increase sales.

Thus supply and demand have provided a great deal of information. The shopkeeper needs to know about the desires of his customers and potential customers.

He needs to know their demand for various quantities of lemonade. He needs to know the price for lemonade charged by his competitors. He needs to know what to do to alter demand and persuade people to buy from himself.

Finally, he needs to try to obtain lower prices.

Answer

There can be no 'correct' answer to a question such as this. However, the answer will need to consider certain factors, and draw a conclusion. The contents should include:

- the factors relating to the demand and supply of lemonade together with an explanation of the use that the shopkeeper could make of each factor
- a conclusion which, perhaps, recommends to the shopkeeper the best actions that can be taken to increase sales.

Example 2, page 147

Question

How should a government correct the problem of inflation?

Advice

You really need to plan your answers to questions of this type.

Look at the question carefully:

- 'How should' means that you are going to have to consider the possibilities and offer a solution.
- 'correct' means that you must look at the various measures that could be used.
- 'the problem of inflation' means that you are going to have to explain what problem is caused by inflation.

Answer

There are many possible answers that it is not helpful to offer just one. However, an analysis of the question suggests that the content should include the elements on the following page

What might be included:

- The problem of inflation, i.e. rising prices within one country, will make that country's goods uncompetitive. More foreign goods will be bought, and fewer domestic goods exported, causing problems with economic growth, unemployment and the balance of payments.
- There should be a brief account of the causes of inflation, i.e. cost-push and demand-pull.
- There should also be possible solutions, i.e. a prices and wages policy and the reduction of demand within the economy. A consideration of the various methods of demand management, including fiscal and monetary policy.
- One must provide a conclusion which offers a solution to the problem.

Example 4, page 149

Question

Assess the impact that Budget decisions could have on the two institutions that you have identified.

Advice

Assess means, once again, that you are required to make a judgement.

The two institutions were the Royal Mint and the high street banks.

What could be the impact upon them of Budget decisions? Think about the alteration of taxation, which could affect the level of spending.

What does the Royal Mint do? It manufactures the actual coins and notes that we spend, so if the Budget encourages spending, then more money may need to be produced. If the Budget discourages spending, then less money may need to be produced.

What do the high street banks do? They act as the bankers for individuals and firms. If the Budget encourages spending, then more money will pass through the accounts of individuals and firms, so they will be busier. If it discourages spending, then less money will go through the accounts, so they will be less busy.

If individuals and firms have less money, however, they may need to borrow more money in order to pay all of their bills, so there may be an increased demand for loans and overdrafts.

On the other hand, if there is less money available, the banks would be taking a risk that these loans may end up unpaid, so there could be a reduction in the loans and overdrafts actually given.

In this way, you have worked out what could happen to the institutions. This is your assessment of the possible effects of the Budget.

Now draw a conclusion, and you have answered the question.

You must remember

- to look at the wording of the question
- to decide exactly what the question requires
- to plan your answer
- to draw a conclusion.

Index

absolute advantage 58–59
advertising 30
Aggregate Monetary Demand (AMD) 48, 49
assets 87
   frozen 52
   liquid 52
   marketable 70
   real 70
average costs 44
average revenue 44

balance of payments 23, 60, 85–88, 97, 130–131
   problems and solutions 61–62
balance of trade 86
balanced budget 54
balancing item 87
bank deposits 66–67
bank notes 65–67
Bank of England 52, 53, 90
   banker activities 107
   market operator activities 107
   policy maker activities 107
   role of 108
banks 106
barter system 89, 94
base rates 53
basic need for survival 74
benefits 82, 83, 95
bibliography 138
bills of exchange 106
Board of Directors 101
border checks 25
budget 83
   deficit 54
   surplus 54
building societies 106–107
business organisations 99–103

capital 2, 47, 69, 72, 73, 122
   circulating 72
   fixed 72
   interest on 47, 69
   social 72
capital account 85
capital gains tax 113
capital goods 4
capital intensive production 4
central government, *see* government
change in price of a substitute 30
change in quantity demanded 29–31
change in quantity supplied 32
channel tunnel 14
cheque 67
choice 3–5
circular flow of income 47–51
circulating capital 72
climate 14
   in demand 30
coins 65–67
command economy 5
commercial banks 106
commercial economy 12
commodity trading 23
Companies Acts 101
complementary goods 30
complete balance of payments account 87
Confederation of British Industry (CBI) 104
consumer goods 4, 73
consumer protection 111
consumer services 72
consumers, households as 72
consumption 47, 72, 73
   household 73
contraction
   demand 29
   supply 32
Cooperative Wholesale Society 101

cooperatives 101
corporation tax 82–83, 113
cost of labour 32
cost of living 79, 121
cost of raw materials and equipment 32
cost-push inflation 93
costs 10, 11, 13, 15, 43–47
   average 44
   economic growth 121–124
   external 121–124
   factor cost 78–79
   fixed 43
   marginal 45
   opportunity cost 3–4, 57–59, 73, 136
   social 121–125
   total 43
   variable 43
Council Tax 114
coursework
   application 138
   approaching firms 141–142
   approaching local dignitaries 141
   assessment objectives 138
   assistance 135, 142
   choice of title 136
   choice of topic 135–136
   data analysis 139
   data presentation 138–139
   evaluation/judgement 138
   general requirements 134
   guidelines 134–143
   information evaluation 140
   interviewing people 142
   knowledge/use of information 138
   library 141
   marking criteria 134, 137, 138
   newspapers and periodicals 141
   notes and books 141
   organisation 137–138
   points to remember 140
   presentation 137
   select/organise/interpret 138
   setting 135
   sources 143–145
   specialist publications 141
   useful addresses 143
   visits 142
credit 66
credit cards 66, 67
currency exchange 89–93

current account 67, 85–87, 130–131
customs duty 114
customs unions 25
cyclical unemployment 95

debt interest 83
defence expenditure 83
deferred payment 66
deflation 62
demand 28–31, 94–96
   and government policy 31
   change in quantity demanded 29–31
   changes of 29
   climate in 30
   contraction in 29
   decrease in 30
   effective 28–29
   extension in 29
   factors affecting 30, 135
   fashion in 30
   increase in 30, 121
   season in 30
   taste in 30
   unlimited 2
demand curve 29
   individual 29
   perfectly elastic 38, 39
   perfectly inelastic 38, 39
   perverse 29
   slope of 38
demand-pull inflation 93
depletion of resources 122
depreciation 62–63, 72, 79
devaluation 62–63
developed economy 130
developed nations 8
direct controls 52
direct taxation 49, 113
diseconomies of scale 15
disposable income 49, 73
distribution 5, 47
division of labour 9–10
domestic ratios 57
double counting 77
durables 73

economic behaviour 8–27
economic growth 97, 120–133
   advantages 120
   costs of 121–124

definition 120
problems of 120
trends in 130
economic indicators 131
economic problem 1–7, 47, 93
   choice 3–5
   scarcity 1–2
economic prosperity 125–126
economies of concentration 14
economies of scale 10–13, 15
economy
   control of 110
   definition 3
   open 49
   tertiary based 14
   three sector 49
   two sector 47–48
education 111
effective demand 28–29
elasticity 38–43
   factors affecting 39
   measurement of 38–39
elasticity of supply 40–42
electronic cheques 67
employee cooperatives 101
employers' associations 104
employment, full 93, 129
energy sources 13
enterprises 2, 47, 69
environmental health services 111
equal opportunities 125
equilibrium 33–36, 48, 49, 130–131
Europe 14
European Coal and Steel Community 116
European Commission 117
European Council of Ministers 117
European Court of Justice 117
European Economic Community 116
European Free Trade Association 116
European Parliament 117
European Union 22, 25, 62
   as trade group 117
   origins 116–117
   structure 117
examination
   allocation of marks 145
   exact requirements 146
   guidance 144–154
   points to note 146
   reading instructions 144

   sample questions 147–154
   selection of questions 145–146
   time allocation 144
exchange controls 25
exchange rate 25, 61, 89–91, 131
   fixed 62, 90
   flexible 90
   floating 62, 91
   problems 91
   types of 90–91
Exchange Rate Mechanism (ERM) 91
excise duty 82, 114
expenditure method 77, 78
expenditure patterns 72–74
   firms 72
   household 72–73
exports 14, 24–25, 49, 61–63, 78, 85
extension in demand 29
extension of supply 32
external costs 121–124
external diseconomies of scale 15
external economies of scale 14

factor cost 78–79
factors of production 2, 69, 121
fashion in demand 30
fiat currency 67
final goods and services 77
financial institutions 48, 106–110
fire services 111
fiscal policy 53–54, 94, 96
fixed capital 72
fixed costs 43
fixed exchange rate 62, 90
flexible exchange rate 90
floating exchange rate 62, 91
forces of location 13, 15
foreign currency 25
Foreign Exchange Market 89
free trade areas 25
frictional unemployment 95, 96
frozen assets 52
full employment 93, 129
funding 52
further education colleges 14

GDP, see Gross Domestic Product (GDP)
General Agreement on Tariffs and Trade (GATT) 25, 62, 117
GNP, see Gross National Product (GNP)

government
  control of trade 24–25
  decisions 3
  expenditure 49, 50, 53, 72, 83, 96, 110
  intervention 81–85, 90
  policy and demand 31
  revenue 82, 83, 112–113
  role of 110–112
  securities 52
  subsidies 25, 33, 78
gross domestic fixed capital formation 21
Gross Domestic Product (GDP) 77–79
  per head 21
gross income 49, 78
Gross National Product (GNP) 79, 120, 124
  growth trends 130
  per capita 124, 126, 131
  per head 124
group behaviour 8–10
growth, see economic growth

habit forming goods 39
health
  expenditure 83
  problems 121, 122
heavy industry 13
hot money 90
households
  as consumers 72
  disposal of income 47
  expenditure patterns 72–73
housing 111
hyper-inflation 93
hypothesis 137

import barriers 62
imports 22–25, 49, 61–63, 78, 85
income 47, 68–69
  and substitution effect 30
  circular flow of 47–51
  disposable 49, 73
  gross 49, 78
  international 20–21
  method 77, 78
  National 77–79
  net 49
  policy 95
  real 48
income distribution 82, 121
  international 20

national 17–19
income elasticity coefficients 40
income elasticity of demand 40
income tax 82, 113
indirect controls 52
indirect taxation 113
individual demand curve 29
individual supply curve 32
inflation 51, 79, 93–95, 129
  mild 93
  policies to cure 94–95
  problem of 94
  runaway 93
information services 15
inheritance tax 113
injections 48–50
institutions 99–119
  see also financial institutions; international institutions
insurance companies 107
intended savings 48
interest on capital 47, 69
interest, profits and dividends (IPD) 86, 87
interest rate 48, 53, 62, 96, 131
International Bank for Reconstruction and Development (IBRD) (World Bank) 117
international income and wealth distribution 20–21
International institutions 116–119
International Monetary Fund (IMF) 60, 85, 117
investment 48, 53, 72, 73
invisible account 87
invisible balance 86
invisible trade 86

Japanese yen 89

Keynes, John M. 73

labour 2, 69
  costs 32
  division of 9–10
  relations 14
  supply 14
labour intensive production 4
land 2, 47, 69
leisure facilities 111
leisure time 125
Less Developed Countries (LDCs) 1, 8, 20, 21, 56

liabilities 87
libraries 111, 141
life assurance 70
light industry 13
limited companies 100, 101
limited liability 100
limited supply 2
liquid assets 52
list of sources 138
local government 83
   expenditure 111
   revenue 114, 115
   role of 110–111
location of firms 13–15
London Stock Exchange 35
long run 40
low priced goods 39
luxuries 39, 73, 74

management and production 33
manufacturing output 131
marginal cost 45
marginal revenue 45
market 33–36
   demand curve 29
   economy 5, 81
   forces 5, 81
   influences on location 14
   open market operations 52
   price 33–36
   supply curve 32
marketable assets 70
mass production 9–10
merchant banks 106
merit goods 53–54, 81, 125
mild inflation 93
mixed economy 5
momentary run 40
monetary policy 52, 62, 94, 96
money market 52
money supply 53, 66–68
money system 8, 9, 65–68
   characteristics of 66
   functions of 65–66

National expenditure 77, 78
National income 77-9, 82
   composition of 69
National Insurance contributions (NICs) 82, 113
National output 77

nationalisation 99
natural disasters 32
natural rate of unemployment 95, 97
necessities 39, 73, 74
needs 1–2, 77
net income 49
net investment 72
net National product 79
non-durables 73
non-taxable allowance 113
normal profit 43

open economy 49
open market operations 52
opportunity cost 3–4, 57, 58, 73, 136
opportunity cost ratios 59
organisational behaviour 10–17
output
   increase in 121, 130
   National 77
output method 77
overcrowding 122

par value 90
partnerships 100
pension funds 70
perfectly elastic demand curve 38, 39
perfectly inelastic demand curve 38, 39
performance 128–133
perverse demand curve 29
planning permission 111
police 111
pollution 121, 122
pounds sterling 89
power source 13
price elasticity coefficients 39
price elasticity of demand 38, 39
price mechanism 28–37
prices
   change expectations 30–31
   effect of exchange rates 62
   factors affecting 135
   stable 93, 129
principle of multiples 12
private enterprise 5
private limited companies 100
private sector 100
private wealth 126
privatisation 99–100
production 3–4, 47, 69

after specialisation 57–59
and management 33
capital intensive 4
labour intensive 4
possibilities 58
possibility frontier 57
taxes on 33
with specialisation 59
without specialisation 57–59
products
  weight-gaining 14
  weight-losing 14
profits 10, 43–47, 69, 72
progressive taxation 82, 113
property 70
proportional taxation 82, 113
public corporations 99
public goods 53–54, 81, 125
public limited companies 100, 108
public money 54
public sector 99
Public Sector Borrowing Requirement (PSBR) 49, 53, 54, 83
Public Sector Debt Repayment (PSDR) 53, 54
public services 110

quality of life 73, 125–128
quantitative controls 52
quintile groups 18
quota system 24

rail transport 14
rate of interest 48, 53, 62, 96, 131
raw materials 13, 14, 22, 32
real assets 70
real income 39
real savings 48
regressive taxation 82, 113
regulation 82
rent 47, 69
Research and Development (R and D) 13, 15
reserves 85
residual unemployment 95, 96
resources 2-4, 21, 56, 121
  allocation 35
  depletion of 122
  scarce 47
retail establishments 14

revenue 43–47
  average 44
  marginal 45
  total 43
rewards 47, 69
Ricardo, David 56
risk 12
roads and road transport 14, 111
rule of increased dimensions 11
runaway inflation 93

savings 47–48
scarce resources 47
scarcity 1–2, 93
season in demand 30
securities 108
self-sufficiency 9, 94
services and service specialists 13, 15, 86, 87
shares and shareholders 100, 101, 108
short run 41
Single European Act 117
Smith, Adam 9
social capital 72
social costs 121–125
social policies 110
social security 83
social services 111
sole trader 100
special deposits 52
specialisation 8–9, 57–59
speculation 90
stable prices 93, 129
standard of living 56, 69, 79, 124–125
Stock Exchange 100, 108
strikes 33, 103
structural unemployment 95, 96
subsistence living 9
substitutes 30, 39
supply 31–33
  changes in 32–33
    quantity supplied 32
  contraction of 32
  elasticity of 40–42
  extension of 32
  weather in 32
supply curve 32
  individual 32
supply-side policies 97
support services 14

tariffs 24, 116
taste in demand 30
taxable income 113
taxation 50, 53, 54, 96, 112–116
    capital gains 113
    corporation tax 82–83, 113
    Council Tax 114
    direct 49, 113
    income tax 82, 113
    indirect 113
    on production 33
    production 33
    progressive 82, 113
    proportional 82, 113
    regressive 82, 113
technical economy 12
technological unemployment 95, 96
technology 4
    changes in 32, 35
tertiary based economy 14
Theory of Comparative Advantage 56–59
three sector economy 49
total cost 43
total revenue 43
tourism 14
trade 85
    gains from 56–64
    problems of 60–64
    reasons for 56
trade fairs 24, 62
trade pattern 21–24
trade unions 103–104
    functions 104
    membership 104
    number of 104
trade war 62
transactions account 87
transfer payments 69, 78, 86, 87, 95
transport facilities 14
Treasury 52
Treaty of Maastricht 117
Treaty of Rome 116
two sector economy 47–48

unbalanced growth 122
unemployment 51, 83, 95, 121, 129–130
    and working population 129–130
    causes of 95
    cyclical 95
    natural rate of 95, 97
    policies to cure 96–97
    problems of 95
    residual 95, 96
    structural 95, 96
    technological 95, 96
    voluntary 95
Uniform Business Rate 114
unitary curve 38, 39
unlimited demand 2
unlimited liability 100

value added method 77
value added tax (VAT) 33, 82, 114
variable costs 43
VAT (value added tax) 33, 82, 114
visible balance 86
visible trade 86
voluntary unemployment 95

wages 32, 47, 69
wants 1–2, 77
waste 15
wealth 9, 68–71
    composition of 70
    distribution of 70
    international distribution 20
    national distribution 20
    private 126
wealth of a nation 21
Wealth of Nations (Adam Smith) 9
weather in supply 32
withdrawals 48–50
working capital 72
working population and unemployment 129–130

zero price 81